D0169141

The Outside Child
In and Out of the Book

Christine Wilkie-Stibbs

Routledge
Taylor & Francis Group
New York   London

CHILDREN'S LITERATURE AND CULTURE
JACK ZIPES, SERIES EDITOR

Routledge
Taylor & Francis Group
270 Madison Avenue
New York, NY 10016

Routledge
Taylor & Francis Group
2 Park Square
Milton Park, Abingdon
Oxon OX14 4RN

© 2008 by Taylor & Francis Group, LLC
Routledge is an imprint of Taylor & Francis Group, an Informa business

Printed in the United States of America on acid-free paper
10 9 8 7 6 5 4 3 2 1

International Standard Book Number-13: 978-0-415-97800-2 (Hardcover)

Visit the Taylor & Francis Web site at
http://www.taylorandfrancis.com

and the Routledge Web site at
http://www.routledge.com

CONTENTS

SERIES EDITOR'S FOREWORD

Dedicated to furthering original research in children's literature and culture, the Children's Literature and Culture series includes monographs on individual authors and illustrators, historical examinations of different periods, literary analyses of genres, and comparative studies on literature and the mass media. The series is international in scope and is intended to encourage innovative research in children's literature with a focus on interdisciplinary methodology.

Children's literature and culture are understood in the broadest sense of the term "children" to encompass the period of childhood up through adolescence. Owing to the fact that the notion of childhood has changed so much since the origination of children's literature, this Routledge series is particularly concerned with transformations in children's culture and how they have affected the representation and socialization of children. While the emphasis of the series is on children's literature, all types of studies that deal with children's radio, film, television, and art are included in an endeavor to grasp the aesthetics and values of children's culture. Not only have there been momentous changes in children's culture in the last fifty years, but there have also been radical shifts in the scholarship that deals with these changes. In this regard, the goal of the Children's Literature and Culture series is to enhance research in this field and, at the same time, point to new directions that bring together the best scholarly work throughout the world.

Jack Zipes

PREFACE

Children's literature has necessarily, if not always consciously, reflected the culture of the time in which it was written. This was no less the case at the end of the twentieth century, when the cusp of a new century brought both a new era of uncertainty and a new world imperium that promulgated simplistic, binary, and adversarial interpretations of difference and created and exacerbated divisions into in-groups and out-groups, haves and have-nots.

In the latter part of the twentieth century, a wave of new realism in children's and young adult literature written in English-speaking countries, provoked partly by new ideologies and changed international and intranational relations, and partly by the examples of innovative writers, gave voice and visibility to a range of previously silenced and taboo subjects. These included, for example, gender and sexual identities, homelessness, the Holocaust, and levels of criminality including narcotics, theft, and violence. This literature inscribed all manner of representations of outsider subjectivities, and these are reflected in some of the children's and young adult fictions in this book that were written either just before or after the end of the millennium. They embody the change in world order and ideology directly in their settings, some more by the prophetic resonance which hindsight gives them. Others that precede the millennial changes embody the perennial issues of poverty, neglect, and the effects and consequences of war that have long been the locations of outsiderness but that assume particular significance when they are read again, as here, against the backdrop of these new inscriptions of difference and Otherness. Whatever their varying degrees of self-conscious intentionality, these fictions all inscribe child outsiderness in relation to prescribed normativity, institutionalized power, and insidious hegemonic ideologies. They are read here against changed social and economic structures in globalization that compose the singularly significant and defining event of the age: the depletion and erosion of, and competition for, the world's diminishing resources; the emergence of newly realized global resistance to Western hegemony that variously is seen to wreak havoc on the economic and political infrastructures and is directed at power elites in the form of global terrorism; the increase of socially and economically disinherited domestic underclasses with rising inner-city poverty, petty criminality, and violence; a rising tide of nationalism, and racist opposition to the mass movement across borders of economic migrants, asylum seekers, or refugees displaced by wars, corruption, oppression, economic exploitation, or natural catastrophe against the ecopolitics of climate change and plundered natural resources; the widening poverty gap and the rise of "fat cat" executives; the collapse of the fabric of principled responsibility and fair play in public and private life symptomatized in the very public 2001 collapse of the U.S. energy company Enron for willful, institutionalized corporate fraud; failed parenting across the social spectrum; the rise of the so-called clash of civilizations; the pressures to conform; and newly pressing issues of bodily inscription. The child or young adult characters of these fictions—from Malorie Blackman's terrorists to Jacqueline Wilson's impoverished, abandoned, and neglected children—are shown to be caught up at some level in the effects of this global climate and are in every case positioned as outside and powerless in relation to those systems that produce, sustain, and reproduce the privations of their daily lives and living.

The turning point for this new era's climate of uncertainty that dramatically raised the profile of in-group and out-group specifications and became the impetus for this book came with the November 2000 U.S. elections when the Bush administration came to power. I remember a sense of deep foreboding that, while recognizing the world as a no less safe place to be than before the elections, it was now in less safe hands than it may have been before, because the only superpower was now in the grip of this new administration and at liberty to unleash its ideology unfettered upon the world in the shape of the "Project for the New American Century" and the drive for "American global leadership." It was an ambitious policy for American domination in the world by the group of neoconservatives whose members were now in and influencing the new Bush administration. It was a project that had been long in the making by those who, long before the events of September 11, 2001, had spoken about the need for a "catastrophic and catalyzing event like a new Pearl Harbor" (Project for the New American Century 51) on the back of which to launch its policy of global domination to the American people. The events of "9/11" may well also have been long in the making, and the attack on the World Trade Center, though unquestionably and world-shatteringly tragic, gave President Bush the opportunity to launch "the war on terror" from public platforms and to hitch it to the ideological ambitions of the Project for the American New Century that he located in his January 2002 State of the Union "axis of evil" speech. It upped the rhetorical ante by grouping together the previously unconnected nations of North Korea, Iran, and Iraq in a fictive alliance that effectively divided the world into "pro" and "anti"-Western alliances in a typically too simplistic "us and them" logic clothed in the equally too simplistic sound bite that "you are either with the terrorists or you are with us." The messianic language is palpable: the switch to an "axis of evil" as the catchphrase that President Bush's speechwriter, David Frum, had originally framed as an "axis of hatred," and the resonances of his sound bite with the biblical "he who is not with us is against us," was deliberately and effectively targeted in the United States to appeal to the evangelical Christian Right that comprised Bush's biggest and loudest electoral support group. It found immediate sympathy around the Western world with a like-minded sound bite generation headed up in the United Kingdom by the Blair government that, with astonishing hubris and an affront to the democratic principles on which it purported to be operating, ignored the tens of thousands of people who assembled on the streets of London (and around the world) to protest in the buildup to the Iraq War that, though the threat to national security might or might not be real enough, this was the wrong kind of "war" for this new kind of threat.

So the world of the children growing up in the new twenty-first century post 2002 was now neatly and officially split into two camps on the back of a cataclysmic event and an opportunist national address by a world leader that immediately projected Anglo-American foreign policy back into the Cold War mentality: of the necessity or reality of "the enemy without," a duality of "insiders" and "outsiders" that comprised the new political landscape, and an imagined and objectionable Other against which to define oneself. In one of the most unstable points in history, the neocon ideology of Otherness launched an era of new certainties onto the world that were very quickly normalized. More than this, it filtered down with extraordinary speed through populist newspaper and media coverage to unleash a flood of new antagonisms toward "out-group" individuals and collectives who were deemed not quite to fit with the more clearly marked prescriptions of in-group definitions, and "political correctness" was consigned as the passé penchant of the "loony" Left. These new definitions of "out-groups" extended in newly emboldened and overtly polarized ways to include "gays," migrant workers, asylum seekers, and all forms of "alternative" lifestyles, and heightened the demonization of minority groups of all descriptions that included children and young people. While, to be fair, on the one hand the UK Blair government has done more than any other UK government in recent history to legislate in favor of minority rights and child protection, and to raise more children out of poverty, it has at the same time, and on the other hand, done little to shift the ground of the simplistic binary logic on which it launched its own particular brand of "the war on terror." And new policies of domestic intolerance emerged in the form of a new criminal justice bill and the introduction of Anti-Social Behaviour Orders (ASBOs) directed at unruly "youth" that have effectively criminalized a socially disinherited generation of young people living in the inner-city and "sink" housing estates who, ironically, garner newfound power to themselves by "terrorizing" their local neighborhoods in their efforts to earn their out-group ASBO "badge of honor." Many of the children's and young adult fictions that feature in this book respond to, reflect, or have anticipated the microeffects of these global events on the child subjectivities they portray.

There is nothing new in history, or in literature, about the outsider in relation to social and political institutions and the discourses of power that operate to produce them; and children's literature has long been a forum for championing the cause of the underdog—with a prototype in S. E. Hinton's *The Outsiders* (1967), and with a more recent popular example in the muggle-world existence of Harry Potter. Far from shying away from politically or socially sensitive issues, children's literature has often pioneered narratives that have addressed them. However, while the genre has been pushing forward into previously uncharted territory to represent all manner of previously ignored outsider child and young adult figures as a bold reflection of the shifting terrain of life and living in late postmodernity (and in some cases deploying pioneeringly experimental narrative forms in which to represent them), and while a number of notable critical studies have preceded the idea of the proto-outsider—for example, Roberta Seelinger Trites's award-winning *Disturbing the Universe: Power and Repression in Adolescent Literature* (2000); Hamida Bosmajian's *Sparing the Child: Grief and the Unspeakable in Youth Literature about Nazism and the Holocaust* (2002); Clare Bradford's *Reading Race: Aboriginality in Australian Children's Literature* (2001); John Stephens's edited volume, *Representing Masculinities in Children's Literature and Film* (2002); and aspects of Robyn McCallum's

Ideologies of Identity in Adolescent Fiction (1999)—there seemed still to be a space in the critical field and contemporary sociopolitical climate for a study in which to bring together a disparate range of fictions featuring a wide range of child figures that could be represented and theorized under a collective terminology of "outsiderness." The term eschews previous inscriptions of the condition as "marginalization" and "exclusion" in an attempt to resignify a particular manifestation of the out-group condition in the dialectic of the textual landscape of the new postimperialism from which it emerges. Also, in recognition of the growing complementarity between the disciplines of children's literature and childhood studies, of which Roni Natov's *The Poetics of Childhood* (2003) is the precursor, I have risked the juxtaposition of the narratives of the lives of ontological outsider children and young adults against the textual constructs of outsider children and young adults in the books, not to merge them into a seamless whole, but to position them in sharp relief against each other and to read both sets of narratives through interpretive theoretical frameworks. The aim has not been to offer a philosophical treatise on the "outsider" in the existential mode of Albert Camus and others so much as to examine the conditions in which the idea of outsiderness is created, sustained, maintained, and naturalized: to unpack it, to "freeze-frame" it, to defamiliarize it in the Formalist sense of "making strange," and to interrogate what alternative modes of thinking are possible in relation to it. Judith Butler has spoken about the need for an "interrogation of the terms by which life is constrained in order to open up the possibility of different modes of living; in other words, not to celebrate difference as such but to establish more inclusive conditions for sheltering and maintaining life that resists models of assimilation" (*Antigone's Claim* 4); and this is the theoretical "spirit" in which the matter of outsiderness is reviewed in this work.

Against this sociopolitical background and within these theoretical frames of reference, the categories of outsider children in the different chapters are considered under more particular headings, some of which have particular meanings in relation to the bodies of theory that inform the chapters. The boxed inserts are intended to be freestanding exemplars of "out-book" outsider children and young adults (or are child-related instances of outsiderness portrayed in, for example, media or government reports) that resonate with the "in-book" representations of outsider children and young adults. However, following the ambition of this work to dismantle the divisive dualities of binarism, I am anticipating that, through the reader, the two sets of inscriptions will provoke the kinds of plurivocal discourses in which the narratives of the outsider children in the book will speak with the narratives of outsider children out of the book in interesting and innovative ways. I hope this book will go some way to facilitate those kinds of conversations.

ACKNOWLEDGMENTS

Many people have helped this book on its way: thanks to the patience of Matt Byrnie and then Max Novick at Routledge New York, and for their helpful suggestions and interest in the project; to the University of Warwick for sabbatical leave to begin my work on the book; to friends and colleagues at Warwick for their support and interest in the project; to Richard Flynn at Georgia State University and Jan Susina at Illinois State University in their capacity as editors of *The Children's Literature Association Quarterly* and *The Lion and the Unicorn*, respectively, for their helpful comments on earlier versions of some parts of chapters 4 and 6 that were published in those two journals; and, not least, deep appreciation and gratitude to Dr. Chen-Wei Yu for meticulously formatting the references.

1

OUTSIDER

In the television pretrial of Michael Jackson, the United Kingdom's *Channel 4 News* conducted two off-the-street, ten-second interviews with two men in Jackson's home state:

> Half man, half woman; half black, half white; Michael Jackson is what happens when you fix it 'till it's broke.
>
> He's black; he's white; he's not even gendered—he's tripping over too many taboos—let's bring him down. ("Off the Street Interview")

If these views are representative of a wider opinion about him, it appears that Jackson is here being defined in the popular imagination as interstitial. He is situated ambivalently between categories: neither this nor that. He is unclassifiable, unnamable, positioned as being between races; between genders; between—by implication of his trial—sex and the law; and between the expectations of adult probity and childish naïveté. Jackson is a borderland figure: the quintessential, self-constructed hybrid that defies easy classification and provokes a mix of reactions (Mercer 247; Willis 77–97). His indeterminate status is further emphasized by the fact that he also lives in the place he calls "Neverland," evoking, by association, the Neverland of J. M. Barrie's fictional fantasy located in a liminal dreamspace between waking and sleeping, fantasy and reality, and figuring the quintessential man-boy–boy-girl–child character, Peter Pan—whose creator, J. M. Barrie, like Jackson himself, also was implicated in the lives of small boys and a seeming refusal to grow up.[1] Jackson not only is emblematic of the demonized girl/man-child, but also may be a symptom of a contemporary zeitgeist incapable of tolerating nonspecificity. The resolution to this particular manifestation of intolerance, apparently, is to "bring him down"—a phrase that resonates all too easily with another popularized sound bite to "take him out"; in any case, to render him invisible. Such views are not new in the history of public reactions. But they are newly enabled, supported, and covertly encouraged by newly reiterated political, ideological, and legislative discourses emerging from a contemporary global consciousness that is willing to voice them with impunity from open platforms where once stood (or may have been believed by many to have stood) the bastions of tolerance and political correctness, and intolerance is the by-product of its own process.[2] They give legitimacy to ever more closely defined and refined articulations of "Otherness," located in and sustained by an "insider"-"outsider" binarity ("you are either with us or against us"). These kinds of discourses disavow the polymorphous, the polyvalent or "perverse," or, indeed, any matter that is not neatly situated at the extremes of its own logic and does not have "outsider-ness" as its inevitable consequence. Julia Kristeva argues that a society, like an individual, can only reject that which it already recognizes, so that what we exclude as a society or a nation is interior to our very identity as a nation or society (*Etrangers* 183–184). When the argument is appropriated to the individual, she comes up with the suggestion that the "stranger" or the "foreigner" is in me. In other words, difference is the very condition of subjective identity; outsiders are, and only can be, the inventions of insiders—projections of what they find repugnant or alien within themselves. Difference is, therefore, the source of outsiderness and the location for this study. Michael Jackson epitomizes difference, and I am suggesting that he is both metaphor and metonymy of this emerging nexus of biopolitics; he is perceived as a lacuna in the binary modality, and is identified only as regressive, abhorrent, and depraved: most definitely "Other," and most certainly "Not-I."

Political and cultural theorists—such as Judith Butler, Ernesto Laclau, and Slavoj Žižek in their *Contingency, Hegemony, Universality: Contemporary Dialogues on the Left*—are now, quite properly, challenging the binary status quo because, among other things, of the way it naturalizes certain kinds of social power and produces certain preferred types of hegemonic subjectivities on the basis of what these critics argue to be a series of culturally prescribed foreclosures; it determines certain norms and is dialectical in its effects. Butler writes,

> Norms, are not only embodied … but embodiment is itself a mode of interpretation, not always conscious, which subjects normativity itself to an iterable temporality. Norms are not static entities, but incorporated and interpreted features of existence that are

sustained by the idealizations furnished by fantasy. ("Competing Universalities" 264)

In my reading of the narratives that feature in this book against this sociopolitical landscape of new certainties, I raise the question about possible alternatives to the binary logic that excludes by process of foreclosure, in an attempt to reimagine and revalue the "in between" in ways that bring prescribed alterity into the frame of signification; and even if the question is not entirely resolved here, it seems to be a sufficiently important project simply to raise it.

The metaphors of exclusion are various. For some, the "Others" are those who fall between binary categories, the "interstitials"; for others, they belong inside the category "Not-us" or "Not normal." In yet another metaphorical approach to them, they are those who inhabit and haunt the very boundaries of categories, and must be kept at those boundaries, inadmissible to the center. Anne Scott writes about outsiders inhabiting "borderlands" (4–5), where categories overlap or merge. Michel Foucault would seem to treat the boundary as an interstice—an overlap of the inadmissible boundaries of two categories. Foucault would classify Jackson in his category of the "abnormals" and as an "ambiguity" who (at least in the popular imagination) inhabits life as some kind of monster, a human monster. The abnormals are, by definition, "boundary" creatures who inhabit an indeterminate space and do not fit neatly into predetermined categorizations or classifications. The monster of Foucault's theorization is defined as being of "double individualities," represented as a "double violation" by transgressing not only social but also, more importantly, *natural* laws. The human monster, he says, "combines the impossible and the forbidden and its behavior transgresses 'juridical regularities'" ("Abnormals" 51). The "abnormals" emerge from historical circumstances and appear under many different guises ranging from "monsters" who commit "unnatural acts" to the "incorrigibles" who transgress penal or regulatory laws. I should suggest that these unnatural acts of "monsters" are most commonly recognized as molestation, particularly child molestation; murder, particularly child murder; and abuse, particularly child abuse. The "incorrigibles," on the other hand, are described by Foucault as being "in need of correction," for which the remedy is to be at least partially disqualified as a legal subject via some kind of restricted freedom. Correction may take the form of confinement or exclusion under the law, or may be a set of corrective training methods: "the army, the schools, the workshops, [or, in more recent history,] ... in families themselves" (Foucault, "Abnormals" 52).

It will have been noted that the appearance of the abnormals in Foucault's theorization is made possible only by the rush for classification and that, almost inevitably, these abnormals are situated in a class at what would be the negative end of a spectrum based on an assumed, even if somewhat unspecified, normativity. If the monster is inscribed in the "abnormal," we might confidently assume that in a class at the other end of this spectrum is inscribed the "angel." The term is already familiar to the disciplines of both women's studies and children's literature, in the "angel-monster" instantiation of women and, more specifically in this context, the "angel-monster" child which I consider in more detail in later chapters.

Mary Douglas suggests that what is extreme, and occupies the margins of categories, is what is most troubling and dangerous. So people at the margins of categories, whether binary or more various, are the most vulnerable within, and dangerous to, any society or social group; they attract the greatest degree of social and political attention and are, not surprisingly, the most demonized (Douglas 4).[3] Margins are not interstices, but these are only parts of different intellectual conceptualizations of the same social circumstances. Whether they are "marginals" or "interstitials," in both sets of inscriptions the most vulnerable and demonized members of societies lie outside the categories of recognized normativities and reside in "outsiderness." The outsiders are often associated as polluting and/or are related to danger or threat, particularly in relation to the body. Ideas about and attitudes toward notions of outsiderness are conjectured in classifications, especially binary classifications, that are locked into a dualist logic that is inherently hierarchical in relation to categories of dominance and submission. Dualism has been described by Val Plumwood as "the logic of colonization" (41),[4] in which structures, she argues, mutuality and equality are anathema. So there is no doubt that in these new articulations of Otherness, the self-assumed insiders regard outsiders as unquestionably of less worth.

Clearly, new conceptual frameworks that articulate less circumscribed views of the kinds of alterities inscribed in outsiderness are required and will be argued for here. So this study asks the following: how far is the condition of outsiderness perpetuated, sustained, and reproduced by the very discourses through which it is uttered, and how far is it possible to radically reposition and resignify outsiderness through more diverse and more contemporary theorizations? Would such a project regard notions of ambiguity and contradiction more favorably than does the quest for mutuality and equality that has dominated the liberal discourses of the past decades?

These questions have been variously addressed and applied to adult behaviors in relation to instruments of power and the enunciation of power in a range of institutional contexts. But the questions become especially interesting when they are addressed to children, whose status between the uterus and the adult effectively already defines them as transitional beings, and as outsiders in regulatory practices. While it may be argued that all bodies, irrespective of their chronological age, inhabit a transitional, nonessential status, it is in the literal and metaphorical spaces of the especially fluid status of the concept of the child's body that opportunities open up for exploration of a different kind of mind map, a different signifying space, in relation to outsiderness.

One approach may be to draw into focus the space between the "insider"-"outsider" binary polarities and the way it is described in critical terminologies. That space, or interstice, sits at the vulnerable margins of and between neat categorizations. Its status raises the question of how, at the outer limits and middle ground of specified normativity, a more complex pluralist reality can be rendered in concrete terms. In other words, how might we differently conceive, understand, and articulate this position we now recognize as being "outside" normative categorizations in ways that move the discourse away from the margins, and away from the "either/or" logic it sustains, into a kind of pluralist logic? A logic of "both/and" not only tolerates ambiguity but also articulates a nominal discourse in relation to it. So, while part of my purpose here is to introduce a degree of instability into the otherwise stable insider-outsider paradigm, my more radical aim is also to conceive a mind map that dissolves the outer reaches of the binary spectrum—to neutralize the idea of outsiderness in favor of a more atomized, more particularized logic. Donna Haraway argues for modes of positionality other than the hegemony of relativism in which the subject is essentialized and naturalized, advocating instead *location*, that is, "non-equivalent positions in a substantive web of connections" (191). Such a project may also go somewhere to achieving what Kristeva has described as the need for the "demassification of the problematic of *difference* [original italics]" ("Women's Time" 209). Kristeva's approach would acknowledge difference without attempting to totalize it, or annihilate it, or reconcile it; it would disintegrate what she describes as the violence directed toward the other "in its very nucleus" (209). Here, too, we may profitably draw from some of the conceptual frameworks deriving from postcolonial and "queer" theories that aspire to antimonolithic frames of reference. Postcolonial theory, for example, derives from the deconstructionist mission to question the premises upon which monolithic assertions, assumptions, and "truths" about individual and collective identities have been built up; it aims to articulate what Shaobo Xie has termed the "multipositionality of identity" (2).

In relation to queer theory, Rebecca Rabinowitz says, "Queer theory's project is to offer a new language in which ... fluidity and gaps are described as powerfully ambiguous and useful rather than simply ironic and unusual" (22). Eve Kosofsky Sedgwick refers to queer theory's "open mesh of possibilities, gaps, overlaps, dissonances and resonances" (8). She goes on to describe how the queer terminology has permeated disciplines other than gender: "the term spins outward along dimensions that can't be subsumed under gender and sexuality at all: the ways that race, ethnicity, postcolonial nationality criss-cross with these *and other* [original italics] identity-constituting, identity-fracturing discourses" (Sedgwick 9). She shares the view of Judith Butler and others that "queerness" is beyond gender, and is, in the words of Alexander Doty, "an attitude, a way of responding, that begins in the place not concerned with, or limited by, notions of a binary opposition" (xv).[5] In his bid to avoid straitjacketing the necessarily elusive quality and fluidity of queer theory's project, Doty adds that queer theory "has been set up to challenge and break apart conventional categories, not to become one itself" (xv). He echoes Teresa de Lauretis, who describes "queerness" as "both interactive yet resistant, both participatory yet distinct" (iii), and Lauren Berlant and Michael Warner, who describe the capacity of queer commentary to take on varied "shapes, risks, ambitions and ambivalences in various contexts" (344).

These kinds of thinking seem to open up at least the possibility for another kind of discourse, another way of looking at and speaking about the conditions that currently circumscribe and define child-outsiderness. However, the term "queer" that is deliberately selected to unsettle preexisting gender inscriptions carries its own connotational baggage that is problematic even within the gay-lesbian-gender discipline or community itself, not least because of its discursive history as a weapon of oppression and term of abuse (Doty 4).[6] And as with any kind of labeling or terminology, especially in the academy, there is debate about what exactly the term "queer" includes and excludes. Therefore, because I wish to map out a distinctive space for child-outsiderness that is analogous to but different from the queer project, and because outsiderness is not here being exclusively located in the questions of sexual identity or sexual preference that are queer theory's first priority, I am faced with the need to coin another term of reference by which to identify my child-outsiderness project. "Outsider theory" springs most readily to mind as a nomination that will both properly capture the kind of fluidity that characterizes the queer project and support the multitheoretical explications of outsiderness in focus here. It also seems appropriate to ask if a project that seeks to somehow neutralize the extremes of the insider-outsider binarity might not give rise en route to other equally theoretically and ontologically problematic subject or identity positions, by seeming to homogenize at the cost of another expedient that seeks to celebrate difference. For this, I must return to Kristeva's views about the need to acknowledge difference without attempting to totalize it, and to de Lauretis, who says (in the context of queer identities but which I am here appropriating to "outsider theory") that "the speculative premise ... is no longer to be seen simply as marginal with regard to a dominant" (iii). And in this regard, she urges "a mode of functioning that is both interactive yet resistant, both participatory yet distinct, claiming at once equality *and* [my italics] difference" (de Lauretis iii). It is arguable whether these oxymoronic positions are both achievable. Equally, it is debatable if the outside child and the groups of outsider children, currently circumscribed not only by the power structures in which they are located but also by their relative immaturity, are able to achieve the same degree of agency as the adult audience to whom de Lauretis addresses her message. However, it is conceivable that the adults who inscribe them in the narratives in focus here might be better placed to reinscribe their conception and perception of outsiderness with the help of the ramifications of the outsider theory that is subsumed in all these theoretical positions.

There is also an inherent and paradoxical complication in this approach that is effectively a poststructuralist drive for pluralism, and it lies in the seemingly unavoidable need to elide commonality. In promoting the idea of the particular, and in valuing difference, the identity or behavioral characteristics that individuals have in common might be overlooked; and I am not altogether convinced by Xie's argument that such a move to acknowledge commonality as well as difference is simply to "subsume ... marginalities into the imperialism of the same" (3). As part of the outsider theory being proposed, I should want to argue that there is scope for holding both views simultaneously in the same project, and that such an approach might thus provide a protection against the pitfalls of binarism and dualism that are being challenged by the project.

WHO IS "THE CHILD"?

The term "the child" is, as ever, problematic. Like the similarly problematic term "the body" (see chapter 5) and its related constructivist terminology "childhood," it is a discursive category riddled with indeterminacies; at the same time, it essentializes and homogenizes all and individual children who emerge from different and competing histories and ethnicities under its collective label. It has an uncertain economy, globally, and a different age definition depending on who or which institution is doing the defining. "The child" may variously signify any kind of being in the process of becoming an "adult"—wherein lies one (if not two) of the many other difficulties of determination— and is also the subject of numerous essentialist and nonessentialist debates.[7] In temporal terms, definitions of the state of being a child may refer to any being between birth to five, eight, eleven, or sixteen years old in education-speak, or a person below the age of eighteen years in United Nations-speak (United Nations Convention on the Rights of the Child [UNCRC] Article 1). In the United States, the death penalty for sixteen year olds was abolished in all states but is still available for eighteen year olds in those states that retain the death penalty. In the United Kingdom, a sixteen year old is old enough to acquire condoms over the counter or from a dispensing machine and may be prescribed contraception without parental knowledge or consent; sixteen year olds in parts of Europe may have sex with people their own age but legally are too young to have sex with people older than eighteen years (and conversely); at sixteen they may marry and have children, but in the United Kingdom are not old enough to vote or hold an adult library card. Article 38.3 of the UNCRC states, "State Parties shall refrain from recruiting any person who has not attained the age of fifteen years into their armed forces," but in the Democratic Republic of the Congo, among other places, children below the age of eleven are recruited and trained to kill with guns, at least in the so-called rebel armies. So, while the materiality of the child as an embodied being cannot be defined as adult, the experiences and definitions of what it means to be a child are mutable. Slavoj Zizek points out that various statutory statuses have been accorded to children in today's changed world:

> A series of processes are in motion in which children are increasingly being accorded the same freedoms as their elders at increasingly young ages: in divorce, they are allowed to influence the decision on which of the two parents they will live with. Children can now sue their parents in the world. (*Ticklish Subject* 343)[8]

He goes on to point out that these changes render not only childhood but also parenthood differently; parenthood, he notes, is "no longer a natural substantial notion, but is always-already politicized" (*Ticklish Subject* 349). Being a "child" means that the lived bodily experiences are mapped out in chunks of linear temporality between a number of arbitrarily determined, but fixed, points that are scrutinized at every turn in the progress toward an unspecified but collective understanding of adulthood that is synony-mized with maturity. Beyond the upper parameters of the prescription, these cease to function as a first principle: "the child's body, and indeed the child's identity, become microcosmically analogous to the total body of the social" (Christensen, James, and Jenks 207). So ideas about who is "the child," and about its related constructivist category "childhood," continue to be slippery and contentious, and continue to be the subject of endless debates, interrogations, and drives for definitions.[9] It is not my intention here to revisit these debates, so much as to acknowledge and build on them. However, in relation to these debates, the "child" in focus in these pages is further complicated by the fact that it is on the one hand a fictional construct with a problematic ontology and on the other hand a flesh-and-blood reality whose ontology is not in doubt. I argue that both converge via a process of narrativization in the discourses through which they appear—a simultaneous ontological and epistemological complication, joined together in the mind of the "reader" through an uncertain doctrine of mimeses, which is also precisely the point at which the Formalist notions of *fabula* and *sjuzet* converge in the act of narration, but which I am here repositioning in a poststructuralist context. Despite, or because of, the illuminations, contributions, influences, and affects of poststructuralist, postmodernist, deconstructionist, and postmillennium interrogations of the field of literary studies, I continue to regard the question of the dialectic between art, life, and subjectivity as a relevant ground for debate and argu-ment, even though the ground and the position from which the questions are raised may be continually and significantly shifting locations and ter-rains. In *Reading Race*, for example, Clare Bradford identifies the slippage between fictional characters and "reality," and the questions pertaining to the ontological status of both: that they can only ever be a representation and an illusion of mimesis constructed through the ideological fabric of the language in which they are represented and expressed in the literature (139). It is in this space that I am reading the focus texts as compellingly metonymic of the contemporary political climate, so that any discussion of the literature invokes the sociopolitical context that has provoked them and is the nexus between the narratives of fiction and narratives of the material world. So this is the ontological terrain in which the question of outsiderness is being explored here.

NARRATING CHILD-OUTSIDERNESS

"Child-outsiderness" is the term used here to refer to an alterity inscribed into narratives about children located at the margins of, or in between, definitions, or groups, or ideologies, or events, or experiences, or situations, by circumstances of historical or geographical distance; sexual, cultural, or racial orientation; belief systems; or bodily appearance (which includes dress as well as being disabled or disfigured). Child-outsiderness, as defined in the context of this work, manifests itself in the child who is adopted, in care, orphaned, homeless, a refugee, seeking asylum, part of a diaspora, immigrant, displaced, or dispossessed; is the victim and/or survivor of violence, abuse, poverty, neglect, or war; or is silenced, rendered invisible, or specially controlled and silenced by certain power structures, ideologies, or belief systems. The concept of child-outsiderness is different from, and more than, the mere "Other" (though the latter is subsumed in it), because, unlike the "Other" of psychosocial theorization, which is by definition locked into the subjective, self-Other binarity, child-outsiderness incorporates into itself also the pluralist context and the third-person objective view of that condition: not simply observing difference as Other, therefore, but also observing the observers and definers of Otherness and difference, the geneses and process of Otherness and the emergence and existence of subjectivities within these spaces so defined. All the child subjects who are included in this work, whether in or out of the book, are outsiders in the sense of the above definitions, and it has been challenging to consider the degrees of difference between their various positionings on the spectrums or binarities, or various statuses by which the condition is usually defined.

The chapter headings of the book are my attempt to impose a degree of categorization upon their individual conditions of outsiderness in an effort to identify, theorize, and situate the different qualities of outsiderness that the child subject experiences or in and by which it has been represented. Why, for example, do novels that address issues of adoption appear in a number of different chapters when, positionally and experientially speaking, they are ostensibly the same? The same could be asked of novels featuring child refugees and novels that depict children in situations of war. Conversely, why does any given novel appear under any particular chapter heading when it might with equally good reason have appeared under another? These were the questions I needed to wrestle with in arriving at my decisions, and are the reason why, while positioning novels as focus texts in any given chapter, I have in some cases revisited these same texts in different chapters to consider them from a different stance, or through a different "lens." A decision about where to place each particular text has been taken for the most part in relation to what I perceived to be some important theme, irrespective of the novel's dominant subject matter, in relation to the theoretical positions I felt best explicated that theme. The decision about where to situate a particular text is also based on narrational perspective(s), or viewpoint(s) or focalizations assumed in the text insofar as they have influenced the perceptions of outsiderness in relation to the character's position (they may not necessarily always be the protagonist or dominant subject of the narrative). In all these senses, the texts and theories are used commutatively to explicate the repositioning of child-outsiderness. There is much to be debated, also, about the differences between fictional and nonfictional texts. For example, Andrea Reiter in her *Narrating the Holocaust*[10] is preoccupied with the question of the effects of different generic styles in relating the unifying experience that was the Holocaust. Arguably, the differences of style and the presentation of the subject and subject matter between, for example, a "report" and a fictional narrative might be anticipated as a clear distinction between the "flat characterization" of the nonfictional texts and the "transparent" characters of the fictional texts.[11] However, on closer inspection, it emerges that the lines of demarcation between the two are not quite as clearly drawn as one might imagine for reasons that will become clearer as the book progresses. The texts that appear in freestanding wraparound boxes throughout the book are intended both to stand alone and to extend the points being raised within the body of the chapter, and in general they relate to "out-of-book" experiences or reports or representations of childhood.

It might be assumed at first sight that the narratives used in this work are prescribed by their generic markers: that, for example, the institutional report is of its nature impersonal, objective, and factual, and that the literary text is subjective, metaphorical, and ironic, and carries poetic license to be somewhat "economical" with, or wholly at odds with, the facts. For example, in the epigraph to his book *Boy Overboard*, Morris Gleitzman apologizes to his readers that because he is not an Afghan refugee, he may have "got some things wrong."[12] And there can be no question that the power of literary texts to control the orders and outcomes of events, for example, or to fix it so that the child character in the story does *not* die, is singularly different from that of the biographical account, the diary, or the report in which outcomes are already fixed in and by the reality from which they derive. However, as we shall see, the *generic* markers of the report become blurred, not only in their own right but also when the reports themselves include case histories, and when personal accounts of childhood experiences such as we see in biography, diary, or personal testimony echo the style of first-person narration of fictional texts, and conversely. Equally, I have found that the fictional texts themselves, although dealing with some or other manifestation of outsiderness in a realist mode, are not a homogeneous category, and that they too may be divided into a number of different subcategories. Some of them, in their focus, intention, stylistics, and representations of character, are more akin to reports in their generic characteristics, and without being in any way pejorative I should wish to describe them as "docu-novels." The novels of Benjamin Zephaniah, Elizabeth Lutzeier, and (arguably but less obviously) Elizabeth Laird fall into this category for reasons I shall more fully explain and illustrate through the book while also taking note of their different narrative functions and effects. Briefly, these docu-novels are novels whose priority is to narrate a social circumstance, or which have a message to tell; they carry little, if any, narration of character interiority. In other words, although the narrating voice is strong and is in the third person, it lacks the flexibility that the narrative function of the omniscient narrator would otherwise bring to the text—with all that that implies for readerly engagement. And, although the apparent intention of these docu-novels is to send a social message to its readers, the narrational comment that is otherwise the mainstay of the moral voice in children's fiction is curiously minimal or silent. Third-person narration in these novels stops short of habitually entering the thoughts of the character, although, by use of a curiously distancing narrational device, we are sometimes *told* by the narrator what the character in focus is thinking. Interestingly and paradoxically in this context, therefore, focalization is restricted in these docu-novels to external characterization, with "flat characters," and in these respects they share more in common with the government reports and policy documents that also feature here.

Even so, and despite their mutual focus on outsiderness in the selection of narratives that feature here, the superiority of the docu-novels over the documentary style of reports and policy documents at evoking readers' sympathy has the effect of making the fictional child characters of the former more "real" to the reader than the ontologically real child or children that are the subject(s) of government and policy reports, and is arguably the single distinguishing difference between the literary and nonfictional texts. More conventionally in terms of generic markers, the narrational style of authors such as Anne Provoost and Nina Bawden deploys a degree of interiority by use of omniscient narration as a focalizer that takes the reader intimately into the inner thoughts of the character(s) and is concerned with the kinds of mental processes that mark out these characters as conscious beings. Murray Knowles refers to what he calls Nina Bawden's use of "mind-style" in *Carrie's War* as "a major feature in distinguishing the best of today's children's literature in general and *Carrie's War* in particular" (Knowles and Malmkjaer 116).

In these senses, these kinds of "mind-style" novels share more in common with the biography or the diary than with other fiction because, in their degrees of interiority, they leave little distance between the mind(s) of the character(s) and the mind of the reader. The effect of closing the generic gap between biographical and novelistic writing raises the question about the status of the biography or diary of whether they function as works of nonfiction or works of quasi-fiction, and is also another manifestation of the blurring of conventional, generic boundaries. And there are further questions to be asked, not only in relation to the respective generic styles of biographical and fictional writing, but also between, on the one hand, the fictionalized status of the biographer and diarist in and through the process of writing—especially when the writing is an adult recollection of childhood, or memoir—as compared with, on the other hand, the quasi-ontological "reality" of the fictional characters of the novel. In other words, the styles of narration and their respective degrees of interiority are themselves unwitting markers of an "insider"-"outsider" positionality across the spectrum of narratives used in this work.

THE BODY OF THE CHILD

The child's bodily and spatial existence are arguably two of the most, if not *the* most, regulated, scrutinized, and surveyed sites. They are the focus of a battery of adult-defined, semipunitive, legislative, and regulatory systems administered through the various state apparatuses and Louis Althusser's agents of ideological transmission (the church, the school, the family, and the political-legal systems; 4–7) and such corrective institutions that Foucault describes (*Discipline and Punish* 178–179), defined on axes of "the normal" and "the pathological," and these regulations ostensibly are almost always presented with the singular motive of child protection. All of the official and legislative documentation I call upon share, almost unwittingly it seems, this common theme: of a focus on the child's physical, corporeal existence and vulnerability. All the documents emerge from authority structures, and all refer back to themselves insofar as their validity is legitimized and they are understood within their own frames of reference. Part of the ongoing purpose of this work is to unravel the complex scenes of the child's body—the body construed as "lived body" (*Leib*: "lived from within" = inside/subject) and "object body" (*Körper*: "seen from without" = outside/object) (Leder 1–8), the body as "I" and "Not-I" in relation to point of view and narration, and the body as perceiver and perceived—and to mount a challenge to the dualism upon which basis these perceptual perspectives have been built up.

In his various works, Foucault asserts that the body is a site of culturally contested meanings, a "nodal point" or "nexus" where regimes and discourse of power inscribe themselves: "the body is the inscribed surface of events" (*History of Sexuality* 1:148). But in Judith Butler's essay "Foucault and the Paradoxes of Bodily Inscription," she asks if Foucault's view of the body as a mere "surface" affected by historical and cultural inscription raises the further question of whether this "body" has an ontological status apart from the inscription (601). In her essay "Bodily Inscriptions, Performative Subversions," she elaborates,

> This body often appears to be a passive medium that is signified by an inscription from a cultural source figured as 'external' to that body. Any theory of the culturally constructed body, however, ought to question 'the body' as a construct of suspect generality when it is figured as passive and prior to discourse. (104)

Here, we see that Butler is wrestling not only with the conceptualization of "the body" as a "blank page" but also with the question of its homogenization, in much the same way as the homogenization of "the child" is challenged; she is also challenging the Cartesian dualism of the "culture" versus "nature" debates, and, by implication, their respective laws surface again, particularly in relation to transgression. Foucault's inscription of a bodily surface, which is best understood in relation to skin and other bodily contours, also demarcates a spatial distinction between "inner" and "outer" body which, as Butler points out, makes sense only with reference to boundaries and points of demarcation:

> A mediating boundary that strives for stability.... And this stability, this coherence is determined in a large part by cultural orders that sanction the subject.... Thus the 'inner' and 'outer' constitute a binary distinction that stabilizes and consolidates the coherent subject. ("Bodily Inscriptions" 108)

When the assumed integrity of that boundary is challenged, or when the boundary fails to act as a clear marker between the inside and the outside body (such as, I suggest, in the many manifestations of child abjection that are discussed in more detail in chapter 4, and might well be metaphoricized in the concept of the gaping wound), it gives rise to a phenomenon where identities are founded in and consolidated by ideas of expulsion or repudiation along bodily, sexual, or racial lines (Young 201–204). This process, Butler maintains, institutes concepts of the "Other," or sets of Others, through exclusion and domination.

What constitutes through division the "inner" and "outer" worlds of the subject is a border and boundary tenuously maintained for the purposes of social regulation and control. ("Bodily Inscriptions" 108)

However, if we can begin to conceive of the body's surface less as a marker between inner and outer regions and more as a "borderland," we are able once again to blur the clear lines of demarcation between the inner and outer realms of the body. The "borderland" is described by Scott as being

A place where dualized oppositions are thrust together and yet are not assimilated. The tension they embody cannot be collapsed into a hierarchical relationship in which one agent is subsumed and instrumentalized by the other. In a state of both isomorphic sameness and irreconcilable difference, the borderland's inhabitants are inherently oxymoronic. (9)

The body perceived as borderland in these terms comes some way toward explicating the conditions of outsiderness in relation to its interstitial status. But I should want to extend Scott's use of the term "dualized" oppositions to "multiple" oppositions, and to extend the range of her "the one versus the other" definition of agency to "one versus multiple others." These oppositional conceptualizations do not altogether escape the binary framework upon which they are founded and are persistently problematic, forever hampering the possibility for another kind of discussion. However, in its metaphorical breaking up of the stable surface tension of bodily inscription, the idea of "borderlands" is useful, and becomes even more so when it is appropriated to the body of the child that, as I have mentioned above (also in chapters 4 and 5), inhabits an especially fluid space in the schema of bodily descriptions.

Historically, the body of the child emerges from, and is aestheticized in, a doctrine of presumed innocence. This perception of the child and childhood effectively suppresses and silences the regulatory practices that come into play in the socializing process to delimit, if not to eradicate, all references to proclivities of the child, particularly the onanistic proclivities, that threaten to disrupt the surface tension of bodily innocence (Lingis, "Subjectification" 297). At this innocence end of the spectrum is the "angel" child perceived as dependent, victim, conformist, passive, benign, and malleable; its body is acted upon rather than acting. With only a few exceptions, most of the child figures that feature here—either as protagonists in the literary narrative or as actual case histories—conform at least superficially to this particular inscription of the child. It is a seemingly inescapable source of complication in the way that the child is socially conceived. Perhaps, too, it tells us a great deal about the way in which the adult writers of these narratives conceive of, or have chosen to represent, the child.

This is especially the case in children's literature, not only in relation to its primary audience—the child reader—but also in relation to the adults who are at least metaphorically looking over the shoulder of the child as he or she reads. They are the same kind of adults who also write and are the audience for policy documents and government and other official reports. However, as with so many binary inscriptions, the doctrine of presumed child innocence is, as always, problematic. It is found wanting in numerous real-life examples of transgressive child behaviors that consistently undermine its credibility: in, for example, the ten-year-old Kalashnikov-wielding resistance fighter of Liberia; and in the names of the child murderers Jon Venables, Robert Thompson, Mary Bell, Willie Bosket, or Amy Fisher—the latter known as the "Long Island Lolita."[13] Subversions of the doctrine of innocence emerge also in a host of literary children such as the enigmatically evil and innocent "Flora" and "Miles" of Henry James's *The Turn of the Screw*; "Jack" and "Roger" of William Golding's *Lord of the Flies*; Vladimir Nabokov's "Lolita"; and the character of "Tulip" in Anne Fine's *The Tulip Touch* (see chapter 4), which Fine wrote in response to the murder by Venables and Thompson of baby James Bulger to interrogate the whole question of the childhood evil–innocence debate. These instances of transgressive innocence are among the few examples of seriously wicked literary child protagonists that are more than outweighed by discursive representations of angel children in children's literature.

These examples of "transgressive" children in relation to normative prescriptions can be read as the "abnormals" of Foucault's definition. They are the child figures whom Foucault would perceive to have crossed the boundary of "natural law," and whose evil actions are taken to be the outward enactment of corrupted inner "souls," signified through perverse bodily inscriptions and behaviors. On the basis of the myth of childhood innocence, they are much maligned in public perception and pronouncement. In contrast, child figures such as the character "Stanley Yelnats" of Louis Sachar's novel of penal servitude, *Holes* (see chapter 4), would qualify as one of Foucault's "incorrigibles" because, unlike the child murderer, he has transgressed only *social* law for which the retribution is bodily subjection through hard labor. Unlike the "abnormals," who are beyond the pale, the "incorrigibles" are seen to be redeemable. This spectrum of child behavior is another marker of the functioning of the inner and outer bodily realms played out on and through bodily surface, but it seems that questions about the child that are founded on a doctrine of presumed innocence will continue to be debated so long as the idea of the child is socially conceived as occupying the either/or extremes of the spectrum.

Ultimately, then, in these connections, the notion that these child figures are either "in" or "out of" the book becomes in itself immaterial. Whenever children are seen to have transgressed the boundaries of regulated behavior, they provoke shock waves of disbelief and revulsion in the wider population—giving rise to literary censorship in the case of literary children or censure of actual children. The weight of the state then comes crashing down upon them with little or no concession to their otherwise protected status as children, or their right to innocence; the nations begin to bay for their blood, and the mechanisms of discipline and regulation come into play in the shape of enclosed spaces: the state penitentiary, the boot camp, house curfew under Anti-Social Behaviour Orders (ASBOs, a UK Labour government initiative acronym), "on-remand" (often in the United Kingdom in "adult" state prisons when the ascribed young offender institutions are already too full), or, in cases of suspected terrorism by the U.S. government, incarceration in Camp Delta at Guantánamo Bay. We might well ask with Alphonso Lingis if such punitive measures both create and condone the behavior they seek to exclude.[14] More particularly, we might consider the possibility that the partiality invoked innocence–evil axis, through which lens the child has been at least historically constituted, is itself the problem that has provoked such rampantly reactionary attitudes toward, and demonizing of, those children who cross the sacred threshold of innocence, rendering them beyond the pale. Julian Petley, for example, reproduces a howl of newspaper extracts, all of them unequivocally condemnatory, in the wake of the James Bulger murder and asks,

> Does this therefore mean that our culture is now finally able to deal sensibly with children as real, complex flesh-and-blood human beings, as opposed to abstractions of "innocence" or "evil"? (103)

And he concludes that the answer is "No." Children in trouble, he says, have been defined as "different," "alien," "other," "evil," and "wicked." He quotes the words of the trial judge of the Bulger murder case:

> Children should not be presumed to be innately good. In the lexicon of crime there is a metaphysical evil, the imperfection of all mankind; there is physical evil, the suffering that humans cause each other, and there is moral evil, the choice of vice over virtue. Children are separated by necessity of age from none of these. (104)

All of these are negative epithets. But, even here, when Petley's singular intention is to debunk the myth of monstrous children, he unwittingly fertilizes the innocence–evil paradigm in which children have been historically inscribed by a refusal to locate them anywhere other than with either evildoers, at one extreme of the polarity, or victims, at the pole of innocence: "Children," he says, "are far less likely to be monsters than the victims of monstrous poverty, homelessness, neglect, sexual abuse and other forms of violence ... from the planet 'inner city' or the planet 'outer housing estate'" (103–105). My point here is not to promote the idea that some children are either innately monstrous or angelic, so much as to make the point that our ways of describing and, more importantly, of representing their various behaviors are circumscribed by the conceptual framework of the either/or binary paradigm with which I began and in which "rule breakers" find no legitimate or nominal place or space simply to be.[15]

The question of "nature" and "natural law" surfaces again in these arguments and is interesting, not least because the historiographies of "nature" and "the child" have intriguingly close resonances with each other, and become especially interesting when they are antonymically juxtaposed with the idea of the "unnatural" and with "unnatural acts." Xie points out how, in Western discourse, culture or civilization is always opposed to nature or primitivity: "Culture refers to norm, canon and modernity; nature designates whatever is unwholesome, irrational, coarse, uncultivated, remote" (5).[16] He points out how both Edward Said and Catherine Hall (in relation to postcolonialism and Western imperialism) have reported how primitivism (for which read, "nature") has been synonymized with the child in the most pejorative of terms (13–14).[17] Even so, the Romantics upheld the supremacy of goodness and innocence in relation to "nature" and the child; and while Western discourse encodes breakers of "natural law" as "monsters," it simultaneously espouses the purity of the "natural life": life as it is lived at its closest to "nature" (and iconicized in the image of the "beautiful" child)[18] as the desirable alternative to life lived as tainted and fettered by materialist Western consumerism.

The myth of the child that bears little or no relation to ontological reality has been variously identified as the desirably innocent and most natural "noble savage" that "served as a model for all that was admirable and uncorrupted in human nature" (White 150),[19] and is also simultaneously regarded as the "savage" to be brought into line with cultural norms. "Nature," then, has an interestingly pluralist pedigree and has been appropriated to the child, who inhabits both ends of the angel-monster, innocence-evil spectrum. "Nature" in all its signifying associations may, then, be regarded as a neutralizing agent in the insider-outsider paradigm in which the question of difference becomes ambiguous.

In chapter 4, I bring together these various strands of the "nature" and "natural" debates and their related antitheses that are waged across the body of the child, to explore how the chasm between the seemingly diametrically opposite instantiations of the "angel" and "monster" child may be defused in a theory of abjection; and how, instead of their mutual experience of polarization at the outer margins of outsiderness discourses, they not only are resignified in relation to each other, but also are particularized and repositioned in the discourses per se. This is not merely another rendition of relativism, but also an attempt to unseat the dualism of the insider-outsider discourses in which the child appears to have been inextricably located. In broad terms, this study seeks to dismantle geopolitical and biopolitical polarities, and to reinstate the proximal view as the knowledge base upon which to conjecture "the child" as an unfinished, heterogeneous, mutable, messy, unfixed, diverse, and complex project that simply dissolves the very possibility of outsiderness as an ontological category.[20] It achieves this, I argue, by the juxtaposition of diverse narratives that collectively refuse to distill notions of "the child" and "childhood" into the faceless realms of mere statistics, legislation, and bureaucracy that characterize policy making and are the source of "I"–"Not-I" dichotomies upon which the discourses of "outsiderness" rely.

2

DISPLACED

It is a commonplace that we care for others unequally, in proportion to how much we think we know about them, how easily we can imagine ourselves to be in their plight, or how likely we judge it that we should find ourselves in their situation. It is hard to empathize with people who seem Other, and it is hard to sympathize with those we cannot empathize with. It is even harder to empathize with people whose identity we do not even recognize, and to whom we do not ascribe an identity as worthy as our own. White explorers, exploiters, and colonizers called themselves "discoverers" of territories new to them because they could ignore the fact that the inhabitants they drove away, enslaved, or massacred were human. Soldiers and marines have long been encouraged and trained to regard enemy combatants as inhuman, dehumanizing them through euphemisms such as "soft targets" or "collateral," and to treat them not as selves, but as parts of a corporate homogeneous Other, or as "the enemy," or as "abnormals" in Michel Foucault's wider definition referred to here in chapter 1. A U.S. marine in *The War Orphan* says of his civilian casualties, "They're all gooks.... We have to give the colonel a body count" (R. Anderson 15). It is also too easy, and comfortable, to ignore victims of Third World wars, oppressions, droughts, or disasters, and treat them as mere statistics, if you are not such a victim, or never have been, or cannot feel you might be. In the contemporary world, host cultures like those of the West are often presented with the physical presence of such victims, in the roles of refugees or asylum seekers, some of whom may be the unrecognized victims of the West's exploitation. When the former periphery begins to fold back into the former center like this, people who are usually ignored impact physically on those who would ignore them and destroy the boundaries between a national culture's "inside" and "outside." In the terminology of my first chapter, the inadmissible boundaries encroach on the "normal" center. Those who were out of sight, out of mind, and out of conscience become at best a nuisance to the "host culture." In *The Colonial Present*, Derek Gregory describes the way that victims of contemporary neoimperialism in Afghanistan, Palestine, and Iraq, civilians as well as military, are dehumanized in their oppressors' perception and subsumed into physical concepts of the Other such as "targets" or "body counts," or metaphysical concepts such as "Terror" (62–72). The deaths of civilian victims, for example, are uncounted and unrecorded. Despite protestations to the contrary under international law, seemingly little attempt is made to avoid them. They are not described in the Western press, and they are neither grieved for nor celebrated. They are not perceived in the way that the objects of ethnic hatred or nationalistic enmity are perceived: they are simply null, beyond even the interstitiality of a Michael Jackson or the liminality of "abnormals." Taking a hint from Giorgio Agamben's *Homo Sacer* (1998), Gregory compares the worthlessness of victims of neoimperialism to that of the *homo sacer* of Roman law, a being whom it is worth neither killing nor sparing—it simply does not matter.

The very language in which we construct our world derogates and diminishes the displaced entrants into our richer countries, whether willing or unwilling. Media reports of the ("scandalous") failings of the United Kingdom's Home Office (the government department with responsibility for UK immigration) in the first half of 2006 made it clear that asylum seekers are people who it is a good thing to expel. Certain media reports and power elites typically recourse to divisive discourses of criminality or implied racial pollution to describe such people to try to garner public support for their views or policies.[1] Because of a history of visual as much as verbal imagery, the words "asylum seekers" and "refugees" may connote anything from willful exploiters of liberal regimes to apathetic, helpless, degraded, supine, and useless persons, similar to the way that they are described in Beverley Naidoo's *The Other Side of Truth* as "starving people, with stick-thin children ... [and] dusty bundles ... trying to escape famine and war" (75), who at best deserve our pity.[2] In Rachel Anderson's *The War Orphan*, the war orphan Ha says (or thinks), "Internee. Refugee. Just words.... We're still prisoners.... We were nothings. Units. Numbers on ID cards.... We had no present, and no future, and even the past was beginning to disappear" (116–117). Jamal, the Afghan boy seeking asylum in Australia in Morris Gleitzman's *Boy Overboard*, who becomes the focus of a liberal campaign to free him in Gleitzman's sequel novel, *Girl Underground*, is imprisoned in detention centers, first on an offshore Australian island, and then in the middle of the Australian desert, and, in that second novel, he regards himself and his family as prisoners: "'*They are so sad because the Australian government won't tell us how long our prison sentence is*'" (emphasis in original) (54). "Immigrant" (as distinct from "migrant") may connote an invader of what is popularly believed to be an overcrowded fortress island, or country, that because of them is periodically threatened by crimes and infectious diseases brought in by outsiders, and where any social change is perceived as change for the worse and is associated with population change.[3] For a generation of Britons, "asylum" has connotations of mean and forbidding psychiatric institutions in which people considered to be less than sane were incarcerated for years.

In the children's young adult (YA) novels that are discussed in some detail in this chapter, child characters who are categorized either as asylum seekers or as refugees or "illegal" immigrants—for one reason or another—are shown being treated by members of the "host" society as if they are not fully human; as if they are properly objects of other people's perceptions rather than the subjects of their own perceptions; as if they are Others, not Selves; and as if their identities can be ignored, dismissed, or unrecognized. The way the novels give readers an entry into, a belief in the reality of, and sympathy with those identities is a corrective to the tendency to objectify these subjectivities as outsiders. Only creatures recognized as human can have human rights. A living part of our Western culture which does directly influence thinking about treatment of refugees and asylum seekers is our acceptance of the human rights of people in society. These are asserted in the Universal Declaration of Human Rights and the International Covenants on Human Rights, cited in the United Nations Convention on the Rights of the Child (UNCRC). According to UN General Assembly Document A/RES/44/25, its 61st plenary meeting on 20 November 1989 reaffirms that "children's rights require special protection and call for continuous improvement of the situation of children all over the world, as well as for their development and education in conditions of peace and security." But since the Enlightenment, Western democracies and constitutional monarchies, including the states whose past and present imperial conquests shape the demography and economy of the present world, have granted their citizens some rights only in return for implied duties. 'This assumption is in the French Revolution's 1795 Declaration of the Rights and Duties of Man and the Citizen, the OAS's 1948 American Declaration of the Rights and Duties of Man, and the 1918 Soviet Constitution... .'[4] However, those who cannot perform the duties which earn their rights but may have performed those duties in the past or be expected to perform them in the future are effectively granted rights because of a past or future usefulness to the state which is ascribed to them. So, notionally, in welfare economies, children are subsidized by the state as an investment in their future social usefulness; in nonwelfare economies, they occupy an ambiguous role in relation to their duty to contribute to the local or domestic economy, or in unstable regimes to take up arms in factional warfare, both of which circumstances give rise to incidents of child labor and child soldiers. Such incidents raise wider questions about definitions of "childhood" inscribed in such works as the UNCRC, as a fanciful Western- (and adult-) defined ideal conjectured in the model of industrialized nations that bears little, and in some cases no, relation to the realities of the life experiences of subjects below the age of eighteen years in non-Western, nonwelfare, nondemocratic, sometimes subsistence economies, societies, and regimes whom the United Nations has defined as "children."

For the purpose of the present Convention, a child means every human being below the age of eighteen years, unless under the law applicable to the child, majority is attained earlier.

UNCRC Article 1

Until and unless they are ascribed refugee status, asylum seekers, who include children, have no citizenship, economic means, labor credit or investment value, or relevant cultural capital; cannot work legally, receive state benefits, vote, or easily volunteer for charitable work or forms of national voluntary service; and so on. They cannot perform duties or pay taxes, so they do not even have some of the rights traditionally granted to useful servants and slaves. Refugee status confers little better by way of experience or attitude in the systems of privilege: "A refugee is an unwanted person who makes claims on the humanity of others without having anything to give in return" (R. Anderson 180). In many respects, it is as if the law does not exist for them.[5] So we see the children in the books described and discussed below receiving help as charity but not as their right. Any power or autonomy they achieve is only achieved as a reaction to their initiatives rather than as a proaction by a host state which recognizes their human rights and their entitlement, as children, to the "special care and assistance" cited from the Universal Declaration of Human Rights and specified in the preamble to the UNCRC (Clause 4). The dates of publication of some of the books in this chapter that precede the date of the UNCRC might have explained the abuses that we see being perpetrated on the fictional child asylum seekers portrayed in them, but current reports relating to events like those portrayed in the Gleitzman books, for example, that refer to the state treatment of asylum seekers arriving in Australia,[6] suggest that the practices of abuses of children's human dignity and rights in a policy of detention (referred to as "reception and process-ing") continue to the present day in that country and in other industri-alized countries that are the magnet for asylum-seeking populations. To gain recognition by the authorities, the asylum-seeking children of those books have to defy their cultural and moral expectations and make a nuisance of themselves by running away from a children's home (*Refugee Boy*), accosting a TV presenter (*The Other Side of Truth*), or resorting to "criminal" acts (*Girl Underground*).

> "I was in detention centre about seven months while I haven't done anything, so now, when I got out I got friends but I'm by myself. They asked me, 'where are you from?' I say I'm from Spain because I can't face say that I'm from Afghani-stan … if you come from Afghanistan, if you say, 'I'm from Afghanistan' then it's true that you are the person in deten-tion centre."
>
> **—Teenage boy found to be a refugee**
> *Australia (82)*

> "I believe you [Australians] are nice people, peace seekers, you support unity. If you come to see us behind the fence, think about how you would feel. Are you aware of what happens here? Come and see our life. I wonder whether if the Government of Iran created camp like Woomera* and Australians had seen pictures of it, if they would have given people a visa to come to Australia then."
>
> **—Unaccompanied child refugee, formerly in Woomera**
> *Australia (55)*

> *One of the ten Australian immigration detention centers.

"When a person goes away from his place, he leaves a part of himself behind" (R. Anderson 104). To have been physically removed from their home, especially if that move is involuntary, unaccompanied by loved ones, out of comfort into discomfort, or to a different climate or language environment, is the most drastic sense in which a child is cast as an "outsider." [7] Such a displacement, perhaps even more for a child than an adult, takes away kin, ancestry, habits, memories, and all those material, historical, and political determinants of culture which create and sustain identity. The habits, customs, beliefs, and values, and the familiar contingencies of a child's perception which constitute the defining and protecting envelope of both their selfhood and their sense of outside reality, are all destabilized or destroyed. So children positioned as outsiders may have to reconstruct themselves as people at an age both beyond and before the innocence and maturity which better equip them to do so. The yearning for a true home, gained or regained, is a theme of the discussion of adopted and fostered children in the chapter 5.

This chapter discusses outsider children who are diminished and destabilized and have their identities and self-images threatened because they are refugees, asylum seekers, migrants, or children of an involuntary diaspora. The main examples are from children's YA novels which, though *fictional*, are based on real and/or typical cases known to their authors, and exemplify how such children from former colonies of European or Eastern European powers, previously and preferably ignored by their colonizers, are sidelined, isolated, and minimized in and by liberal Western society. The dislocation they experience, and the consequent devaluation of their legal, moral, and linguistic statuses, all threaten their physical and psychological welfare and their self-esteem, and are seen to be at odds with the declared intentions of these societies—all of whom (with the initial exceptions of Somalia and the United States) are signatories to the UNCRC—to give special consideration and protection to children, irrespectively of their citizenship status, race, or creed. They are works of literature, not case histories, but they do more than exploit for the purposes of entertainment the sorts of distressful situations in which some real children find themselves. Literature at its best is what most convinces us of the realities of other people's identities and selfhoods, so that these novels, responsibly written and attempting authenticity, act as powerful and memorable case histories which are as true as, or truer than, factually accurate ones. They are "proximal" evidence, in the terms of my introduction, to set alongside the "distal" statistics on child-outsiderness. So, although published as literature, and despite postmodernist disavowals and dissolution and decentering of the subject in literature, these novels are no doubt intended to help their relatively privileged young readers to believe in, sympathize with, and even be angry about such children's unnecessary misfortunes. But, however strongly it engages a reader, a book cannot produce such a complete empathy with a fictional subject as the fictional Simon comes to feel for his fictional adopted brother, Ha, in *The War Orphan*, because the emotions that readers experience in engaging with texts arguably are secondary emotions such as pity and anger, not primary sensations like pain. And child readers do not feel the pain of fictional characters even though they believe in them, any more than they get sick when reading about too much hamburger consumption. Nevertheless, the reader feels *for* the characters, if not *as* the characters, and this has been the traditional, liberal, moral argument for fiction, from Matthew Arnold through F. R. Leavis to, most recently, John Carey.

SEEKING ASYLUM

As none of the books is written by a refugee or asylum seeker, and none by a child, each purports to "speak for the subaltern," to use the terminology in which Gayatri Spivak criticizes those who benevolently appropriate the voice of the powerless and thereby unintentionally add to their diminishment and silencing ("Can the Subaltern Speak?" 66–111). While this is a salutary consideration, it can be argued that speaking for them is preferable to their both remaining silent and remaining unnoticed.[8] The justification for writers speaking on behalf of displaced children is well put in the epigraph to Morris Gleitzman's *Boy Overboard*:

Dear Reader

This is a story. It's not about an actual family, it's a story I've made up. But I couldn't have written it without help from people who so kindly told me about their own incredible journeys.

Because I've never been a refugee and I'm not from Afghanistan, I may have got some things wrong. If so, I ask their forgiveness, and yours.

I wrote this story to express my sympathy for children everywhere who have to flee to survive, and my admiration for the adults who embrace them at the end of their journey.

Likewise, Benjamin Zephaniah dedicates his book *Refugee Boy* to two actual refugees, Million and Dereje Hailemariam, and he includes poetry written as if by refugee children:

Dear Mother,
I keep shedding tears,
Even in these my tender years I don't have dreams
I have nightmares,
Dear Mother now I cry;
Dear Britain,
I've found refuge here,
But all of us came from somewhere
And can't simply disappear,
Compassion must be shown. (293)

The Mask We Wear

I wore the mask that kept me veiled
From eyes that stare but do not see
For they look at things invisibly
They see the mask but not the me
And I behind the mask live on still
Made of flesh and bones and not of steel
Emotion packed and spirited
Spit back words to wound and scar those who prey

JALLOW-RUTHERFORD

And Elizabeth Laird claims that she based her novels *Kiss the Dust* and *A Little Piece of Ground*[9] on the experiences of actual Kurdish and Palestinian children. In the preface to the former, she writes, "The people in this book are not real, but their story is like that of thousands who have been forced to run away from Iraq across the Zagros mountains." However, that the children in these novels are fictional products of serious adult writers might explain the paucity of references to child culture in the target books, though the game of football that features in more than one of them, if not ubiquitous, may be sufficiently universal as to count as a genuine global cross-cultural uniter of children from diverse ethnic and cultural backgrounds.

Set in prewar Afghanistan, Morris Gleitzman's *Boy Overboard* raises interesting narratological and generic questions. The first-person, present-tense narration, focalized through the protagonist, Jamal, is a far more deliberate representation of a child's viewpoint than the others to be discussed. Jamal has a penchant for interpreting events in terms of his own interests that are simultaneously amusing and poignant, but it also tells a great deal about the particular worldview from which the imagery derives and into which it feeds. For example, when he sees crowds gathering round a stadium he thinks it is for a football match, when it is in fact for an arraignment and execution of women who have offended the fundamentalist Afghan regime (including his own mother—who is dramatically and somewhat implausibly rescued by his father). When his parents tell him they must leave home at once, he thinks it is because he has broken a window with his football rather than because his mother's secret school has been discovered.

> Jamilla grew up in a country where 40 per cent of women had jobs.... But when the Taliban took over in 1996, she was ordered to go home and live the rest of her life in Purdah [seclusion].... Females accused of adultery, lesbianism or reading a book other than the Koran were shot in the Kabul sports stadium before a howling male mob.
>
> But Jamilla could not accept being reduced to the status of a piece of soft furnishing; she set up a secret school for girls in her home, where she continued to teach them to read and write.
>
> **Hari (37)**

When he sees his father surrounded by aggressive armed men, he thinks it is because he (his father) has a defective brake light. And when he hears of Australian gold mines, he thinks they are land mines made of gold. Jamal is obsessed with football. He announces himself in the book's first sentence—"I'm Manchester United" (Gleitzman, *Boy Overboard* 1)—and his exuberant account frequently uses footballing metaphors: moonlight "almost as bright as Manchester United's stadium" (43), crowds in a refugee camp greater than that for "the World Cup Final" (76), and "United Nations men ... dressed like English Premier League Managers" (85).

More tellingly, Jamal's casual use of militaristic imagery is his unwitting demonstration of the violent and militarized landscape against which he, and other children like him whose lives have been dominated by protracted wars, is normalized. At the beginning of the book, Jamal plays football among land mines and sometimes ruined and sometimes active tanks, with his one-legged friend (who lost his leg to a land mine) and his naughty little sister (whenever she can escape the enforced confinement of females in their houses and hitch up her skirts and join in). He says, "as though an American air strike has hit me in the head" (Gleitzman, *Boy Overboard* 3), and "my heart has a missile attack" (8), and maybe there is a buried reference to missiles in "the ball scuds past his fingers" (5). Such imagery continues through the book: as the truck in which Jamal is hiding is searched, he feels "air-strikes going on inside my chest" (73).

For over half its length—and similar to Elizabeth Laird's *Kiss The Dust*—the book concentrates on the arduous journey made by the refugee child in his family's bid for a safe haven in Australia. These two books are structurally different from the others discussed in more detail below, because their main concern is for the process of the flight from harm while the others are focused instead on their central subjects' experiences once they have arrived in the host country; though a partial exception is *The War Orphan* with its fractured, polyvocal, and disordered impressionistic account of Ha's journey from the resettlement camp to Saigon. Also, *The War Orphan*'s narratological complexity is of a different order from that of the others discussed here. Nevertheless, these other fictional accounts focusing on international displacement of some kind fall within my description of the docu-novel, and are narratologically interesting as a group in their own right: Jamal's story is told in the first person and focalized through him, and the emphasis is on *experience*; others that are told in the third person and focalized through a main character emphasize *events*. So, irrespectively of whether they are focalized through first- or third-person narration, the common characteristic of the docu-novel on this evidence is its emphasis on message and event rather than characterization and feeling. An escape, especially one as epic as Jamal's, is an experience of outsiderness, even though Jamal's devotion to football and to his sister, and his clear vision of Australia as the "promised land," enable him to survive, somewhat implausibly, relatively psychologically unscathed.

According to our experience severe stress and trauma related to illnesses in detainees may manifest as a variety of illnesses and disorders. They include anxieties, depressions, acute stress disorder, post-traumatic stress disorder, and social pathology such as violence, suicide and physical and sexual abuse among the detainees. Factors which lead to such illness and which may be usefully addressed are:

- threats to life and reliving them through current triggers and
- threats to what makes life meaningful, which can be just as important as direct threat to life

Australasian Society for Traumatic Stress Studies

In escaping Afghanistan and attempting to reach Australia, Jamal and his mother, father, and sister endure desperate car drives, border crossings, confinement in hiding places and an overcrowded camp, flying and sailing (both for the first time and both unsafely), storm, piracy, being held to ransom, family separation, and finally arriving at a destination which they first believe to be Australia but is in fact an immigration detention center on an offshore Pacific island. In response to Jamal's question prompted by his bitter disappointment at not being welcomed with open arms and unmitigated joy by his host country, a government official tells Jamal that there has been a reelection of the Australian government which had (correctly, as it turned out) "'thought they'd get more votes by keeping you out'" (Gleitzman, *Boy Overboard* 179). It is the story of thousands of people who flee daily from persecution by oppressive regimes. But any children (or adults for that matter) who have read about and vicariously shared in the plight of these literary children are less likely to anonymize the images they see on TV of crowded, open-topped, wooden boatloads of filthy, malnourished, dehydrated, emaciated, and exhausted people awaiting asylum off the coast of Australia, or film footage of dead Kurds in the wake of the massacre of thousands of them by Saddam Hussein's regime.

"I want to tell you that actually I spent about fifteen nights in the ride to Australia. I was in a small boat if you want to call that a boat, because it was smaller than that, with lots of difficulties. When I saw [we were] getting near Australia I was becoming a bit hopeful. When we passed Darwin I got to the detention centre[;] as soon as I looked at these barbed wires my mind was full of fear. That was the time that I experienced fear."

—**Unaccompanied Afghan boy found to be a refugee**
Australia (55)

I get letters from kids saying, "I see refugees on television and I thought they're a lot of scroungers, but this book really opened my eyes, and I went to the library and I read something else"—and that's great, that's what I really want to do.

Mahamdallie

In contrast with the story of Sade in Naidoo's *The Other Side of Truth* (discussed below), Jamal has a precocious responsibility for his younger sister, who contrasts with Sade's little brother, Femi, in personality as well as sex: little Bibi's irrepressible contentiousness (she is a virtuosa of scatological invective and stone throwing) and immodesty (she beats the boys at football) frequently embarrass and endanger them. Femi, on the other hand, is silent, possibly traumatized by his experiences of witnessing the shooting of their mother by agents of the Nigerian government which had just hung Ken Saro-Wiwa—the bullet that was clearly intended for their politically active journalist father. Femi keeps the loss of his mother and motherland, and his cultural displacement, locked deep inside his disturbed psyche. Like Sade, Jamal suffers a diminishing but refining of the physical tokens of his originating culture. He retains, just, his football ball, a constant source of pride and concern (rescued from under tank tracks and the sea at the quayside) that is used as a token of sharing in the making of friends with other children, and exemplifies once again the symbolism of football as an intercultural reference point and locus of a commonly understood "language": kids who do not speak each other's language know implicitly the language of football, irrespectively also of their cultural differences and divisions. He has learned that, in order to buy their sea tickets at hugely inflated prices from the mavericks who control the boats, his mother has traded the jeweled candlestick which is an heirloom and believed to be an ancestral protective talisman. To the end, his ancestry remains the constant and continuing reference point against which, with increasing meaningfulness, he defines his sense of self. He is descended from brave warriors on his mother's side and patient bakers on his father's, and the valor of warriors and the patience of bakers are the two single characteristics that determine his ability to survive with a sense of pride in self and family the regimes of power that would otherwise silence and annihilate him and erase his history by enforced process and programs of assimilation.

The depressing truth, however, is that in spite of their desire for self-determination, will to succeed, and single-minded ambition to "arrive" such as we see in these narratives, the experiences of self are shaped ultimately by the relations of power and domination, rather than by any individual subjective will, and are an illustration of how these experiences of subjection affect not only their relationships to self but also the responses to them by anyone coming into contact with them in such diminished and diminishing conditions as they are in. So we see how spatial proximity to centers of power is a fundamental determiner of individual cultural identity and self-identity.

The grim [detention] centre ... is a last staging post for failed asylum seekers about to be ejected from Britain.

For Manuel and Antonio, that meant being returned to Angola the next morning, where Manuel's parents had been murdered and his sisters raped and killed. Manual, a political activist ... had lived in fear of being sent home for four years....

Manuel had failed in his efforts to defend his asylum case in person, his pidgin English being no match for his cross-examiners in court, but he understood enough about the British system to know that if his 13-year-old son was an orphan, he would be allowed to stay and finish school.

He wrote one last exhortation: "Be good, son, and do well at school." He then gathered up a bedsheet and walked out of the cell. A little way down the corridor, he was caught on CCTV unwinding the sheet and fixing one end to the stairwell. The other end was tied around his neck....

His father's sacrifice was not in vain. Antonio has been placed in foster care and allowed to stay in Britain, at least until he has finished secondary education.

Elliott and Brennan (16)

Benjamin Zephaniah's *Refugee Boy* is focalized through the protagonist, Alem, but the emphasis is on events rather than character. It is another example of the ways in which a young asylum seeker arrives and survives in a host country as a nonentity who must remake himself and his identity against the odds, and is an effective indicator of the material and legal difficulties that such a young person might endure. Alem's parents are educated people, voluntary peace workers, and Pan-African in their beliefs, but by birth they are Ethiopian and Eritrean respectively. So they are endangered aliens in both countries at the time of the war between Ethiopia and Eritrea.[10] That war drives them from Africa, eventually kills Alem's mother, and has its terrible absurdity represented at the (atypically literary) beginning of the book by a brief scene of violence repeated with the nationalities reversed. The father brings Alem to England and well-meaningly abandons him there—possibly in the mistaken belief that unaccompanied children will have greater rights of protection and easier access to refugee status. But Alem's right to stay is contested. It is further jeopardized when his father rejoins him, then finally secured only when and because his father is killed, so that Alem is officially an orphan—and thus becomes more entitled to the "right to remain." The novel details hardships (as in a children's home and a sordid bedsit), humiliation (it was written at a time when UK asylum seekers did not have the right of other benefit recipients to receive benefits in cash, but were fed via vouchers), fear of arrest, and the unpredictability of passport controls and asylum hearings in which they are only "cases." Alem's story is tragic, but the tragic events that overtake his life are seemingly minimized against his atypically successful ability in asserting his right to be recognized. He is clever, mature beyond his fourteen years, English speaking, and apparently invulnerable physically, with an established and confident self-identity, and he falls among immediate contacts and a relatively benevolent school whose collective understanding and goodwill are a cushion against the law's attempts to diminish him. Like the other children featured in this group of novels, he has many attributes of the "angel child," but he also is an example of a child who can, in the terms of Teresa de Lauretis, be "both interactive and resistant ... participatory and yet distinct" (iii). The novel is undoubtedly intent on presenting refugee children in a positive light and offering hope of success, but it could also be said that the relative ease and seemingly unproblematic process of absorption and acceptance into the host country do not ring true with what is known to be the actual lived experience of asylum-seeking children generally. Almost all Alem's assistance, comfort, and understanding come from the charity of the rainbow coalition of his immediate personal contacts, in which he seems remarkably fortunate, and certainly more fortunate than his parents had been with theirs in Africa. The social worker is sympathetic; a volunteer Refugee Council (with an Ethiopian worker) is tireless in its efforts on his behalf; school is welcoming, as is the (Scottish) hotelier on whom he is abandoned; and he has loving (Irish) foster parents. The multiethnic composition of London is represented in a positive light, and his friends and helpers have an almost diagrammatic representativeness. There is a sympathetic Palestinian refugee and an Indian teacher, his best friend is the child of Chilean refugees, and the supporters who make fluent public speeches and organize a concert and demonstration to oppose the deportation of him and his father include an Ethiopian-born East Londoner and a Rastafarian who claims Ethiopia as his spiritual home. Apart from the almost uncontexted shooting of Alem's father, there is only one serious incident of racist abuse in the book, when, until the police stop them, some youths shout and spit at a demonstration that is being held on behalf of Alem and his father. The effect is to imply that people are benevolent, even if the society which they constitute is not. It is like the paradox of there being institutional racism in institutions made up entirely of people who are not believed to be personally racist by either themselves or others. It also suggests that asylum seekers can cope by their own efforts and the personal kindness of those they meet fortuitously, without achieving or needing the rights that children are otherwise accorded. It may also carry misleading messages to the young readers from the majority communities who are its primary audience that the experience of unaccompanied asylum-seeking children like Alem will have an easy transition into the culture and countries into which they arrive, and obviously cause them to become complacent.

Such extraliterary judgments are not inappropriate for a novel that seems more than most children's YA novels to have more didactic than literary ambitions. It does have some humorous incidents, mostly arising from misunderstandings of English culture, but it also has passages of seemingly narratologically intrusive information used for didactic purpose, such as the following: "Spaghetti was one of Alem's favorite foods. The Italian army invaded Eritrea in 1882, and then in 1935 they entered Ethiopia. Unable to conquer the country, they were soon chased out, but they left behind tanks, unexploded bombs and spaghetti" (Zephaniah, *Refugee Boy* 23).[11]

Its central character is no doubt fictional, or a hybrid of real case histories, but the novel bears all the characteristics of the "docu-novel" in ways that I have described here and in chapter 1, with its emphasis on events and message, rather than character. Although the novel is focalized through Alem's sole viewpoint, the third-person narration is an unusual form of hybrid that mixes the voice and viewpoint we might expect of first-person narration but that reports on, rather than entering, Alem's thoughts. His inner feelings are only hinted at and seem more dominated by his curiosity and intellectual ambition than by any self-doubt or distress at his misfortune or anger at his treatment. His reactions to his parents' deaths are described very much from the outside—an ominous silent period with a desire to be alone, a sudden violent outburst of grief, then a relatively quick recovery. At the same time, it lacks the distance of the "third-person objective view" that would otherwise emphasize Alem's status as an outsider. One effect is that although the novel is effective in representing the external conditions of Alem's legal, social, and economic plight, his inner condition is relatively unexplored. He is a "flat" character, and one wonders if this is the most effective form of narration in which to represent such traumatic experiences as those of unaccompanied asylum-seeking children and young people. Articulate and confident of his own identity, worth, and moral integrity, he is a voracious autodidact (he reads George Orwell's *1984* on Christmas Day), and at school, though he makes friends easily, he "wasn't going to let friendships get in the way [of education]" (Zephaniah, *Refugee Boy* 131). He soon becomes, he tells us in an afterword, "a lover of literature, a budding architect, a friend, a symbol of hope" (290). His headteacher praises him to the school assembly with the words "He values education. Within a very short period of time he has excelled in the classroom, his interest in literature and language is passionate, his quest for knowledge is relentless, and I have never met anyone who has had a bad word to say about his behaviour and attitude" (275). The blurb describes him as "a brave young man who despite all that happens to him, maintains a shining spirit of courage throughout." Throughout this, he is never bullied at school in ways that might otherwise be expected to be the fate of the high school "geek." Readers may be glad for Alem's success. But, as a politics of representation, the image (and the message) appears to be one of success by a rapid process of assimilation into the dominant discourse and idealized Western models, as Alem rapidly transforms from his refugee status to something of an uneasy product of the conflicting social and cultural realities he encounters, which may well be the actual strategy by which the immigrant subject survives and succeeds in the adopted culture that is itself already plural—no longer as the essentialist monocultural subject they might have believed themselves to be, and are believed to be, but as the newly emerged palimpsest subject who bears the imprint of past, present, and future identities into which "outsiderness" as a negative construct effectively dissolves. In the words of Gareth Griffiths, we might well be seeing him "embrac[ing] his hybridised position not as a badge of failure or denigration but as part of that contestational weave of cultures which recent critical theory argues is the inescapable condition of all postmodernist experience" (240). At the same time, he is naïve and benign in the extreme: he cannot understand why children smoke, when practical jokes are played on him he "soon learned that it was nothing personal" (Zephaniah, *Refugee Boy* 131), and when some bigger boys at the children's home steal his food he behaves with calm reason and courage (then runs away). Benign, conformist, and victim—attributes all of the "angel child"—Alem appears to be the colonizer's model subject: superficially at least, he is transmuted into the quintessential young British gentleman, the impeccably moral son of his meek, high-minded father, and one is left to wonder at what cost to his ethnic identity and origins his success has been achieved. One wonders, too, if there is a hint of irony in Zephaniah's description of his character's rapid rise through the ranks of the meritocracy—that appears to have been a far more positive experience than Benjamin Zephaniah himself seems to have enjoyed when he was pitched into East London secondary schools (Zephaniah, "Interview" 10). But there is nothing in this novel to suggest that that is in fact the case. Alem seems the least psychologically threatened of the fictional children discussed in this chapter, despite the tragedy of his displacement and double orphaning. Ironically, it is his father's death which saves him from deportation, apparently out of compassion rather than because of a change in his legal status by being orphaned that would in fact have given him the right to remain. It appears from this novel that the asylum-seeking child has a better chance of being treated as a human when without a parent than with one.

MIGRATING VOICES, CHANGED IDENTITIES

Sade, the twelve-year-old girl at the center of *The Other Side of Truth*, Beverley Naidoo's 2000 Carnegie and Smarties Award winner, also endures an episode of flight from her African country. She, too, is abandoned in England, is rejected by immigration procedures, is fostered, makes friends with other refugee children, and is reunited with her father, all experiences similar to those of Alem. However, the texture of Beverley Naidoo's novel is richer. It is varied not only by exchanges of letters, and an "African" opening, but also by Sade's need to cope with two personal problems apart from all those of being an asylum seeker. One of those problems is that she is accompanied throughout by a younger sibling (a staple relationship of many flight and exile novels for children), who reacts to their ordeal and expresses his grief by retreating into a quasi-autistic and mute state: he becomes "a little stone" (Naidoo 154), outside even his immediate company and foster family. So Sade has to take on a precocious responsibility and selflessness that deprive her of her chance to experience the kind of ideals of childhood to which she would be otherwise exposed, and to grieve: she has adult duties without being accorded either adults', or children's, rights. Thus the boundaries of officially inscribed definitions of childhood, and of what it means to be a child, as conjectured by Western norms, are again brought into sharp focus and are challenged. Sade's trajectory differs from Alem's in the way the telling of her story begins and ends. The novel begins with the shooting of her mother by agents of the Nigerian military government. They object to Sade's father's fearlessly critical journalism. Sade witnesses the shooting, and parts of the description of it are repeated throughout the book, as she remembers the horror, dreams about it, and cherishes her few mementoes of her mother. Like Tara in Elizabeth

Laird's *Kiss the Dust* and Alem of Gleitzman's *Boy Overboard*, Jamal experiences the erosion of possessions, living standards, health, dignity, and independence to become reliant on the kindness of strangers. She is progressively deprived of these mementoes and tokens of her past life and her identity, starting with a little bag sewn by her mother which UK customs slash open in a search for drugs, as if to demonstrate that in entering the United Kingdom, she has lost her right to private property and the right to be presumed innocent. The presumedly innocent child assumes a different coding when he or she is displaced into another and hostile space. She is morally disorientated by a typical transformation of grief into guilt, as she begins to dwell on the (few and trivial) ways she had upset her mother during their life together in Nigeria. At the end of the book, in a conventional if qualified happy ending, Sade's father, like Alem's, arrives in England, is at first imprisoned, then is released and allowed to stay after his children retrace their first nightmare journey through London to doorstep a well-known, liberal TV news presenter who then acts on their behalf.

> Children have long been identified within the international framework of human rights as deserved of special consideration (UDHR Art 25b) because of the nature of childhood, being a time of evolving capabilities, or relative vulnerability to abuse and exploitation, a critical time for survival and development.
>
> **Child Rights Information Network**

> No child shall be subjected to arbitrary or unlawful interference with his or her privacy, family home or correspondence, nor to unlawful attacks on his honour and reputation.
>
> **UNCRC Article 16**

Sade, like Alem, survives to establish a matured identity through her own endurance and determination and through the efforts of others. However, although in some ways *The Other Side of Truth* is a more optimistic narrative than *Refugee Boy*, it is more realistic in its description of the difficulties which Sade and Femi have with everyday life than is *Refugee Boy* in its depiction of Alem's difficulties. Sade and Femi's situation as nonpersons is emphasized when they arrive in England with false names—the first erosion of their identity—only to be abandoned in Victoria Station by the woman who has been paid to pretend they are her children. Trying to find the uncle who should have met them, they have a nightmare quest through London at night, being attacked by a derelict and losing some of their luggage. Sade is constantly cold and ill clad at first, a naturalistic touch but also a metaphor of her dejected, rejected, and denuded condition. They feel they are being criminalized when they have to give fingerprints, and Sade gets an objective view of herself and her brother as "Other"; she is shocked to find that they are thought of as those "refugees" she has always envisaged as "starving people, with stick-thin children … [and] dusty bundles" (Naidoo 75)—becoming themselves a reification of the stereotypes she has anonymized.

Sade too is displaced by her very experience of isolation. She is cut off from all relations, with her mother dead, the phone in their Nigerian home cut off, and the uncle they expected to meet them in the United Kingdom disappeared. It takes two attempts to find her and her brother a satisfactory foster home with a golden-hearted Jamaican couple who finish up lodging and feeding the father, too. Perhaps there is further study to be done in relation to children's literature about the stereotyping of foster parents who are themselves the product of colonial migration, substituting their homes for the loss of the homeland of another generation of displaced persons. Sade approaches school with a justifiable and justified anxiety, is mocked for her name and origins, is prevented by bullies from studying, and is forced into theft by girls who threaten to hurt her little brother. Her self-esteem, self-confidence, and honesty are comprehensively threatened by the people and circumstances she encounters. Her other "personal problem" is the moral dilemma referred to in the book's title. Her father's pride and principle, and what earns the Nigerian government's enmity, are that he always tells the truth. But to get his children out of the country, he has to arrange the deceit of their false passports. He himself later escapes from Nigeria with a false passport, but that deception, which helps him evade a Nigerian prison, is what lands him in a British prison. Sade and Femi have been schooled in honesty, but they are forced to lie about their names in order to escape, and then to lie about their surnames in England to protect their father (which deceit on their part, by another irony, delays their father's finding them when he gets to England). Her experience of being bullied at school forces her into reluctant deceit. She has to lie to a teacher about the homework the bullies have destroyed, and lie to her foster parents and social worker about the theft she has been forced into and the bullying in general. Her father has taught her to stand up to bullies, but it was his standing up to the Nigerian military government bullies that got her mother murdered. Thus we see a gradual erosion of deeply held social and moral values in the face of bullying and oppression, and learn that the "other side of truth" is lying to survive. Her Somalian friend's parents, the shopkeepers from whom she is forced to steal, avoid trouble by accepting abuse and exploitation and emblematize the colonizers' "model" subjects: of generational silently suffering immigrants who may feel that abuse is the price to be paid for the "privilege" of their immigrant status. Grieving Femi only breaks his pathological silence when he is finally able to tell "'Mr Seven O'Clock [News]'" the truth that they have been smuggled. As an illegal immigrant, then, Sade has lost not only her family, the child-centered childhood she once enjoyed as a member of her secure middle-class family, and her self-esteem, but also what she has been taught to believe is her moral integrity in which cause her mother has been killed.

At her mother's death, Sade's voice "was lost somewhere deep inside her" (Naidoo 2), and the newspaper for which her father has written so offensively to the military government is called *Speak*. Language is the vehicle of culture and central to individual identity. There have been wars over what should be the official language of states and regions, and ethnic groups and communities; and acts of genocide or self-immolation committed either in the struggle to retain their language, or by other dominant groups' determination to extinguish it. There has been dissent, sometimes bloody, at the imposition of a language upon local education systems or place names and road signs by state powers or stronger ethnic groups; as a fluid and discursive site, language is nevertheless a site that encodes identity and demarcates the proximity of the speaker to centers of power.[12] Jane Miller, in a study of bilingual and multilingual children, gives examples of where children can find it only proper, or even only possible, to speak of some subjects in one of their languages. One example is of a girl who can only talk and maybe only think about sex in her second, "public" language, and not in her first, "home" language. The centrality of language to identity, and the diminishment, isolation, and humiliation of children placed in a position where their language is devalued, unrecognized, and inoperative, is powerfully dealt with in Elizabeth Lutzeier's *Lost for Words*, in which Aysha, another twelve year old, is brought to London with her mother from a happy life in their extended family in rural Bangladesh. They are brought by a father whom Aysha hardly knows and who turns out to have been far less economically and socially successful in England than they have been led to believe.

The migrations of Alem, Jamal, Sade, and their families were forced: they are true exiles, pushed from, and unable to return to, the countries which were once, but can no longer be, their homes. Aysha's status is different: she and her mother are economic migrants, and their displacement has been forced upon them by the father, who has been pulled to the postimperial center by the hope of wealth, but they discover for themselves what he has not told them: that even in a globalized world economy, wealth is less geographically or socially mobile than the labor which generates it.[13]

The novel is a conventional and often touching story of triumph over adversity, told from the protagonist's viewpoint and often in indirect free discourse (see quotation below). As with the previous story, writing from the viewpoint of the naïve outsider child effectively represents that child's vulnerability. But also, because children are not cultural or political analysts, even third-person narration which is focused through their perception obviates any credible plausible analysis or critique, within the text, of the society from whose culture and customs the child is excluded. And the novel form necessarily emphasizes the differences that the actions of the individuals may make to their lives at the expense of the differences made by the larger political and economic forces which are the subjects of different sorts of written discourse. Aysha's story is of one spirited girl overcoming the diminishments of outsiderness by enforced displacement with little help from anyone except an amiable English schoolgirl, Angela, who, with a dysfunctional home and learning difficulties, is herself represented as an outsider child. To be friends with an illiterate and innumerate English girl who is an object of amusement, pity, and contempt lowers Aysha's esteem with classmates. As a child who herself has only limited and restricted uses of her own native English language, Angela nevertheless gives Aysha the benefit of her knowledge of the underground language of swearing by warning her off the linguistic vulgarities she unwittingly learns from the other students. She gives Aysha a teddy bear, an ironic symbol of the cultural imperialism from which the "teddy bear" has emerged. Then Angela suddenly disappears, having been taken into care, and we are left to wonder what other untold stories of exclusion and abuse lie behind Angela's brief appearance in the narrative. She leaves Aysha with a scrawled address that Aysha cannot read.

Like *Refugee Boy* and *The Other Side of Truth*, the book treats the difficulties encountered by its unsophisticated and unquestioning subject as givens, but it is interesting and important because it does give due weight to the part played by language difference in the inhospitability of the host "culture." If they cannot speak, they cannot represent themselves in mainstream cultural superiority and privileges. If they cannot speak, they exist invisibly in spaces of constructed silence. London can be seen by willing immigrants from ex-colonies, as well as by suburban and provincial British-born teenagers, as a site of emancipation, with its "ability to thrust people from different backgrounds and social spheres into sometimes fractious, sometimes harmonious co-existence ... [in a] restless, clamorous agglomeration of exiles, migrants and refugees from suburbia and the sub-continent alike" (Sandhu 146). The diaspora is by definition an ethnoscape of shifting cultural spaces and disarticulation. But the liberating opportunities of metropoles are usually celebrated and enjoyed by those who have succeeded in them: for those who do not succeed, they can be the cruelest sites of unsupported failure. In London Aysha and her mother are perpetually cold, ill housed, and ill fed; reliant on the reluctant charity of another Bangladeshi family; and virtually abandoned and imprisoned by the father, who is out all day doing or seeking badly paid work. Aysha had hoped that the consolation for her uprooting would be that in England she would go to school as is her right. Despite her immigrant status, she is a child whose rights are protected by and codified in international law, but she is a nonperson in the metropolis: with no right to a home, she has no right to an education; and with no address, she can have no school. Her father has insufficient time and language and cultural knowledge to negotiate a school place for her. She and her mother are expected by her conventional father to live entirely privately, and, having no English at all, they are entirely dependent on him. She suffers from what David Mitchell, although speaking of a fictional upper-class Dominican migrant to the United States in Julia Alvarez's *How the Garcia Girls Lost Their Accents*, calls "loss of cultural privilege in the transition from a social context she understands to one she does not" (173). The disruption of her realities, of her memories, of her surroundings, of her position in an extended family, of her images of her parents, and of her language—these disruptions all threaten her sense of reality, self, and self-worth.

States Parties recognize the right of the child to education, and with a view to achieving this right progressively and on the basis of equal opportunity.

UNCRC Article 28

Although the graphic accounts of life in London are less literary and engaging than the Bangladeshi-set opening, they do graphically detail the ignorance, prejudice, and hostility met by immigrants; the terrors of getting lost and robbed; the racist attacks and even firebombings which they see happen to other immigrants; and—again—the disgustingness of rented rooms, and temporary and bed-and-breakfast accommodation, that are the breeding ground for so much child poverty, social division, criminality, and abuse. In one of the last of these squalid bedsits, they briefly have the company of another, widowed, Bangladeshi woman who can both talk to them and also, because she has some English, give them some support and protection. Like so many of their first acquaintances, she disappears, a motif that emphasizes the inconsequence of immigrant identity and personhood. Essentially homeless, even when they do have accommodation, they cannot establish or expect a network of family, friends, and acquaintances.

With her intelligence, adaptability, and energy, Aysha slowly builds a life for herself and her mother, albeit a diminished one. She accommodates to the hostile society, and by the end of the book has aspirations to succeed in it. Unknown to her father, Aysha goes shopping and begins to learn some English words. Later, she takes her mother with her, and, when they are placed in a "hotel"—another squalid single room from which they are excluded between ten a.m. and five p.m.—they learn to keep warm in big shops and the library, where there are some books in Bengali. Like so many of the other narratives of displacement in this chapter, we have no reason to suspect that because this account of the diminished circumstances of an immigrant family, and the loss of cultural rights, recognition, and heritage that comes with immigration, is fictional, it does not have a corresponding reality.

On 6 July 1999, Victoria and Kouao moved into his [Manning's] flat at 267 Somerset Gardens. The flat was really no more than a small bedsit. There was a separate bathroom and kitchen area, but only one room for all three people to sleep in. The bedsit contained two sofa beds. Manning said Victoria slept on one of them, and he and Kouao slept on the other. This arrangement continued until October, when Victoria's sofa bed was thrown out and she began to spend her nights in the bathroom.

Laming (3.28)

Almost half of all black Caribbean children in Britain live in poverty, but the situation is even worse for Bangladeshi and Pakistani children. 61% of children in these groups live in the most acute poverty, in households whose income is in the bottom fifth.

Holloway

When the humiliating search for a school for Aysha succeeds, she, who had been famed in Bangladesh for her volubility and reading skills, is classified as having "NO LANGUAGE." At her first school, she is unable to demonstrate or use her gift for math because she does not understand the verbal instructions. She is even mocked for her origins and accent (in Bengali) by a more established and Anglicized girl who is also of Bangladeshi origin. Because she can only communicate in Bengali in the intimacy of her nuclear family, her very mother tongue is diminished:

> She was having to make her own words, to remake her language, her very own language, out of the two languages that other people had thrown at her. She was remaking her own world. She could never go back to Bangladesh for good. She had two languages and she didn't quite belong in either of them. And she had two homes, both places where she didn't quite belong. (Lutzeier, *Lost for Words* 137)

As Aysha adapts to England, English, and English schools, she develops, as do most immigrant children who grow up partly outside the home, a social identity at odds with her home identity and culture. Similarly to the way that Tara in *Kiss the Dust* offends her traditional grandmother's expectations of a young woman by not wearing a chador, for example, Aysha begins to fall foul of the expectations which her father and other Bangladeshis have of a young woman such as she is becoming. It is as if in the threatening alien environment of their diaspora, perhaps exhibiting the "group contrast effect" (Harris 91), the men recreate a nostalgically simplistic, conservative, unchanging, and unadapting version of the values which were shaped by the different social and material circumstances of a different location. She meets her salvation in a Bangladeshi woman doctor, whom, with the doctor's approval, she adopts as a role model. Because Aysha is intelligent and resilient, and sustained by her ambition to emulate the doctor, she eventually negotiates all of the ostracism, being ignored, what becomes disabling nostalgia for Bangladesh (her beloved grandfather is now dead), and her father's unwelcome expectations. She survives the symmetric threats to her self-esteem from the two contradictory cultures she is suspended between. Because Aysha has been seen with a man (she helped a man with learning difficulties over the road to the Day Centre), her father threatens to send his womenfolk back to Bangladesh. To their own surprise, both Aysha and her mother resist, because each can now imagine an improved and preferable life and acceptable identity for themselves in England. The novel ends with a new school term and a confident Aysha taking a new girl under her wing, another Bangladeshi with "NO LANGUAGE." But, once again, the story is of paradigmatic optimism and success via dogged refusal to be subsumed into the inhospitable system that would exclude, silence, and erase their existence and that tells us nothing of the thousands who are ground down by the poverty and daily grind of their experiences of being immigrant, or refugee or asylum seekers, and who do not beat the system but simply despair.

The outsider children at the centers of all these novels could be disparaged as "too good to ring true"—and so they are: they do no wrong that they are not forced into, and there is no mention of pop music, or of play other than football, and little or no narration of the kinds of interiority that would render them credible. They are young people who would never be called "youths," but rather they are thoughtful, amenable, sensitive, solitary, self-determined, self-motivated young people such as Terry Eagleton claimed are the intended products, as well as readers, of the "respectable" children's literature such as is endorsed by awards, teachers' recommendations, academic discussions such as this book, and the "adults … looking over the shoulder of the child as it reads" (4–7). The identities of the protagonists, though bruised and matured in Sade's case, and transformed in Aysha's, come through as essences of their personalities, rather than entirely as the complex, changing, protean sets of reactions and interactions that characterize the identities of real people. There is a problem in this, then, of the genre itself being an agent of the dominant center, despite the obvious intratextual attempts by the genre's authors to critique and deconstruct the center and to expose the plight of those who by becoming so dispossessed and displaced from their former centers of ethnicity and identity are positioned in relation to it as voiceless and powerless.

In all of these narratives, children displaced from their homes and homelands are seen to have reduced and weakened rights in spite of the arsenal of international law that is designed specifically to strengthen and protect the rights of the child. Their self-defining links with their cultural origins—kinship, language, and values—are stretched and broken, and their cultural identities are seen to be either hybridized or subjugated beneath a veneer of others' identities, which they either aspire to or have thrust upon them in the bid to survive the transition. Terry Goldie might describe it as "a process of indiginization" (232) borne of the necessity to belong. More precisely, it disturbs and displaces the centrist discourses of "ethnicity" that situate refugees, asylum seekers, and immigrants *as* "outside" and polarized into the "savage" and the "civilised" mind (Petersen and Rutherford 185). The message of hope that the reader might take from these narratives of outsiderness, if there is one, is the idea of the palimpsest: of cultural and ethnic identities not as monoliths but comprising histories of cultural superimpositions eroding the very idea of essentialist discourses that would dictate, determine, and command a center of dominance to be aspired to or assimilated into.

The child shall be registered immediately after birth and shall have the right from birth to a name, the right to acquire a nationality and, as far as possible, the right to know and be cared for by his parents.

UNCRC Article 7

3

ERASED

In 2005, right outside of London's National Gallery and in the shadow of the one-armed admiral of *Nelson's Column* in Trafalgar Square, the sculptor Marc Quinn installed on the "Fourth Plinth"[1] a sculpted torso of an armless, pregnant, naked woman; and it caused a furor of debate as good people wrestled to justify, deny, or contain their repugnance at being confronted with such a sight in one of London's main streets, nearby one of its major centers of Art.

One of the differences between the armless, naked woman on the plinth and another sculpture in the public domain—the armless, naked Venus de Milo—is that the former was fashioned from a real-life model (Alison Lapper, who was born with shortened arms as a consequence of her mother's taking the pregnancy drug thalidomide) and the latter was born of the classical imagination with only an aesthetic relation to any real woman; but, like the former, Venus de Milo's arms were shortened as a result of historical accident. The former, though fashioned in white marble like the Venus de Milo, is a protuberant body, while the latter is a classical, smooth-lined, fissure-free body. The former disturbed sensibilities, and the latter elevates them. Alison Lapper said of her sculpted image, "I regard it as a modern tribute to femininity, disability and motherhood. It is so rare to see disability in everyday life—let alone naked, pregnant and proud" ("Fourth Plinth").

So, where are all those disabled bodies from everyday life that, as Lapper herself must know from her own experiences, are rarely seen in public? And how come disability becomes remarkable, enters into the public discourse and consciousness, and startles the sensibilities only when it is placed on a plinth in the middle of a London street and experienced by many as an object of discomfort and unease? Could it possibly be that the dismembered sculpture's relational position in space—on show, looked at, defiant, and in this case reproductive—signifies differently and, more to the point, more threateningly than the normally occluded spaces that disabled bodies more usually occupy, just outside the line of vision of the averted gaze and conjectured as passive, retreating, inactive, dependent, and powerless? Or was the sculpture's appearance on the plinth a violation of the normative public spaces mapped out for those bodies that aspire to the Lacanian fantasy of wholeness in their postmirror phase development—of which the image of dismemberment is a too stark reminder of the fine and fragile division between their own specular image of completion and the ever present threat of bodily disintegration and chaos (Lacan 5)?

In Maurice Merleau-Ponty's view, the subject discovers its own visibility through the gaze of another (143); and in Michel Foucault's view, the body has significance only when it is either powerful or economically useful (*Discipline and Punish* 25–26). Embodiment has become a sociopolitical statement in Western consciousness, and from the moment of its birth the body of the child is in training, through sets of overt and covert systems of regulation, surveillance, coercion, and practices, toward an endpoint of socially prescribed perfection designed to maximize the body's power, use value, and function in the world within these sets of prescriptions.

Debates about what exactly the body is are as extensive, rich, and varied, and as fluid and flexible and well trodden, as debates about what the child is.[2] And, as with the child, they very often seek to pin down the body to singular, or at best binary, definitions, or to refute the attempt to pin it down. Here, however, the strands of the debate about childhood, and the strands of debates about the body, meet in the body of the child, but are not necessarily doubly complicated by the fact of their coalescence. Criticism relating to the body of the child, as with that relating to bodies per se, is still located in the "Self" (or mind, or identity) versus the materiality of the "body"; it is about the relations between "embodiment" and experience—and whether or not the idea of embodiment successfully expresses the dual aspects of bodily inscriptions as both *Leib* and *Körper* (denoting the inner body and outer body; Leder 1–18; Ots 116–136). They are about constructivism and essentialism, and about the child's body as product or process, as subject or object, as actor or acted upon, and as performance or inscription. Each one of these debates is a thesis in its own right, and all of them hover around the perennial return to the issue of "Cartesian dualism," that is, this split between body and mind, between inner and outer Self. But what seems to be an inescapable point of return, and is especially relevant to these narratives of erasure in this chapter, is the particular relation of the body to the world, and of the body *in* the world as a *determiner* of meanings and experience, "the condition through which it is possible to have relations with objects in the world" (Fraser and Greco 44). Put another way, the body as a semiotic system is "successful" and is determined in the degree to which it negotiates the complex sets of encodings and decodings prescribed by, in, and for the corporeal training. It is difficult to argue therefore for the separation between body, mind, and experience, or between these and the question of the Self. The idea of "embodiment" to which these particular sets of arguments aspire is an interestingly fluid concept in the debates about corporeal definitions in which the body is conceived as neither essentialist nor constructivist but as continuous dialectical production. The child as embodiment is "performative" in Judith Butler's definition, not only in relation to questions of gender and sexuality on which her thesis focuses and which will be revisited later in this chapter in consideration of Shyam Selvaduria's *Funny Boy*, but also in relation to its performance in social spaces generally that, in turn, determine how the individual body is *permitted* to perform, or not, in accordance with its power position in the hierarchical schemas of corporeal values.

This chapter focuses on narratives of child and young adult bodies that are erased from the "gaze" because they fail to signify in what Kroker and Kroker describe as the "fantastic simulacra of body rhetorics" (22), and because the lens of prescribed normativity *is* the norm. They are erased—actually or figuratively—by being physically disfigured, as in Robert Cormier's *Heroes* (1998) and Benjamin Zephaniah's *Face* (1999). Both of these narratives are about young boys with recently mutilated faces. Or they are erased because they are ignored, as in Jacqueline Wilson's *The Illustrated Mum* (2000) about the impoverished life of two sisters in the shadow of their manic-depressive mother who is addicted to tattooing herself: tattoos become the ultimate expression of the aestheticized body as inscribed surface for this mother and function as both performance and erasure, in which process the two girls are inexorably caught up and subordinated. Or they are erased because they are unable to effectively communicate, as in Mark Haddon's *The Curious Incident of the Dog in the Night-time* (2004) about the existential and subjective effects of Asperger's syndrome on the fifteen-year-old character Christopher, whose mind-body mechanisms disconnect and collapse into what Christopher himself aptly describes as "white noise" (8) and as "the crash," as in "CTRL + ALT + DEL, and shutting down programs and turning the computer off and rebooting so that I can remember what I am doing and where I am meant to be going" (178). It is a physical expression and symptom of his autism that the Krokers might describe as "panic noise," because Christopher's inability to synthesize and filter his sensory experiences affects him equally and as profoundly as the phenomenon of "information over-load" affects the postmodern subject of their thesis. Or they are erased by being shamed, as in Selvadurai's *Funny Boy* (2004), set in 1970s Sri Lanka, about the boy character, Arjie, who is ostracized by his family when they recognize and react against Arjie's early-childhood predilections for female company and clothing. Like some of the other bodily inscriptions that have so far featured in this work, these children's and young adults' bodies are figured as *projections* of late postmodernity's existential crisis as "the enemy without," but they also function in the narrative as "the enemy within": as the *introjection* of all that is disavowed by the dominant rhetoric of the social body and is hidden from view or silenced.[3] And although a recently liberal renaissance has accorded them a modicum of voice and visibility, such bodies as these still struggle for expression, representation, recognition, and understanding, and to materialize—as the Alison Lapper comment quoted above bears witness. But, as Jonathan Katz points out in his essay "Dismembership" (which title is most surely apposite to the bodies under erasure that are in focus here), silencing does not imply silence! Katz goes on to say, "Indeed, what silence permits is the emergence of other meanings and readings that evade the grip of orthodoxy or authority. Silence opens up the process of artistic signification to alternative or 'other' purposes" (175). We might equally apply the same sentiment to the issue of erasure: that it does not necessarily, in this conjecture, imply invisibility. It is the return to the "queered" bodies discussed in chapter 1 here: of bodies that, as Katz says, "engage against the grain of our knowledges" (181). They shift the ground and break open the hegemony on which the binary systems of knowing depend. Jacques Derrida would class them as the "undecidables" (Spivak, "Translator's Preface" lxxvii) because "they operate like ball-bearings in a binary system, overturning first in this direction, and then in that, so as to keep the binary itself from being re-established" (quoted in Katz 181).

> The adults talked about a healthy diet, taking exercise, not smoking, drinking alcohol in moderation, reducing stress, and having a happy and healthy environment. In their interviews the children drew (lots of) fruit and vegetables, and pictures of bodies swimming and generally doing physical activity. The older the child the better able s/he became at identifying what was currently thought to be good or bad for health.
>
> **Backett-Milburn (81)**

Anne Becker points out that the self-disciplined body—as distinct from Foucault's "disciplined" body and as part of the difference between agency and being acted upon—carries the most kudos in the world because it is the outward mark of inner self-regulation and self-control (101). With it comes the ability to exercise power over others, and also the ability to control the social spaces that these kinds of regulated bodies occupy. This may be one explanation of why slender, groomed, adorned, fit bodies, kept intact by regimes of body management, are the preferred model of perfection in Western sensibilities, because they are the medium through which control is conveyed and exercised in frameworks of discipline and regulation. Children are in training to aspire to the fit body image through all manner of private and public regulatory agencies. The point is that the "successful" body is encoded in sets of benchmarked orthodoxies that sanction conformity and pathologize other modes of behavior and values then deemed to be deviant or disordered. Subjectivities are not only, then, embodied; they also are encoded in and by the bodies they occupy through these predetermining parameters that confer or erase the power to perform, and to influence or erase individual identity. In contrast, indiscipline is located in uncontrolled, "oozing," "leaky," indeterminate, protuberant, and incomplete bodies that threaten the stability and closure upon which the regimes of regulation rely.[4] So the unfit, mobile, "overweight," uncoordinated, heterotopic body, like that of the developing child, and bodies that are deemed to be incomplete or dysfunctional by being, for example, dismembered or disabled, are rendered undesirable, improper even, and unwanted. They occupy a minor role, are often invisible, or are erased in the scopic and performative system of values. They are often associated or synonymous with unruliness and disorder. It is this latter category of bodily inscription and representation that is in focus here, and the fantasies of otherness they encode.

We could argue that all children so defined occupy such a space; that childhood is by definition the systematically differentiated position of disorder in its condition of mobility, unfixedness, and the kind of bodily indiscipline that accompanies the childhood necessity for play, for example, by its not having fully negotiated the rules of social engagement, or because "the child" may not yet be fully able to take full control of its gangling, ever changing body and behaviors. The younger the child, the less likely they are to participate in adult and, we should remind ourselves, Western-defined, social-class-oriented prescriptions toward bodily perfection. Thus, so long as the conditions of childhood as they are and have been so defined endure, the ideal body of the child in these senses is continuously in process toward achieving greater control to become more powerful. Inevitably, many will fall short of the ideal. It is not so much that children are erased physically from this milieu of orderliness and control, but that their opportunities to occupy positions of power in the systems of knowledge that produce the meanings and definitions are delimited by their temporal immaturity and inexperience. The plethora of policy documents, some of which are documented in this work, that lay down the conditions and protectionisms for "the child" in public, private, and social spaces is evidence of the collective child's relative absence of agency in that process. Children are social actors—are performative—then, only in the extent and degree to which they are *able* to properly subscribe to the modes of specification and institutional structurings that dictate and proscribe their embodied childly behavior; and in the degree to which they may be permitted to change the base rules that define them both *as* children and as bodies in training. Such relations of domination to subordination become ever more complicated when the embodied child is perceived to be not fully engaging the bodily spaces of childhood that have been mapped out for it, or where the training is seen to be ineffectual, to have failed, or to be inapplicable: as in matters of disability, dismemberment or disfigurement, or what is perceived to be sexual deviance—the terms themselves are conjectured on the basis of binary inscriptions marking out the negative spaces excluded from the domain of the normal body and gaze, and Grosz points out that such a conception has "no choice but to cast those different enough from the definition ... into the arena of the pre, proto- or non-human" (Grosz, *Space* 211).

As the children of the commune, our role was to run free, to be uninhibited, to say yes, to look beautiful, innocent, uncorrupted. For our hair to billow out in the wind as we ran. But some of us were not always like that.

Guest* (108)

* From *My Life in Orange*, an autobiographical memoir and a tale of childhood isolation, misery, and neglect in the shadow of his mother's seeking "heaven on earth" in the 1980s "guru" Bhagwan communes.

ENCODING AND DECODING BODY AND VISIBILITY

This apparent inability to successfully process, internalize, reproduce, and interpret complex codings, encodings, and decodings is what motivates the narrative of Mark Haddon's *The Curious Incident of the Dog in the Night-time*, focusing on the autistic character, Christopher, whom Haddon situates metafictionally in the first-person narrative that is filtered through Christopher's sensibilities: about the story he is writing about himself, and the curious incident of the dead dog. It is a "murder mystery novel" (Haddon 5), marked out in prime-numbered chapters because, Christopher tells us, the mathematical patterns of prime numbers remind him of life: "Prime numbers are what is left when you have taken all the patterns away ... they are very logical but you could never work out the rules" (15). An entire system and spectrum of semiosis are brought into the frame to produce an alternative mind-bodyscape that is entirely internally consistent and logical within Christopher's own unrelentingly literal frames of reference. They affect and determine his bodily positionings in and responses to the world, as well as signify his behaviors back *into* the world in ways that render him continually to be misread, misunderstood, and misconstrued by those adults he comes into daily contact with: as alien, in fact, through the lens of "normative" inscriptions through which they gaze on him. In common with some other children with Asperger's syndrome, Christopher is a mathematical genius; he knows every fact there is to know about the intricate patterning of math, and the physical universe; he is good at "chess and maths and logic" (178), the irony being that, for Christopher, logic is an inappropriate and intransigent tool through which to "read" the complexities of everybody else's everyday lives and embodied messages that the narrative reveals to be anything but logical in his perceptions.

He has learned a great deal about a great many other subjects, and he has received exemplary training in the codes of social behavior from those who have care of him. These social trainers include his parents and his exemplary mentor, Siobhan, who has the knack of explaining the world to Christopher like no other human being he comes into contact with—though she functions as an absent presence in the narrative and never comes into it directly. He knows, for example, that he must always tell the truth, but he knows also that this rule is not always uniformly applied to particular situations, such as:

> you are not allowed to tell old people that they are old and you are not allowed to tell people if they smell funny, or if a grown-up has made a fart. You are not allowed to say, "I don't like you," unless that person has been horrible to you. (60)

He knows about "stranger danger" (45); but everyone is a stranger if, like Christopher, you don't like people you have never met before (45). He learns every single detail of his life by rote and is wholly incapable of reasoning the transferability of the rules to situations other than those he has learned by heart. Equally, he knows the literal facts of metaphor and rhetoric, but has no understanding of their figurative import, positioning them on a par with lies "because a pig is not like a day and people do not have skeletons in their cupboards" (20). Christopher has been taught to live by the rules—of truth, of loyalty, of respect, and of fair play—and to keep his promises. He is quite literally a model of success regarding his ability to learn the social rules of engagement. By any other criteria, he would rightfully have earned a prestigious bodily space in the power and knowledge systems in which he has been trained, but his being on the spectrum of autism marks him out as different and powerless. He is not entirely powerless, however, because the insidious irony of his autism means that, in practice, he is able to exercise absolute control over those others who are charged with overseeing his behavior: a lethal cocktail of his dependency versus their exasperation; his absolute intractability versus their anger, frustration, and irritation; and his single-minded pursuit of an idea—such as to find out who killed Wellington the dog—versus adult attempts to prevent him from getting to the truth of the matter. It produces a catalogue of expletives, bewilderment, and bemusement, and leaves in its wake a devastating trail of wrecked relationships and lives. So, those who would be powerful in the normative systems are effectively neutralized by this character who unwittingly usurps the codes of social engagement in a social hierarchy in which his psycho-physical status has been inscribed as marginal, and is an example of the emergence of alternative meanings when the orthodoxies of power are overturned by an otherwise silenced and powerless "Other."

Through the character of Christopher, the gaze of the erased is rerouted to scrutinize the matrices of normativity and their distantiating effects in the systems of representation; and these systems are found wanting. Those adults who, since his birth, have worked to inculcate the rules of social engagement into Christopher's addled mind—as mentioned, of fair play, truthfulness, consideration for other people's feelings, nonviolence, and all the other codes that define the normalcy to which he has so painfully tried and failed to aspire—are exposed as foppery when Christopher discovers that those "Others" who dictate the rules do not even remotely subscribe to them themselves. Through his own research and observations, he establishes that his father was the person who had murdered Mrs. Shears' dog, Wellington, with the pitchfork found at the scene of the crime of which Christopher himself had at first been accused. His father had lied to him that his mother was dead. His mother has in fact deserted them both to live in London with Mr. Shears, with whom she has been having a long-standing affair. Christopher discovers this fact when he finds the forty-three letters his mother has sent to him since she eloped with Mr. Shears, hidden in a box in his father's bedroom. His father had snatched from him and hidden the book Christopher had been writing to solve the mystery of the curious incident of the dead dog: "the bloody dog," his father had kept calling it. The grown-ups shout at him, threaten him, and betray him; his father punches him in anger; and his mother drags him from his home with his father to live in a cheerless bedsit with shared bathroom facilities.

When Mr. Shears, drunk, invades his bedroom at the London apartment that he now shares with Christopher's mother, he curses into the half-awake Christopher's ear:

> You think you're so fucking clever, don't you? Don't you ever, ever think about other people for one second, eh? Well I bet you're really pleased with yourself now, aren't you? (Haddon 252)

Christopher, clearly, is singularly unclever about the rules of this particular social game requiring the kinds of self-reflexive capacities that Mr. Shears is equally unable to subscribe to but that he projects onto Christopher. Throughout all this befuddling morass of contradictions, Christopher is slowly beginning to realize that the adults who police his autism-induced behavioral deficiencies are demonstratively as unclever as he at subscribing to the rules they would impose upon him, and this is the basis on which the narrative disrupts and reveals unstable meanings embedded in the discursive rules of normativity through which these now intriguingly Othered "Others" "appear" in the world. Another example of the bewildering inconsistencies and contradictions embedded in the rules comes when his father tries to convince Christopher that he loves him dearly soon after the incident in which he has struck Christopher in his fit of anger, and after Christopher has discovered the hidden letters from his mother, and after his father has confiscated Christopher's book.

> I love you very much, Christopher. Don't ever forget that. I know I lose my rag occasionally. I know I get angry. I know I shout. And I know I shouldn't. But I only do it because I worry about you, because I don't want to see you getting into trouble, because I don't want you to get hurt. Do you understand? (108)

And he does! But such are the mysteries of the codes of love that Christopher comprehensively fails to grasp them.

In one way or another, all the narratives in this section expose the fragility and instability of the codes and structures upon which the socially regulated norms of bodily behavior function. The gaze of the otherwise erased is refocused to disrupt, scrutinize, and reveal those negative spaces of "Otherness" as a legitimate forum from which to interrogate so-called normative values.

Dr. Rowan Williams [Archbishop of Canterbury] says a new generation of young parents fail to offer the right example to their children who, in turn, are becoming "infant adults." It is understood that the Archbishop fears we are creating a society where adults, having not been properly cared for as children, are themselves unable to bring up their own offspring. The Children's society is concerned about a climate of 'fear and confusion' amongst young people. It points to higher levels of depression and mental illness in the country, than elsewhere in the European Union.

Watson

In Jacqueline Wilson's *The Illustrated Mum*, the focus is on the children's mother, Marigold, through the eyes of her daughter, Dolphin. Marigold behaves like a child and is inadequate by every normal standard or criterion of motherly performance, including her own, but, exceptionally, not Dolphin's. Despite all the petty injustices and acts of cruelty that Marigold perpetrates on Dolphin and her older sister, Star, and despite her thoughtless, feckless, self-possessed, self-obsessed, self-absorbed, but beguiling behavior, Dolphin worships her mother, Marigold:

> "You're the best ever mum. Please don't cry again. You'll make your eyes go all red." (Wilson 10)
> "I know sometimes, well, I act a bit wild and screw up. But would you say I'm a really bad mother?"
> "No, of course not, You're a lovely mother." (52)
> "I love you, Marigold," I said, putting my arm round her slim waist.
> "I love you too, Dolly Dolphin," she said, and she hugged me close. (59)

The three of them live on a knife-edge of poverty, near starvation, and unpredictability, and the girls exist in a permanent state of highly charged anxiety as they await their mother's next outrageous performance—either by her neglect of them (she stays out all night without thinking to tell her daughters where she has gone or when she will be back) or by her overindulgence (she binges them on masses of her homemade cakes to assuage her guilt at being a self-confessedly neglectful and inadequate mother, using money they do not have while the girls traipse around in threadbare but eccentrically glamorous clothing and worn-out shoes that she fails to see). Dolphin is mocked, sidelined, bullied in school, and, typically of many other "Othered" subjects who inhabit the negative spaces of outsiderness, pathologized in terms of dirt, filth, and disease: "I could catch a terrible disease off her. She's *disgusting* [original italics]" (33).

If the flip side of erasure is performance, then Marigold is the spectacle and her two daughters are cast in the role of the passive, invisible, and insignificant spectators of her show. The narrative vacillates across these points of appearance and erasure, functioning like Derrida's proverbial ball bearing, overturning the fixed points of the binary and calling them into question. Marigold is clinically sick, and her behavior is manic—moving between high points of hysterical exuberance and excess through all the shades of emotions into the slough of despond and despair. She is an uncanny exaggeration of a great many other mothers, not classed as manic or depressive, who may perform their daily lives on this spectrum of high point–low point of emotion and neglect and who may, or may not, feel themselves to be inadequate by the standards exacted by prescribed motherhood. And though she breaks all the maternal rules that would render her beyond the pale and position her as not even a "good enough" mother by any normative measures, there is a tenacity of warmth and love between Marigold and her two daughters that endures through it all and is the disruptive return gaze that destabilizes the easy rush to condemn her.

> Brushing my hair, folding my clothes, taking care of myself—all the things I used to do with my mother—now made me feel sad. I began to avoid doing them.… I began to run everywhere on tiptoes. I refused to care for myself. My nails grew long; my hair was unkempt. When I wet the bed, I pretended I hadn't. When I was discovered, I refused to change the sheets. I refused to dance, refused to sing, refused to celebrate.
>
> **Guest (108–109)**

> I would walk through the huge, long, low marquees, running my eyes along the hundreds of benches, pushing my way through the crowds and thousands of sannyasins arriving for their evening meal, looking down each row under the huge green canvas canopy. After dark, much of my time at the Ranch was spent wandering through those crowds looking for my mother. There were times when evening drew in, I felt I had spent my whole life on tiptoes, looking for my mother in a darkening crowd.
>
> **Guest (196)**

> A group of 110 eminent teachers, psychologists, children's authors and other experts have written to a newspaper urging the Government to act, warning that the demands and restrictions of the modern world are denying children the opportunity to grow up at their own pace. The group includes Jacqueline Wilson, the children's laureate, Philip Pullman, a celebrated writer, Baroness Susan Greenfield, the director of the Royal Institution and Dr Penelope Leach, a child care expert. They write: "We are deeply concerned at the escalating incidence of childhood depression and children's behavioural and developmental conditions."
>
> **"Children Are Being Poisoned by Modern Life"**

Marigold confirms her identity and causes herself to appear as both subject and object through her bodily inscriptions that are a simultaneous act of self-definition and self-immolation, pleasure and pain. Each of them is a mini-narrative of her life that she reads and rereads and retells like a storybook of events that confirm her existence in the world and to herself, and through which she separates out and fetishizes the different bits of her body parts; and, as if to emphasize the point, these are also the illustrated chapter headings of the book: for example, "Cross," "Daisy Chain," "Micky/Heart," "Star," "Marigold," and "Serpent." When Dolphin and, eventually, Star end up "in care," they find themselves in the bosom of a jolly earth mother who instantly dispels all their accumulated fears of separation from their own mother that have bound them together as a "family" through thick and thin. But it comes at the cost of Marigold's ultimate attempt to erase herself out of existence completely in a harrowing scene in which Dolphin finds her, naked, in the bathroom having painted herself from head to toe in white paint (and in this context, her attempt to erase herself in white is an eerily paradoxical reminder of the defiant *appearance* of the white sculpted body of Alison Lapper):

> I couldn't believe what I saw. She was white all over. Even part of her hair. Her neck, her arms, her bare body, her legs. She'd painted herself white with the gloss paint. There were frantic white splotches all over her body covering each and every tattoo, although the larger darker ones showed through her new white skin like veins.
>
> I put out my hand to touch her, to see if it was real.
>
> "No. Don't. Not dry yet," said Marigold. "Not dry. Wet. So I can't sit down. I can't lie down. I can't. But that's OK. It will dry and so will I. And then I'll be right. I'll be white. I'll be a good mother and a good lover, and Micky will bring Star back and we'll be together for ever and ever, a family, my family and it will be all right, it will, it will, it will." (Wilson 158)

She has made herself into a freak spectacle. But, at the same time, by this act of attempting to obliterate her tattoos that are the collective narrative of her life and focus of self-definition, she also has obliterated her performance of self. The moment of her self-erasure, however, becomes the moment of her own redemption when she is whisked off for medical treatment in a state hospital, and Dolphin and Star are taken into temporary foster care until such time as Marigold has responded to her treatment. By this time, both of the girls have found their respective fathers—Mick and Michael—but their ambition to achieve their fantasy of a two-parent, happy family unit proves to be elusive in practice. The one constant in their life is to be Marigold: "It didn't matter if she was mad or bad. She belonged to us and we belonged to her" (Wilson 223).

So, Jacqueline Wilson reinstalls the status of motherhood in the sphere of filial love through the uncritical viewpoint of the child while, at the same time, the legitimacy of Marigold's love for her children would be questioned by the censorious voice and viewpoint of the establishment that would condemn her to the same space of negativity to which Marigold has condemned herself. It is a difficult and controversial point of departure about which there are as many questions as there are answers. However, to have interrogated the profile of "appropriate" motherhood from this subjective position of the child is to provoke and disturb the ground that has been staked out by the boundary markers of ideal motherhood to which Marigold aspires but judges herself to have failed.

This said, there comes an optimum point along this continuum of love and neglect when the establishment intervenes in the filial view of parental "normalcy" for the perceived long-term good of the child, who is otherwise powerless and voiceless in the process. The care, concern, and high degree of agency accorded to Dolphin and Star by the welfare worker who eventually places them in state care are exemplary of its kind. But it does not beggar belief that the very real experiences of poverty, neglect, and emotional traumas that Dolphin and Star endured went unseen by the social institutions that are set up to police the boundaries of neglect and deprivation, not least because the children themselves were practiced in the art of evasion and self-erasure, of making themselves invisible in those domains of scrutiny and censure that they quite properly feared would have them removed from their mother and placed into the kind of state "care" that they had anticipated, arguably quite rightly, to be the worst kind of fate for them and is the ground across which a great deal of public debate about child protection is conducted:

> "Marigold, we have to tell her everything"s fine. We can't have her phoning the welfare people, can we?"
> "Why not?" Marigold said, her voice sounding flat and far away.
> "Because they might put me in a home!"
> "Maybe you'd be better off," said Marigold. "That old bat was right. I'm not a fit mother." (Wilson 156)

"ACTING IN CONCERT"

To return to the point:[5] we see in these narratives the stalking ground of erasure, the territory that Judith Butler has identified in which bodies are built as a series of exclusions, and fail to properly materialize "precisely because they stand outside the criteria of selection" (Katz 173).

> This delimitation ... marks the boundary that includes and excludes, that decides, as it were, what will and will not be the stuff of the object to which we then refer. This marking off will have some normative force, and, indeed, some violence, for it can construct only through erasing; it can bound a thing only through enforcing a certain criterion, a principle of selectivity. (Butler, *Bodies* 11)

Butler describes such bodies as "extra discursive" (11) in the sense that they are, as Katz says, "that which cannot be spoken.... It is literally the unmarked, the unsaid, refusing the boundary between the known and the excluded. A knowing beyond the authorized: 'queer' knowing" (Katz 173).

In Shyam Selvaduria's *Funny Boy*, Arjie inhabits this kind of queer knowing from his very earliest childhood, and before he has the language enough or is old enough to own or communicate the kinds of self-reflexive understandings of "self" that are believed to be the axiom of such knowing. The narrative is structured in islands of memories:[6] the recollections of an age of innocence retold by a much older, much more knowing and disillusioned Arjie. He is ubiquitous in the narrative: secretly eavesdropping and spying on the adults to whose most secret conversations, behaviors, and beliefs he is privy. The early memories cluster round a series of "spend-the-days" when Arjie is six years old. These are family gatherings at his grandparents' house, with aunts, cousins, and uncles. The land surrounding his grandparents' home is iconically divided into two territories, "the girls'" at the back of the house ("the back garden, the kitchen and the porch" [Selvaduria 3]), and the boys' at the front of the house ("the front garden, the road and the field" [3]); that is how and where the cousins spend their days in this entirely child-governed space out of sight and out of mind of the adults. While his female cousin Meena chooses to spend her days playing cricket with the boys, seemingly without consequence or social sanction from the boys that may be a reflection of the relative insignificance of girls in this particular community at this time, Arjie chooses to play with the girls, and to take the lead in their imaginative games: acting out, and dressing up in "saris, blouses, sheets and curtains" (4) from their grandparents' dirty-clothes basket. During these days of uninterrupted play, Arjie indulges his fantasies of otherness in magical games of transformation and transfiguration, especially the game of "bride-bride" in which he always gets to play the part of the bride. The ritual of his becoming the bride is performed seriously and sensuously, played out in front of the (symptomatically cracked) full-length mirror belonging to one of the maidservants through which Arjie surveys his gradual conversion from "boy" to "woman" while reveling in the sheer delight of looking at himself: no longer a game now, but the experience of a newly emerged subject of and in feminine desire. Held in the power of his own gaze, he is caught up in his power too to enact a different identity through his movements, expressions, and sensibilities.

> The sari being wrapped around my body, the veil being pinned to my head, the rouge put on my cheeks, lipstick on my lips, kohl around my eyes—I was able to leave the constraints of myself and ascend into another, more brilliant, more beautiful self, a self to whom this day was dedicated, and around whom the world, represented by my cousins putting flowers in my hair, draping the palu, seemed to revolve. It was a self magnified, like the goddesses of the Sinhalese and Tamil cinema.... I was an icon, a graceful, benevolent, perfect being upon whom adoring eyes of the world rested. (4–5)

Butler talks about gender as "a kind of doing," a societal performance, "a practice of improvisation within a scene of constraint" ("Introduction" 1). And it is here, in these hidden, unspoken spaces, these "queer" spaces that are out of sight and sound of the regulatory scrutiny and sanction of the adult members of his polite, middle-class Sinhalese family, that Arjie performs gender, desire, and agency. The frisson of excitement that characterizes his descriptions of the material reformulation of his body through these acts of cross-dressing, coupled with the unwitting elements of secrecy and seriousness with which the games are played out, suggests at least an incipient knowing, at least at some level of Arjie's naïve understanding, that these are acts of societal transgression, that these interstices of play permit him to practice and perform an identity other than his societally ascribed gender role of "boy." The power of the gaze in this process is the primary agent of both pleasure and prohibition: as in, for example, the sight of his glittering body and brightly colored face reflected in the mirror of his Radha Aunty's dressing mirror in front of which she, with some glee at her own daring, has painted his face with makeup and bedecked him in her jewelry, saying, "Gosh. You would have made beautiful girl" (Selvaduria 50); and his "almost religious" (15) experience of the pleasure of gazing on his mother while she dresses herself for special occasions "with a joy akin to ecstasy [at] the pleasure of watching" (15). When he accompanies his Radha Aunty to her musical drama group, the musical director, known as "Auntie Doris," fixes him in the feminine gaze, saying, "What a lovely boy. Should have been a girl with those eyelashes" (55). These are the sources and acclamations of the public recognition of his "Other" self that Arjie revels in—though at this stage and age, he has seemingly no self-consciously aware sense of its Otherness. However, as with all the other instances and representations of the gaze, it is Janus-faced and proves to be the eventual source of his undoing in its societal aspect. His undoing arrives fittingly enough in female form in the shape of his jealous cousin "Her fatness," when she intuitively recognizes the force of her heteronormative biopower over Arjie and informs on him to the grown-ups, exposing him as "a pansy," "a faggot," and "a sissy!" (11). Later in the narrative, he is referred to as "a funny one" (14), a "girlie-boy," with "Tendencies.... From the time he was small, he has shown certain tendencies.... You know ... he used to play with dolls, always reading" (166). So, this secret identity that Arjie has hitherto experienced as unproblematically thrilling and natural is made strange, alien, deconstructed, denaturalized, and Othered to *him* through the societal gaze that has been critically turned back on him—objectifying him to both himself and the world. After his girl games have been discovered and he has been paraded in shame before the assembled grown-ups, he is instantly banished from the girls' world, and also from the affections of his father and mother, who force him instead to play cricket with the boys: an outsider in his own family unit. And, as he later discovers, he is an outsider also in the system of heavily regulated gender binarities of the wider Sri Lankan society that is sustained, policed, and reproduced as much by its women as its men in a naturalized heterosexuality in which Arjie quickly discovers he can play no part:

> The future spend-the-days were no longer to be enjoyed, no longer to be looked forward to. And then there would be the loneliness. I would be caught between the boys' and the girls' worlds, not belonging or wanted in either. (89)

At fourteen, his father sends him to the Queen Victoria Academy, which he believes will force Arjie "'to become a man'" (Selvaduria 210). The academy is an all-male institution run on the English public school model with a culture of bullying, victimization, public humiliation, and repressed homosexual relations. Here Arjie loses his virginity to Shehan, a Tamil boy (another transgression because Arjie is Sinhalese and the background to the novel is the 1970s war between the ethnic factions of Tamils and Sinhalese). The act takes place, symptomatically enough, in the darkness of the garage of his parents' home during a game of hide-and-seek with his sister that recalls the earlier occluded play spaces of transgression. He subsequently castigates himself through the (by now) internalized societal values of compulsory heteronormativity that he has so singularly failed to live up to. They have come to haunt him with a vengeance in the form of self-regulatory power and subjection, in which he begins to subscribe now to his father's view (the Law of the Father) that there was something "wrong" with him, that his father "had been right to try to protect me from what he feared was inside me, but he failed. What I had done in the garage had moved me beyond his hand" (262).

How predictable, we might say, that the feminine, cross-gendered child has grown into the homosexual adult. But there are numerous unexamined assumptions at the heart of these easy resignations and assumptions, some of which play unquestioningly into the stereotypes of gender binarity because they naturalize the very notion of gender on which such binary inscriptions endure. In *Undoing Gender*, Butler raises the specter of the untenable premises of them all. She questions, first, "if there is a gender that somehow pre-exists regulation" (41), and she concludes that gender is the *mechanism* by which notions of masculine and feminine are produced and naturalized (42). She problematizes the notion that "feminine traits" and "masculine traits" could ever be regarded as givens that are not already subsumed in societal norms (79); and she challenges the exclusively binary premise of the heterosexual matrix on which gender inversions are based, saying that it misrepresents the "queer crossings" in heterosexuality (80). In this final point that is immediately relevant to the biopolitics of Arjie, she challenges the too simplistic binary inscription of "feminine" and "masculine" attributes in relation to desire: that is, of boys with 'feminine' attributes, and girls with 'masculine' attributes, and the assumption that 'boy traits' will lead to a desire for women and 'girl traits' will lead to a desire for men.

> It would not follow that the "feminine" is attracted to the masculine and the "masculine" to the feminine ... when, for instance a feminized heterosexual man wants a feminized woman, in order that the two might well be "girls together." (79–80)

In light of Butler's deconstructionist thesis in this context, then, of queered gender and sexual identities, and her splitting of the concept of gender from the concept of sexual identity, there may be perceived to be a fundamental inconsistency in the eventual direction of Arjie's sexual orientation. And in these senses, we are left wondering if the narrative of *Funny Boy* goes quite far enough to unseat the binary status quo. Perhaps the too easy inversions—of gender (masculine/feminine) and of sexuality (male/female), coupled with Arjie's unreconciled alienation from his own sexual predilections by the end of the narrative—do not ring quite true, or go quite far enough to shift the ground of the binary inscription. By the end of the narrative, Arjie's grandparents have both been killed in sectarian riots with the Tamil Tigers, his family home and father's businesses have been wrecked, and the family is poised to immigrate to Canada as "penniless refugees." So there is a certain irony in one of Arjie's final comments that he finds it "impossible to imagine that the world will ever be normal again" (308), when it is the fiercely regulated regimes of normalcy that have encoded his difference as an erasure to be banished to the irreconcilable realm of "extradiscursive" space that lingers in the narrative to its end.

LOSS OF FACE

In Cormier's novel *Heroes* and Zephaniah's novel *Face*, the focus is on facial disfigurement. Francis Joseph Cassavant is a returning World War II veteran who has lost his face to an exploded grenade, supposedly in an act of heroism to try to save a platoon of men for which he has been awarded the Silver Star for bravery. In the eyes of the state, Francis is an official hero.

Martin, of Zephaniah's *Face*, is a member of "The Gang of Three" Londoners. He gets badly burned when the stolen car in which he accepts a lift from some friends who are out joyriding crashes and bursts into flames. Martin is an antihero, and this narrative is about the little daily triumphs through which he learns to come to terms with his changed facial features and how to cope with people's changed attitudes toward him. The dedication at the front of the book is to

> All the staff and supporters of Changing Faces. A great bunch of dudes working to raise awareness and increase the resources devoted to the care and rehabilitation of facially disfigured people.

So we must presume that Zephaniah had a particular kind of real-life audience in mind in writing this book, that it is based on the particular real-life experiences of facially disfigured young people, and that his purpose is to educate his readers' responses to disfigurement.

> I think this book was splendid and brightened up my life. I
> am facially disfigured myself aka deformed and have found
> it hard in the past to get through life as it has treated me so
> badly. I feel for poor martin [sic] because I was also called
> 'poxy face' as a child and it is a very cruel thing to say as I
> was also physically abused as well it has taught me that some
> people are sick in the head and they have the problem not
> deformed people I would recomend [sic] this book to any
> deformed person as it makes them feel equal to martin and
> I also think that normal people would be fascinated by the
> story and think about what they would do in this situation.
> Please share this with everyone as I don't mind sharing my
> personal information as it may help people.
>
> **—Baleswaran, a boy from Zimbabwe**

Though both of these novels are about the literal and metaphorical loss of face, in many other respects they could not be more different from each other. *Heroes* is a chilling tale of isolation, anonymity, revenge, and death, while *Face* is about reconciliation, sociality, and hope. In *Heroes* Francis is the first-person narrator who takes us uncomfortably into his innermost thoughts and feelings, experiences and motivation. In contrast, Zephaniah's *Face* is told in his characteristic docu-novel style of third-person narration that, ironically, is not nearly so successful a device for positioning his readers to achieve what is presumably Zephaniah's main purpose and intention, a close empathetic relation with his character.

The loss of face—and, in Francis's case, the loss of facial organs: his mouth, nose, and teeth—positions both characters on the cusp of bodily indefinition, as the convex and concave facial contours collapse into a visceral mass of undifferentiated flesh bearing patches of distorted, discontinuous, or disappeared membrane of skin that was once the marker of inner and outer bodily surface and is now the marker of the grotesque bodily form, as when Martin first views himself in a mirror.

He suffered a silent shock. His eyes were completely red with only minute bits of white coming through.... Then Martin focused his eyes on the skin on his face. It was bright red in places, and brown in others. He noticed pinky white bits, which looked like flesh with no skin cover, where he could see veins.... The contours of his face were jagged. On seeing his lips which were swollen as if he had been in a fight.… He began to really stare at his right cheek, checking every millimetre of it. *It looks like a mountain* [original italics] he thought. (Zephaniah, *Face* 71–72)

The grotesque disturbs boundaries, codes, systems, and identities. Mikhail Bakhtin describes the grotesque body in relation to "excrescences" and "orifices," "mountains and abysses" (318); and he points out that the grotesque body is unfinished and transgresses its own limits:

The stress is laid on those parts of the body that are open to the outside world, that is, the parts through which the world enters the body or emerges from it or through which the body itself goes out to meet the world. (316–317)

Of all the features of the human face, the nose and mouth play the most important part in the grotesque image of the body. (316)

So, the loss of facial features (and, especially in psychoanalytic terms, their connectedness to erotogenic bodily parts) signals a threat of imminent collapse into bodily dissolution and primitiveness, and the kind of regressiveness that is associated with loss of control, ego, and self-identity. It is the realm of the uncanny grotesque[7] that provides the spectacle for horror movies. "The grotesque body is open, protruding, irregular, secreting, multiple and changing" (Russo 8); and these are the terms in which Francis describes his disappeared face—as oozing, secreting, irregular, and cavernous, with "caves" in the place where his nostrils once were.

My nose, or I should say, my caves, runs a lot. I don't know why this should happen and even the doctors can't figure it out but it's like I have a cold that never goes away. The bandage gets wet and I have to change it often and it's hard closing the safety pin at the back of my head. (Cormier 2)

The distorted facial features are an uncanny mix of the cavernous interior body of the female and the protuberant body of the male (Russo 6).[8] It takes us back once again to the queered undifferentiated space that cannot be spoken. Francis inhabits a nonspace, skulking on the sidelines of the streets and avoiding the return gaze of the people who stare at him, and describes himself in nonhuman terms; "No face at all, actually, the nostrils like a snout of an animal, the peeling cheeks the toothless gums" (Cormier 58); "The Hunchback of Notre Dame, my face like a gargoyle" (3).[9] He loiters in the shadows and at the margins, "Not only to hide the ugliness of what used to be my face, but to hide my identity" (3). But for Francis, the opportunity to remain anonymously behind the mask of his bandages and scarves "like a spy in disguise" (15), and beneath his Red Sox cap (2) pulled low over his eyes that are the only remaining part of his former face, suits his purpose well. For Francis is on a mission to kill Larry LaSalle. LaSalle is a former youth leader who—in the days before Francis had lied about his age to enlist in the armed services—had been himself a Silver Star returning war hero, home on leave to the cheering of crowds and into the arms of the Frenchtown dignitaries who had assembled to welcome the return of their homegrown hero back into their midst. He had raped the love of Francis's life, Nicole Renard, while Francis had watched unseen in the moonlit half-shadows of the local youth hall, "The Wreck Centre," that he had supposedly already left much earlier. Hidden from view by his cover, Francis listens to Larry and Nicole's dancing to the tune of "Dancing in the Dark" (67) as it transmutes within his half-sight and sound into a *danse macabre*: a dance of death in which Larry rapes Nicole. Larry had been Francis's hero in his pre-GI days: a model of manhood that he had revered, respected, and aspired to, and part of the narrative is to dismantle the rhetoric of heroism that precedes such people in the public domain of media reports: it carnivalizes them and makes them absurd. Francis had joined the army so that he could die a "hero's" death because he had been too cowardly to jump from the steeple of St. Jude's church following his distress and despair at the rape of Nicole. So we are left to suspect that his act of Silver Star heroism had been in fact a deliberate attempt to kill himself "with honor" to protect the good name of his dead mother and father.

> The scared war. God, but I was scared, Francis.... Heroes, he scoffs, his voice sharp and bitter.... We weren't heroes. Only us, the boys of Frenchtown. Scared and homesick and cramps in the stomach and vomit. Nothing glamorous like the write-ups in the papers or the newsreels. We weren't heroes. We were only there. (50)

Not only does Francis's presence in the narrative disturb the codes of identity and order, but he also disturbs and collapses time as the episodes of his life that have brought him to this point of his vengeful return to Frenchtown are played out in flashbacks and nightmare sequences. Having failed to successfully die as a hero in the war, his decision to kill Larry LaSalle is also another decision to kill himself, a deliberate election of evil in which, like Marlowe's Faust, he effectively chooses to "sell his soul to the devil" and opts for this revenging life-in-death existence in which everything ceases to matter. And, like Faust who burned his books, Francis burns the little piece of paper, the last remnants of his hope for life, bearing the contact details of the only plastic surgeon in the country who could rebuild his face and the list of veterans' hospitals that would put him in contact with his only remaining friend in the world, Enrico.

> The truth is that I don't care whether I heal or not. Because I know that it doesn't matter.... I watch the flames eating up the list of hospitals. *Goodbye Enrico.*
> The smell of the ashes fills the air, a damp incense burning for Larry LaSalle's home-coming. (Cormier 59–60)

When he finally confronts Larry LaSalle with his gun, Francis has not the courage to pull the trigger. But Larry shoots himself instead with a bullet from his own gun. He tracks down Nicole at a convent school and realizes he is forever lost from her love, if not from her affections and sympathy. The ending is befittingly ambivalent: it leaves Francis wavering on the brink between his life and his death, between hope and despair, which is the space of the grotesque. And also within the paradoxical spaces and ambiguities of the grotesque style (that is also the typically despairing style of Cormier's novels in general), the choices are the despair of life and the comfort of death with a strong narrative hint that he will probably decide, or has already decided, to kill himself after all:

> I think of Nicole.
> I think of the gun inside the duffel bag at my feet.
> I pick up the duffel bag and sling it over my shoulder. The weight is nice and comfortable on my back. (Cormier 96)

It is a tale of shattered illusions and dreams exteriorized in the grotesque body: of the inside projected outward into the world reminiscent of Pierre de Nesson's observation that the "worms which devour cadavers do not come from the earth but from within the body, from its natural 'liquors'" (quoted in Harpham 107). We might say in this sense that Francis's disfigured face was the projection of his own bodily pollutants, of rage and revenge, in which process the grenade was but a capricious property.

What a shocking contrast, then, to come up against Zephaniah's *Face* straight after *Hero*, and the abrupt shift of focus from the small-town, friendless, solitary life of Francis to inner-city Martin and his network of supportive friends, supported by a stable, two-parent, supportive family. The message and the moral in this narrative are writ large through the story: of courage in the face of adversity, and of life-affirming self-determination and unwavering optimism. After Martin's face is burned beyond former recognition, the entire family and state machinery move in to support his trauma: twenty-four-hour hospital care from untiring, ever-cheerful, always on-call, unstintingly dedicated medical staff. His parents shower him with gifts and goodies, and friends stick by him to support his recovery from former Martin to new Martin with the badly disfigured face.

Unlike Francis, whose first encounter with his face was from the public reaction to him in the streets of London when he walked out from the military hospital base, Martin confronts his disfigurement in the privacy of his hospital room, in the mirror that he demands from the nursing staff. The context is friendlier than we saw in *Hero*, but the bleak details of disfigurement reflected back to Martin from the mirror are no less grotesque than those ascribed to Francis. He has an immediate reaction of compulsion and repulsion: "Martin was scared by what he saw but he could not look away" (Zephaniah, *Face* 72). And this is also the reaction of his friends when they visit him in the hospital: "Martin noticed that none of the three had looked him in the face while he was looking at them, but the moment his eyes were off them, he could feel them staring" (86), exemplifying that "the grotesque is always a civil war of attraction/repulsion" (Harpham 9).

Zephaniah causes his readers to assess their own reactions to people like Martin, which is a noble enough ambition:

> As far as your friends are concerned, well, they have to figure out their own problems. They have to come to terms with themselves. They also have to think about how they see you. (*Face* 90)

It recalls Julia Kristeva's point (in chapter 1 here) that the "stranger is in me."

Martin tries to convince himself that "despite all that had happened, he was still the same person he had been before" (Zephaniah, *Face* 81), and this is a view of him that is supported by his counselor: "You're still the same guy" (91). However, it must be said that this view is premised on a deceit—either by the well-intentioned Zephaniah as author, or by the people who may have advised him about how they might advise people like his character Martin who are recovering from trauma— because it evades the issue of how the subject is formed and performs in relation and reaction to the ontological appearance and status of its body in the world. The unspoken element of this narrative, therefore, is that Martin, and the Martins of the world beyond the pages of the book to whom the docu-narrative is directed, cannot and will never be "the same person" he was before his burning. He cannot and will not be "the same," not least because, first, it refuses the notion of the nonessentialist subject; second, because it disallows the concept of "the subject in process"; and, third, in relation to both of these, it overlooks the extent to which the subject is the determinate product in determinate circumstances of its lived-body experiences. The space that Martin now inhabits is ontologically and physiologically changed, and the "he" that exists in this space is now differently encoded in relation to it, and it to him: "No law of logic is more fundamental than that p and not-p cannot occupy the same space simultaneously" (Harpham 106). And we perceive just how much the posttrauma Martin has changed from pretrauma Martin, even while he is protesting his sameness to the world:

> Let me explain something to you. Anything I could do before I can do now. There are some things I can do better now, like spotting the patroniser.... *It isn't just about me and how I cope with it, it's me learning to deal with other people's prejudices* [original italics], he thought. (Zephaniah, *Face* 150)

These are not only or simply other people's prejudices, however; they are also other people's fears, and the threat of the potential disintegration of themselves that is posed by their confrontation with the abyss of Martin's disintegrated face in the world. The point is even more graphically illustrated when he comes up against some children in the play park:

> Some of the children jumped back and screamed. Others shouted abuse: *'Ugly man,' 'You're the bad man,' 'Dog face.'* The kids shouted to each other, *'Don't let him touch you, he'll kill you,' 'If you look at him for long you'll go blind.'* Some of them picked up twigs and pieces of paper from the ground and threw them at him shouting, *'Get away, bogey man,' Here's you* [sic] *dinner,' 'You haven't got no Mommy or Daddy'* [all italics are original]. (176–177)

The Medusa, the Gorgon, the Bogeyman: all the mythologized transitional creatures and objects of the monstrous are contained in these unfettered views of the children, and they involve also the deflected gaze, the averted attention, and a turning away from the vision of incompletion that confronts them. In their view, Martin embodies the *unheimlich* (the unhomely), the unparented, and the unnatural ("'*no Mommy or Daddy*'"); he is the primal body that reverts to the earliest childhood experiences of the species and that returns to haunt them. The irrepressible return gaze of the socially erased bodies in this context are a reminder of the power of the child to efface the fragile boundaries of those structures that contain and define hegemonic "normalcy." The message from these narratives is that the gaze of the erased is the return of the repressed, and that it returns not merely to invert the systems of normalcy and negativity in which alterity is inscribed, but also to continually scrutinize, challenge, interrogate, deconstruct, and disturb them in ways that permit the emergence of other meanings and readings that evade the grip of orthodoxy or authority (Katz 175) in a continuous process of rejecting and resisting the binary inscription of the outsider.

4

ABJECT

On the face of it, the range of disparate subject matter in the texts[1] that feature in this chapter appears to have little to unite them. However, notwithstanding the generic spread of the texts themselves—ranging across novels, biographies, diaries, memoirs, and reports—they also feature a number of discrete other differences: child figures who are both abused and abusing, resistant and passive, and who are (as will become clearer as the chapter progresses) individually representative of the innocence-evil, angel-monster spectrum I have discussed and challenged in chapter 1. They feature narrative time that spans approximately eighty years, through times of war and peace, and are geographically located across four countries and cultures. In some of the literary narratives, the past dissolves into the present as memory, imagination, dream, and daydream; in others, generic elements of fantasy give way to realism; and in still others, realism gives way to flights of fancy. These wide-ranging narrative features carry their own particular resonances that are explored throughout the chapter, along with their relative effects. But I bring them together under the umbrella term of "abjection" because the child subjects of these narratives all share in the particular spatiotemporal positioning of their bodies as the type of borderland that both challenges the binary schism and is the condition of abjection. All the child figures in these texts have been made interstitial by being caught up in a cycle of power and subjection to the various institutions or states or apparatuses by the adults who are its agents and who have, or should have, responsibility of care. As such, their bodily and psychic experiences have been subjected to numerous forms of neglect, deprecation, or condemnation and are the tropological expression of all that has been objectified through the process of abjection. Their bodies are what Julia Kristeva would describe in relation to abjection as "the jettisoned object that is radically excluded, which draws towards the place where meaning collapses" (*Powers* 2).

My purpose is not so much to explicate Kristeva's thesis on abjection, which she articulated first and foremost as a philosophical treatise in her seminal work, *The Powers of Horror: An Essay on Abjection*, already referred to above, as to illuminate certain possible readings of these texts against the nuanced appropriations of her thesis to a range of literary and social discourses;[2] this does not, however, preclude, delimit, or undermine other readings of these fictional texts that are not always within the scope and focus of this work.[3] I juxtapose the fictional and quasi-fictional narratives with ones that are drawn from life, positioned in and emerging from diverse ideologies, histories, and cultures.[4] In such a process, abjection is appropriated as both a psychosocial reality and a psychoanalytical literary criticism[5] on which site both sets of ontologies converge in and through narrativization in anticipation that the child figures, encoded as abject in both sets of narratives, resonate with each other in the mind of the reader. As with the other child figures who are "in" and "out" of the book in this work, it is also a move to dissolve and complicate the frames between the narratives we call "life" and the narratives we call "children's and young adult fiction." Kristeva's thesis on abjection is at once specific in relation to its origins and highly transferential for its implications across a wide range of disciplines, behaving like something of a theoretical conduit in the interdisciplinary field. A substantial body of criticism has emerged from Kristeva's work in this area, especially in the fields of feminist, cultural, and childhood studies, and much of this criticism has been concerned with consequences and inflection of abjection. Critical responses have been especially negative in relation to Kristeva's reliance on the Oedipal paradigm deriving from the work of Jacques Lacan on which premise much of the theory is based.[6] Abjection, then, is rooted in the Lacanian psychoanalytical model, albeit one that has been heavily nuanced by, and in, the work of Kristeva herself; and, as we shall see, it continues to be regarded as somewhat intrinsically problematical in light of these subsequent critical interrogations. Kristeva identifies abjection as "the in-between, the ambiguous, the composite" (*Powers* 4), and it is this interstitial status of abjection that I wish to draw into focus and interrogate through these narratives, not the least because the very idea of interstitiality relies on prescribed notions of normativity in which it does not partake.

THE ABJECT BODY OF THE CHILD

Kristeva tells us that the abject has only the quality of being opposed to "I." In other words, the abject is not only the product of subjection (though subjection is most certainly related to it), but also the very process through which the individual self achieves the status of becoming what Sigmund Freud has defined as ego and is at once repulsive and attractive. The child's body, whether it is regarded as the "subject-to-be" or as "being a subject," inexorably is in the polymorphous mode. As such, it is already positioned in the borderland between the presocialized condition and the developed ego and already codified in these respects as abject. The properties of abjection that Kristeva identifies as most threatening the supremacy of subjective ego are fluids that emit from the inside to the outside of the body—blood, vomit, urine, saliva, excrement—and all that endanger it from without: decay, infection, and disease (*Powers* 71). They are most abhorrent because they are the least controllable and most closely related to the presocialized state of the body of the child. Therefore, it is "not lack of cleanliness or health that causes abjection," Kristeva says, "*but what disturbs identity, system, order* [my italics]" (*Powers* 4). It is in this specific that I pitch another critical point of my thesis: that the abject is as much about its social and political as its psychological import. Therefore, the child as abject is, as it were, "the unspoken of a stable speaking position, an abyss at the very borders of the subject's identity, a hole into which the subject may fall" (Grosz, "Body of Signification" 87). The body of the child that is essentialized in this theorization is conceived as a condition of unformedness. It presents an ever present threat to the aspiring ego identity and must, therefore, be disavowed and expelled. By extension, all who are infantilized in and by any such forms of dominant are similarly implicated in abjection, not merely as a psychoanalytic necessity, but also as a social reality.

Anne Fine's *The Tulip Touch*, like so many of the other narratives in this study, is a quasi-memoir focalized through the first-person narration of the now adult Natalie narrating a brief, but formative, period in her childhood experiences, which she spent with her friend Tulip. Tulip is an amoral and openly asocial thirteen year old, whom I believe to be the dramatization of Natalie's presocialized ego (and vice versa).[7] For example, Natalie is forever articulating her symbiosis with her friend Tulip expressed in her inability to act independently of her. Fine has Natalie suggest, "I lost my confidence that all the thoughts I had were quite my own" (76). "You'd think I didn't have a will of my own. And wouldn't you suspect that she'd get bored playing with such a servile shadow?" (77). "She tugged so hard at me. I had to go. But as I stumbled after her, still looking back, I knew I was bewitched. The *Tulip Touch* had really got me this time" (123). "I felt she'd caught me young and sucked me in, and even buried my own feelings so deep, I practically didn't have them" (137). Together these two characters comprise the ego and the id of the human psyche: a semiotic pairing of a two-in-one character that both resolves the narratological problem of complex characterization for the genre's implied child readership, and exemplifies the status of abjection by being neither this nor that but occupying the borderland between two sets of psychical inscriptions. At the same time they are, like the other child figures featured here, a demonstration of the subject's psychic inscription in sociality in quite the way in which Judith Butler has suggested:

> Whereas I accept the psychoanalytic postulate … that the subject comes into being on the basis of foreclosure (Laplanche), I do not understand this foreclosure as the vanishing point of sociality.… The unconscious is not a psychic reality purified of social content that subsequently constitutes a necessary gap in the domain of conscious, social life. ("Competing Universalities" 265)

Nina Bawden's *Squib* is in the Bawden tradition of outsider children, which includes characters featured in *The Finding* (1985) and *The Outside Child* (1989).[8] The title refers to the boy character "Squib," who is so named by the other child characters because his bodily movements resemble a jumping firecracker. We never discover his real name, or indeed if he has one. Squib's role in the narrative, in this reading, is not to be or become a character, but to act as a cipher and catalyst for other phenomena in and through which the narrative functions. Despite his title status, the third-person narrative is focalized through the principal character, Kate. She has a secret belief, wish, and hope that Squib is her lost younger brother, Rupert, who had been swept out to sea several years earlier and whose body had never been recovered. Kate is another borderlander, caught up as she is between the Pleasure and Reality Principles of the Freudian definition: between a lost father and an absent mother, and between the pleasure of her desire for the return of her lost, most probably dead, brother and the pain of her gradual reconciliation to the fact that Squib is not Rupert resurfaced in another guise. Kate is another example of the literary abject in a scenario in which the rootless, unknowable, silent, and, as we discover, physically abused Squib is both the physical embodiment and projection of Kate's grief and mourning, and the material, corporeal expression of abjection through a body that has been starved and beaten, and is itself precariously balanced between life and death. Kristeva says,

"The abject is the violence of mourning for an 'object' that has always already been lost" (Kristeva, *Powers* 15); she is referring of course to the Lacanian subject's originary mourning for the loss of the mother that is here displaced. Squib and the dead Rupert assume a collectively indeterminate status as the narrative enigma that is simultaneously between life and death, at once both subject and object, both in and out of life, and conjures up the image of the corpse that, as a "border that has encroached upon everything" (*Powers* 3), is described as being the most sickening of wastes: the ultimate face of abjection.

Sonya Hartnett's *Thursday's Child*, like *The Tulip Touch*, is another narrative about recollected childhood, focalized through the first-person narration of Harper Flute. *Thursday's Child* is about the struggles of one family to survive the Australian Depression of the 1930s in a parched, outback landscape; they endure the extremes of poverty against all the odds, made worse by a feckless father, an ever increasing family, and little or no source of income. *Thursday's Child* presents a classic instantiation and dramatization in a literary narrative of the ongoing academic debates about abjection as either an a priori psychic condition and necessary affect of ego acquisition locked, as it is, in the binary of the structuralist, Lacanian paradigm; or an expression of social repudiation through which societies and groups generally consolidate their social identities via a series of foreclosures such as Butler describes: "the transvaluation and ejection of something originally part of identity into a defiling otherness" (*Gender Trouble* 132). In such a process, the body (in this case, the collective body of the Flute family) is "synechdocal of the social system per se" (123). The novel has a historically real location in abject poverty. Hartnett points out that she based her novel on the actual facts of the Great Depression: "Before and during the writing of the novel I read a lot about life in this City during the Great Depression" (Hartnett, "Author's Note" 1). But she also admits to using the 1930s Depression as a plot device: "The Depression is, in this novel, a plot device, which seems ghastly, given everything that the Depression symbolises.... But the plot needed its characters to live in a vortex of poverty" (1). Karen Coats writes that such a circumstance of poverty is the expression of "the repressed representations, in that they are unavailable to us, [that] form independent relations among themselves and create material effects in our realities" (22). The Flute family continually hovers on the brink of starvation, sustained only by a diet of watery, wild rabbit stew, the effects of which inscribe their bodies as emaciated, wasted, and collectively abject in the ways I have described: they endure death, dirt, poverty, sickness, and disease that are the express contents of abjection. Members of the family shed tears, not for themselves, but for each other and the hopelessness of the other's life, in which process the subterranean and unspeaking Tin, in this reading, embodies all that is abjected from the body of the family. Tin also is a borderlander, positioned between nature and culture, neither animal nor human: "There was less that was human in Tin.... He was not a boy, but an unowned and willful animal" (Hartnett, *Thursday's Child* 196). He is likened variously to a "cat" (95) and a "snake" (95), and described as bearing teeth and claws and "with a territory he must defend" (196). Tin, moving between the depths and surface of the earth, becomes, during the course of the story, completely feral; he is forever lurking just beneath the walls of the ramshackle family home. From this underworld, like the function of abjection he personifies, Tin poses a continuous and ever present threat to the already fragile stability of the family; he is positioned as a characterization of all that which, in Kristeva's words, "takes the ego back to its source on the abominable limits from which, in order to be, the ego has broken" (*Powers* 15). Tin figures here as an example of Michel Foucault's "abnormals" ("Abnormals" 51). He is an ambiguity and, by definition, a boundary creature, who inhabits an indeterminate space between human and animal and who does not fit neatly into any predetermined mode of categorization or classification. His transition from boyhood to wildness is swift, and a reminder of the much disputed and fragile border between nature and culture in the human condition.[9] He becomes dirty, savage, and uncultured. While his motivation remains a narrative indeterminate, he nevertheless assumes the role of the redemptive noble savage by dispensing natural justice on the lascivious, landowning Vandery Cable, who has raped and exploited his eldest sister. Tin kills him. Already marked as being beyond the reach of penal law, he is now also, strictly speaking, a transgressor of natural law and, as such, slips over into Foucault's category of "monsters" who commit "unnatural acts" ("Abnormals" 51). In the eyes of regulatory practices, he is regarded as being unredeemable. Later in the narrative, there is an ambiguity surrounding Tin's abortive attempt to rescue Caffy after the child has slipped accidentally into one of Tin's many tunnels around the homestead. Readers are left wondering if the dead body of Caffy that Tin eventually offers up to his family has been the result of suffocation or willful murder: either is a possibility in his wild state. Positioned between the two conditions of the maternal chora and the paternal law, he is figured here as an ever present threat to the fragile stability of the collective, cultural life of the ego, which may explain the reason why he must be relegated to an invisible presence in the narrative, and remain timeless. Harper reports, "I never saw Tin an old man or even a young one, so he stays just as a boy in my mind" (Hartnett, *Thursday's Child* 7). As the essence of abjection, the narrating Harper recognizes something of herself in Tin, which is that unacculturated childhood part of herself, "rebellious in her rage" (215), that she no longer wishes to own: "Let his digging take him to the end of the dirt" (95).

Digging and dirt are at the heart of Louis Sachar's *Holes*. Among many possible other readings, it is about the tenacity of youth to outface the oppressions of the Law and its injustices, which are meted out in petty penal servitude, and is about the question of origins and truth. The first-person narrative is focalized through the character Stanley Yelnats, whose palindromic name is as significant for Stanley's nonstatus and nonidentity in the great, so-called civilized scheme of things as the name of his friend and fellow inmate, Zero, whom he befriends at Camp Green Lake boot camp, where Stanley is serving a hard labor sentence for a petty crime he did not commit. Camp Green Lake has no water. The land is barren and unyielding. It is a timeless nonspace with archaic links to a richer, lusher past that continually impinges on the present, and is positioned between two powers: the wily, irrational, and uncontrollable power of Nature, and the authoritarian, centralized, virulent, and oppressive power of the Law. In the context of the interstitial nature of the character of abjection, Nature and the Law are the metaphorical markers of Camp Green Lake's locus between the feminine semiotic and the masculine symbolic. Its inmates, who are caught in the tension between these two extremes, epitomize their status as dejects, by which term Kristeva defines those who inhabit the condition of abjection (*Powers* 8). The irrationality of the nonego that is on the side of the mother continually threatens the supremacy of the pristine ego that is on the side of the Symbolic and the father's law. It has to be said, at this point, that such a negative instantiation of the maternal body, though logical within the frame of Kristeva's thesis, is clearly controversially situated in the wider critical debates of feminist psychoanalytical and cultural criticism.

Johanna Reiss's *The Upstairs Room* is set in 1942 Holland. The story is about the life in hiding of two sisters, Annie and Sini de Leeuw, during the Nazi occupation of their hometown of Winterswijk; it is also the author's fictionalized account of her own life in hiding. The narrative presents Annie's first-person perspective of the time the sisters spend together during the remaining years of World War II in the upstairs room of the home of the Oostervelds, who are a generous, kind, and simple peasant farming family who, like so many other brave people, risked their lives to give Jews shelter. Sini tries to disguise herself as a gentile by bleaching her black hair: "Her hair was long and shiny, but black—the wrong color" (Reiss 36). By this gesture, she unwittingly invokes the Nazi ambition for blonde, Aryan domination, but, by a freak of chemical reaction, this results in her hair turning red as if to metaphorically emphasize her borderland status. Annie has her hair cut short to disguise herself as a boy. Both gestures, and the fact of their being hidden, signal the erasure of their racial, cultural, ethnic, and personal identities that is the manifestation of Kristeva's "jettisoned object(s)" (*Powers* 2) who inhabit "the place where meaning collapses" (2). Sini marks out their days of concealment by a series of "deep dark" crosses of a calendar on the wall of their room, as if to confirm the fact of their existence to themselves and to the world even while signaling their loss of agency and their abject status of nothingness. They embody, and are the expression of, the violence with which the national ego expels the undesirable face from its ranks, conceived and connoted as racially and ethnically defiling or polluting, to achieve free and uninhibited supremacy. The abject, in the words of John Lechte, "is the mud of Narcissus' pool" (160); it is "the moment of narcissistic perturbation" (Kristeva, *Powers* 15). Abjection is conjectured in Kristeva's thesis as the underbelly, the "not-I," the obverse of all that names itself as "I" but cannot be assimilated into the "I" and continually threatens the "I"'s stability. It emanates from, inhabits, and is defined by an insider-outsider correlative: "on the edge of non-existence and hallucination, of a reality that, if I acknowledge it, annihilates me" (2). The abject and abjection, Kristeva says, are "the primers of my culture" (2). The abject, therefore, is not merely or simply the "Other," because it is a borderland state that is both *and* neither, within *and* without "me," as when I eat some kind of distasteful food: "I expel *myself*, I spit *myself* out, I abject *myself* within the same motion through which 'I' claim to establish *myself*" (Kristeva, *Powers* 3). The abject is the problematic of the "hidden face of our identity"; it is "the stranger [who] inhabits us" (Kristeva, *Etrangers* 9). And so, it is in this sense that the abject is paradoxically "both/and," subject and object, the borderland that these child figures inhabit. Their bodies are excluded, rejected, extinguished, mistreated, or hidden; they are all conjectured in alterity and identified in the narratives as being in some way different—though we might well ask, Different in relation to what? There are examples in each of the texts in which the child figures identify themselves or are identified in difference:

> *Squib*: "Perhaps he's only a child," Kate said.… "Too easy," Robin said. "I mean, he's more different than that" (Bawden 7).
> *The Tulip Touch*: "Is that a scarecrow?" Dad peered against the sudden glare. "No, I do believe that it's a little girl" (Fine 11).
> *Thursday's Child*: "That's a wild child you've got" (Hartnett 44).

Holes: "He didn't have any friends at home. He was overweight and the kids at his middle school often teased him about his size" (Sachar 7).

The Upstairs Room: "I asked Rachel why he had done that—spat at us. Because we were Jews, she said. But he wasn't German, and how did he know we were Jews? I asked. We looked different, she answered, darker. Rachel knew so much. No wonder she was a teacher. When I got home, I was going to see how different I looked" (Reiss 7).

In relation to Kristeva's observations about the "stranger" or "foreigner," these child figures are sited as the objects of the abjected contents of their oppressors' individual and collective psyches, as the sublimation and dramatization of the continuous process of ejection that is essential to maintaining both personal and/or national ego supremacy. It is because these child figures embody *ambivalence*, marked out as difference, that they are defined as intolerable by the centrist binary framework of societal classification; they are the tropes and symptom of the collective and the individual face of abjection and the projected sublimation of those aspects of the social and individual consciousness that cannot be tolerated or assimilated. They are also the material affects of power.

It seems inconceivable, therefore, to discuss abjection without also discussing the position and role of power in relation to it. In *The Psychic Life of Power: Theories in Subjection*, Butler draws on the work of G. W. F. Hegel, Friedrich Nietzsche, Sigmund Freud, Michel Foucault, and Louis Althusser to articulate her thesis of power and subjection which, I feel, opens up something of a dialogue with Kristeva's work on abjection: that the subject is produced reflexively out of the power systems, which it simultaneously rejects and depends on, and, further, to which it is "passionately" attached. Butler goes one step further than the cynical dismissiveness to which this notion gives rise—that final responsibility for subordination resides with the subject him or herself—to assert that attachment to subjection is the psychic effect and insidious by-product of the workings of power (*Psychic* 6). Butler points out this has particular resonances with the life of the child as the quintessential subordinate for whom dependency is its primary condition and whose attachment to subordination is therefore fundamental:

No subject emerges without a passionate attachment to those on whom he or she is fundamentally dependent (even if the passion is "negative" in the psychoanalytic sense) ... the formation of primary passion in dependency renders the child vulnerable to subordination and exploitation ... subordination proves central to the becoming of the subject. (*Psychic* 7)

Butler explains that this is one reason why she thinks that the debates about the reality of the sexual abuse of children mistake the character of the exploitation:

It is not simply that a sexuality is unilaterally imposed by the adult, nor that a sexuality is unilaterally fantasized by the child, but that the child's love, a love that is necessary for its existence, is exploited and a passionate attachment abused. (*Psychic* 7–9)

It is easy to see how Butler's theorization of the workings of power, and her thesis of a "passionate attachment" as one of its by-products, might be appropriated to explain the willingness of abused children to protect their abusers that might not always be explained simply in terms of the subsequent reprisals they fear from their abusers. John Bowlby refers to the work of Anna Freud, "An Experiment in Group Upbringing" (Freud and Dann), which describes a group of three- and four-year-old children who might be described as having this same experience of passionate attachment to each other, in a circumstance of absolute necessity, and in the absence of any nurturing other adult:

> They arrived in the bedroom and the social worker asked how I was. I said I was fine far too scared to say anything else for fear of the reprisals that would come after she'd left. She obviously wanted to believe me, because if I was all right then she could get out of the house as fast as possible. I concentrated with all my strength, trying to will her to lift the sheets that hid my broken body, but I could see she was already backing out of the door.
>
> **Lewis (79)**[10]

That an infant can become attached to others of the same age, or only a little older, makes it plain that attachment behavior can develop and be directed towards a figure who has done nothing to meet the infant's physiological needs. (Bowlby, *Attachment and Loss* 1:217)

There are numerous examples, in cases of kidnap and imprisonment, in which the victim forms a passionate attachment with his or her captor or oppressor.

In *The Tulip Touch*, we glean from the narrative asides and innu-
endo scattered throughout the text that Tulip is being at least physically abused by her father and is just such a quintessence of abjection
that is one of the by-products of power misused. Natalie narrates,

> I hated Tulip's house. It wasn't just that the carpets were stained
> and the furniture battered. It was that Tulip herself seemed differ-
> ent, just a shell, as if she had slipped away invisibly and left some
> strange, strained imitation in her place. (Fine 23–24)
>
> I turn the photo in my hand, and try to push the word away.
> But it comes back at me, time and again. I can't get rid of it. If you
> didn't know her better, you'd have said she looked *desolate*. (37)

From Tulip's asides and her obviously well-developed sense of sexual
knowingness that are dramatized in and through the staged scenarios
that Fine sets up to make her point, we must assume that, as well as
being physically abused by her father, Tulip is being sexually abused by
him also.

> Prosecution witness Anthony Urquiza, a psychologist
> who has not interviewed Jackson's accuser, Gavin Arvizo,
> described "child sexual assault accommodation syndrome,"
> in which youngsters become secretive, feel helpless and
> trapped, delay reporting acts of abuse, and finally learn to
> cope with the situation. He said children often underwent
> changes in behaviour because of the abuse, including "act-
> ing out, becoming defiant, name-calling."
>
> **"Frail Jacko Late for Court Again"**

We see this being played out in the chilling incident with the rabbit,
which Tulip is slowly and systematically persecuting:

> Tulip was crooning in the rabbit's ear. "Who's a clever bunny?
> Who's going to be a good girl? Who's Tulip's special one? She's
> not going to make a fuss, is she? Oh, no. She isn't going to do that.
> Because she enjoys it really, doesn't she? And if she starts strug-
> gling, she'll get hurt." (Fine 92)

During her youth, Amy suffered from several traumatic events that would forever change her life. As a young child, she alleged that a family member sexually abused her repeatedly. She experienced yet another traumatic event at the age of thirteen, when a contractor hired to make repairs in the family house raped her as she lay in her own bed.

Bell, "Point Blank. Amy Fisher: The Long Island Lolita"

We see it also in her capacity to insinuate sexuality into what appear to be innocent displays of affection on the part of Natalie's father, although the finely balanced ambiguity of the scene may cause readers to wonder about the extent to which the father—as the double inscription of Tulip's father, also—is behaving altogether innocently:

She came as often as she could, sucking up to Mum, flirting with Dad.

"Good morning Mr. Barnes."
"Morning Tulip, my flower. But I have to warn you that no one gets late breakfast in this hotel even here in the kitchens, without first settling with the Manager."
"What's the price today?"
"Let me see . . . It's Saturday, isn't it? And High Season. So I'm afraid it's going to be—a hug and three kisses."
He'd take off his glasses and she'd count the kisses out onto his cheek.
"One. Two. Three. And the hug. There!"
"Right," he'd say. "Now that you've paid, you must have another sausage." (Fine 37)

In this section, the locus of abjection at the corporeal border between the semiotic chora and the symbolic order is encoded in those two words "sucking," in relation to the mother, and "flirting," in relation to the father, which function here as metonyms of both the presocialized and socialized forms of oral gratification.[11]

Through the hints and glimpses of the narration and the naïve speculations of the other child characters in Bawden's *Squib*, the protagonist is caught up in a cycle of physical abuse at the hands of the woman and man with whom he lives in a dilapidated bus parked on a nearby trailer site on derelict ground from which he is eventually rescued to a happy ending by the children.

> The sad irony is that we have considerable body of evidence relating to the background circumstances of both vulnerable children and the adults who harm them. In a report published last year by the department of Health, "Learning from the Past," a review of serious case reviews, evidence from a random selection of cases indicated that, for example, the age of the primary carer at the time of the death of a child is normally between 21 and 30, that almost half of them have had mental health problems and the majority were in unstable long-term relationships with some degree of violence. Furthermore, they are part of households that experience frequent moves and have, increasingly, drug and alcohol problems.
>
> **Hanvey (2)**

Squib is at once desired by Kate as her "lost object" and rejected by the adults with whom he lives. Unlike Fine, who relies on hints and glimpses and offstage happenings to portray the abuse of the character Tulip, Bawden builds up to the horrific scene of Squib's physical abuse by increasing degrees of detail that give way, eventually, to an unsparing description of the scene of Squib's abuse quite literally in front of the eyes of her child characters and, by extension, her readers:

> Blood was oozing in dark, shiny beads like a row of garnets, but Squib made no sound.... Kate sat Squib on the ground, legs sticking out straight, like a doll's.... His little leg was so thin. So twig-like, she felt it might snap if she handled it roughly. She took off his scratched, patent shoe and rolled down his sock. There was a mark round his leg like a bracelet of bruises; as she touched it, she glanced up at him and his eyes met hers with that strange look.... She thought What is he seeing? And then, He looks so old! Old and wise and sad, as if he knew something she was still too young to know. (Bawden, *Squib* 11)

Mr. Cameron recalled that Victoria would become quiet and reserved when Kouao arrived at the house to take her home. Victoria tended to look down at the floor, rubbing her hands together whenever Kouao was present.... On several occasions, Victoria turned up at Mrs Cameron's house with a number of small cuts on her fingers. When questioned about them, Kouao said they had been caused by Victoria playing with razor blades. Mr. Cameron also noticed marks to Victoria's face, although these were not serious and he thought they could have been caused by ordinary childish rough and tumble.

Laming (26–27)

The *Squib* narrative moves from such examples of suggested abuse to a graphic depiction of it in the scene witnessed by Robin:

The woman was half sitting, half lying across it, her head thrown back. For one heart-thumping second, Robin thought she was dead, her neck broken, but then she began to struggle up and he saw blood pour from her nose. She gasped and fell back again, pressing a cloth to her face. He thought she muttered "Get out," but she was in no state to make him. His pulse slowed down and he looked round, almost calm suddenly. The laundry basket was under the table. He whispered, "Squib!" and dragged it out.

He tore open the strap that fastened the lid and saw him, scrooged up at one end, his pale, cottony head drooping forward. He whimpered and screwed up tighter as Robin touched him, but this was no time for coaxing: Robin bent and gathered him up in a ball. He felt horribly light—all bones, Robin thought, like a big dead bird he'd once found on a beach. (Bawden, *Squib* 95–96)

As I struggled to get free, she picked me up as if I was a pile of old clothes and chucked me across the width of the room. I remember those few seconds hanging in the air, like I could fly, before I crashed down on the window ledge, hitting my head on the corner.

Lewis (26)

FOCALIZING ABJECTION

Focalization is a complex mix of first- and third-person, past and present tense narration. Nikolajeva tells us, "Focalization as a narrative device denotes a limitation of the information that is allowed to reach the reader.... Focalization implies manipulation of the narrator's character's and reader's point of view resulting in our perceiving the narrative 'as if' it were told by the focalizing character" (*Rhetoric* 61). The category descriptors of focalization derive from the work of Gérard Genette (189–94); they are identified there as "internal-", "external-", or "non-" focalized narration; and refer to the degrees of mobility of the narrative voice and viewpoint within the narrative that may also more traditionally be described as first- and third-person narration, respectively. And there are a number of subcategories that are described as "inter-", "intra-", and "extra-" diegetic positions which denote the temporal and spatial proximity between, on the one hand, voice and viewpoint and, on the other, the events of the story. But I find that these categories do little to enhance our understanding of the role of the especially "child" focalization and the especially child or adult readership that form the communication loop of children's literature generally but have a number of particular ramifications for the set of novels that I am grouping here as novels of abjection. This coupling of the child with issues of focalization denotes an especially circumscribed range of readerly information and a uniquely complex set of readerly positions that may be either naïvely complicit or objectively critical, depending on the worldview and experience that each reader brings to bear upon the texts and, conversely, what the texts themselves allow their readers to know. The issues surrounding child focalization become even more pressing when the textual content is dealing with the levels of privation and deprivation that are in focus in this chapter because they throw up unusually high levels of indeterminacy in the text-reader loop in an apparent absence of adult-informed narration that may prove to be a high-risk strategy in this particular context. The child's unmediated voice and viewpoint in literature are always problematical narrative devices because of the unusually restricted worldview made available to its readers through childish sensibilities. But in children's literature, where the primary, target readership is another child, in what I would call "child-to-child" narration, the potential for narrative to miss rather than to make the point is that much greater. An unadulterated example of "child-to-child" narration comes in Johanna Reiss's *The Upstairs Room*. This novel is autobiographical: Reiss makes this point clear to her readers in an authorial note at the front of the book:

> This book is about my life, or rather part of my life, the part that
> took place in Holland during the Second World War. In this book
> I have gone back to those years, when I was a child, and Jewish,
> and therefore undesirable, when I had to hide from the Germans.
> ("Epigraph" v)

Reiss had several choices available to her for writing this narrative,
which could have been written as a straightforward autobiography.
She chose instead, however, to fictionalize the events of her childhood
experiences, to do so through the unmediated viewpoint of her child
character "Annie" (possibly a corruption of, or pet name for, Reiss's
own first name, Johanna), and to view events consistently through the
child's perceptions without any hint of hindsightful adult commentary
that would have been available to her in the choices she made about the
writing process and style in which she chose to write. The first-person
narrator, Annie de Leeuw, relates the events leading up to and during
her own and her family's life in hiding in Second World War Holland.
The narrative describes the period between 1938 to 1945, beginning
when Annie is just six years old and ending when she and her sister,
Sini, are finally released from their hiding place in the upstairs room
of a house in the village of Usselo where the Oostervelds, a family of
Dutch peasant farmers, have saved the two Jewish girls from an almost
certain fate in the death camps. In this "child-to-child" narrative, the
child Annie's naïveté and puzzlement about the events taking place
around her ostensibly become the reader's puzzlement also, as in, for
example, when the grip of the Nazi occupation tightens around their
little Dutch town of Winterswijk and curtails the freedom of Jews. It
is not too difficult to imagine that a naïve child reader of these events
would be wholly complicit with the naïve child character's narration
and may miss the sinister message that a more mature and more experienced reader might read into the bland, unexplained, and uncom-
mented-on statements, charged with childish indignation and pride,
that issue from the fictional Annie's narration. One example is when
the restriction notices are posted on the tree in the village square which
Annie eventually refers to as "the talking tree":

> In the spring of 1941, the tree began to have many announcements
> on it. We couldn't rent rooms anymore in hotels. With mother
> sick almost all the time now, we wouldn't have done that anyway.
> But why did the next poster say that Jews could no longer go to
> beaches and parks? That wasn't fair. (Reiss, *Upstairs Room* 10)
>
> When school started again, I was in the fourth grade, but only
> for a few weeks: Jewish children were no longer allowed to attend

school. I read the announcement at the marketplace and ran home. 'I'm very glad,' I said. 'I hope I never have to go back.' (11)

On the way to school I had started to notice signs saying *Joden verboden* ('forbidden to Jews'). The signs were on the walls of several restaurants and at the movie theater. I never went to the movies anyway.… It was a pity about the restaurants. We used to go sometimes. Until those signs. (12–13)

Annie is proud of the star sign that the Jewish people above the age of six years are required to wear on their clothes. "But the stars weren't so bad. I fingered mine. It made me look grown up" (19–20). This tone of naïve irony is stunningly and chillingly effective to the adult reader, but it risks the possibility that a less well-informed and naïve child reader may miss the point. However, the countercomments of the kind that we would otherwise expect to find embedded in the narrative voice of children's literature to facilitate a naïve reader's wider interpretation are present in this text from two other sources: the author's historical introduction to the story and the utterances of some of the adult characters in the story:

I asked Rachel why he had done that—spat at us. Because we were Jews, she said. But he wasn't German, and how did he know we were Jews? I asked. We looked different, she answered, darker. (7)

The first announcements had made Father angry, but not nearly as angry as the one which said that everybody had to register at the town hall. "Everybody," he yelled. "Only the papers *we* have to carry with us have something extra on them! A big *J. J* [original italics] for Jew!" (11)

Jood [original italics] ('Jew') the star said, in black letters on a yellow back-ground. And they weren't just ordinary letters. No, they had curlicues, especially the *d* [original italics].

Father was furious. "They even make you pay for these things," he shouted, "and textile coupons they want for them, too." (19)

The first-person (internal) focalization here is Reiss's adult attempt to recapture the perceptual field she experienced as a child. But there is a kind of "child-to-child" narration that is third person (externally focalized) and indisputably "adult," but that attempts to mediate a child's viewpoint and carries its own peculiar set of narratological difficulties. We have seen this device used, with greater or lesser success, in the novels of Benjamin Zephaniah, and in the work of Elizabeth Laird, and I have described this distinct characteristic of marrying third-person (by definition, adult) narration with the child's (or young person's) viewpoint as "docu-novel" because I feel that the peculiar distance the docu-novel sets up in the perceptual field between narrator and character is uncomfortable territory in children's fiction. Elizabeth Lutzeier's *No Shelter* is just such an example of this kind of "child-child" docu-novel mediated through the character of six-year-old Johannes that carries an uncomfortable degree of textual indeterminacy between narration and naïve readership: for example, when, in the early hours of a morning of 1943, the Jewish Daniela is forcibly removed by German soldiers from the Berlin apartment Johannes shares with her and his mother, and is packed off in a truck to what a mature reader knows to be the death camps, a naïve young reader may well believe, with Johannes, that Johannes's mother sobs because Daniela did not wish them goodbye, and may well sympathize with the near starving boy's joy that Daniela's departure means that he and his family left behind will be able to eat more food that day:

> Are you crying because she didn't say goodbye? Don't worry. She didn't take any food with her, so now we've got some extra food. We can have plenty to eat today; it's all in a heap on the kitchen table. (35)

And unlike Reiss's novel that was fictional autobiography, Lutzeier's is fictional documentary, which she says in a blurb note was "inspired by people's own stories rather than the history books." And unlike Reiss's novel that carries other narrational devices to facilitate wider interpretation, Lutzeier leaves her narration entirely in the field of her child characters and, by extension, her child readers. Reiss, on the other hand, seizes the opportunity to build into her third-person narration those kinds of narrational comments that would otherwise languish in the naïve and totally subjective view of her child characters, and she thus affords her (child) reader an opportunity for a broader interpretation than the child-to-child readings that would otherwise be the case. The point is especially made in relation to these narratives of abjection, where the naïve view of the child character is often at odds with the enormity of the events being narrated.

LANGUAGE, IDENTITY, AND ABJECTION

Butler relates that the subordination of the subject takes place through language. Language, she says, is the quintessential agent of the subject's accession to subjectivity in the symbolic order,[12] and she goes so far as saying that the subject *is* language:

The genealogy of the subject as a critical category, however, suggests that the subject, rather than be identified strictly with the
individual, ought to be designated as a linguistic category, a place-
holder, a structure in formation. (*Psychic* 10)

If language is perceived as the mode of empowerment and is related to
accession to identity and subjective agency through the paternal authority, and if language is named in patriarchy as the space from which
acculturated subjects may speak their lives, the loss or lack of it marks
out the subject as powerless, silent or silenced, by extension "feminized,"
and a potential victim to be exploited, expunged, and exterminated.

Most of these child figures are significantly silent and, therefore,
are lacking agency in Butler's definition. Tulip's speaking is only ever
reported in the narrative through the framing narrative voice and
agency of the girl character, Natalie, whom I have already situated as
Tulip's superego. Squib, the other abused character in this set of narratives, is also silent: "Squib doesn't talk" (Bawden, *Squib* 17). Tin never
utters a word; communicating only through noises and gestures, he is
truly the quintessential, preverbal child of the semiotic chora. The Jewish sisters, Annie and Sini de Leeuw, are silenced by their incarceration
and are without access to even written language because there are no
books. The subordination of their voice and loss of mother tongue to the
paternal authority of the German language are marked by their need
to whisper their way through the remaining days, months, and years
of the war. They emblematize the Nazi regime's ambition to unsignify
all Jews by being symptomatically excluded from the "Fatherland" of
language that is the domain of the symbolic, power and the law: "I find
myself reduced to the same abjection, a fecalized, feminized, passiv-
ated rot" (Kristeva, *Powers* 185). Zero, of Sachar's *Holes*, only assumes
a credible identity and a proper name on the state registers after his
accession to the written word by being taught to read by Stanley during
their days at Camp Green Lake.

Loss of language is the symptom of the abject status of all of these
child figures who share in the same semiotic space of effacement
through their mutual experiences of becoming hidden or defaced bodies, of becoming "strays," by becoming rootless and displaced, by their
mutual experience of physical incarceration or immobilization, and
by their impotence and curtailed freedom in the face of some form of
oppressive power. Loss of language makes them into nonsubjects who,
symptomatically, lack a proper name. As mentioned above, "Squib"
is so named only by the other child characters because he moves like
a firecracker: "'Squib's not a name,' the bigger ones said. Once in the

beginning, Robin had asked him, 'What's your real name?' but he hung his head and said nothing" (Bawden, *Squib* 7). The name "Tulip" is undermined and mocked for its credibility as a real name by Natalie: "'Tulip,' she said. I couldn't believe that was her name. I thought she must mean the kitten" (Fine 13). Zero is a nickname for a boy who is an official nobody: "'As far as anybody knows, Zero doesn't exist'" (Sachar 208); and "James Augustin Barnabas Flute" (Hartnett, *Thursday's Child* 7) is only ever referred to as Tin; the name identifies him by definition as a nonperson: "Tin Flute."

Most of these child figures also have lost their mothers—by either death or dissociation, which Kristeva has marked out as the primal psychological and corporeal rift that the aspiring ego identity undergoes of necessity. The de Leeuw sisters' mother dies when, with a quite extraordinary calculation, they and their father flee the Nazi occupation and leave her behind at the mercy of a Jewish hospital that is itself being squeezed out of existence by the occupation. Tin adopts his subterranean life when he is displaced in his mother's attentions as the youngest child by the birth of another sibling, Caffy; this is here interpreted as his metaphorical attempt to return to the womb and his refusal of ego identity. Kate's mother is wedded to her life as an artist after the loss of her husband and son, and has no time for Kate. Squib's familial relationship with "starvation Sal" is never defined, but however inadequate, she is inscribed as the primary caregiver; and Tulip has been made into the mother-substitute as her father's sex object. All these examples of metaphoric or literal loss of the mother seem to behave as metaphors for the way in which the abject is positioned, admittedly controversially, between maternal loss and paternal power denied.

In these ambiguous borderlanders who reside in the abject, the abuse of power is incorporated into the very fabric of their bodily existence to bring them to the "no place," which is also "the nothing" of identity and which then returns to the bodily surface as the physical exhibition of the unspeakable properties of abjection in the form of vomit, dirt, sweat, excreta, and blood. They embody curtailed subjectivity that is dramatized as a failed project in their proper accession to language and the symbolic, where the supposedly speaking subject is constituted and is empowered; they are, in Kristeva's words, the "articulation of negativity germane to the unconscious" (*Powers* 7). Above all, they present the singular threat to the stable, individual, and social ego for which the private, public, and political response has been to "bring him (or her?) down," which takes us back to the public display of intolerance to hybridity and ambiguity outside the Santa Maria Courthouse, and to all the other life histories that are documented here as exemplars of abjection.

Despite the call to bring them down, to silence or to repress them, these child figures who inhabit the borderland of abjection and who are the archetypes of ambivalence are also the locus of the most significant meanings relating to social, cultural, and personal identity, from which questions about the collective consciousness speak most loudly not least because, as Homi K. Bhabha has pointed out, that ambivalence functions as one of the "most significant discursive and psychical strategies of discriminatory power" (*Location* 2). Abjection embodies outsiderness in its very condition of rejection, and of its being ejected from the corporate social body. Far from being silenced by the process, however, it returns to the subject as the continuous and stark reminder that what is abjected is the projection of self that is impossible to be disowned.

5

UNATTACHED

Just as geographical displacement provides ready subject matters for writers for children and young adults, so do the loss of a mother and/or father and the consequent removal of a child into a different home. Such children have their "necessity to belong" tested. There has always been a need for the adoption and fostering of children who are abandoned, orphaned, "illegitimate," or deprived of the care of birth parents, or for other reasons, especially those who are deprived of birth mothers. Such children are more likely than others to suffer the ongoing difficulties of not having developed a strong and reciprocated attachment in their infancy, usually to a birth mother.

This chapter focuses on literary and actual children who, for whatever reasons of their being removed from their birth parents and adopted, fostered, or in care, illustrate all the typical behavior patterns of failed attachment in early childhood. "Attachment theory" still strongly influences the understanding and practice of adoption and fostering, ever since it was developed in the 1950s by John Bowlby practicing in England; Mary Ainsworth researching in Canada, then England and Africa; and Harry Harlow working with monkeys in the United States (Bretherton 759). Hence, this chapter is titled "Unattached" inasmuch as these child figures are represented as having failed to develop the necessary early bonding with a significant other in a reciprocal relationship, who may or may not be a birth mother, through which to thrive in relationships and emotional development generally. As part of his attachment theory, Bowlby stated,

> The infant and young child should experience a warm, intimate, and continuous relationship with its mother (or permanent

mother substitute) in which both find satisfaction and enjoyment. (Quoted in Bretherton 765)

The focus, therefore, is on a clutch of paradigm fictions that are typical of this generic type of abandoned, adopted, and fostered children: Katherine Paterson's *The Great Gilly Hopkins* (1981) is an account of a disaffected eleven-year-old girl's adjustment to a new foster home. Jacqueline Wilson's *The Story of Tracy Beaker* (1991) and its sequel *The Dare Game* (2000) are about an equally rebellious child resisting the institutional forms of care in preference to her version of foster care or adoption by a substitute mother. Sharon Creech's *Ruby Holler* (2002) is about a twin girl and boy who are fostered out of an abusive residential care home by an unlikely and unworldly old couple who offer an alternative lifestyle; Cynthia Voigt's *Homecoming* (2003) and its sequel *Dicey's Song* (2003) are stories about the grit and determination of a young girl's search for her lost family and family roots. Finally, Rachel Anderson's *The War Orphan* (1984) is about an intercountry adoption of a traumatized Vietnamese boy and his impact on the birth child of the adopting couple. These are all classics of their type with enduring resonances for the ongoing questions and debates surrounding the fostering and adoption of children who have lost their parents for one reason or another, and function like "case histories" in the children's literature of abandoned children.

In contemporary Western society, the society out of which all the works of fiction in this chapter have been authored and in which conventional nuclear family units are the "normal" site of child rearing, adoption and fostering have become institutionalized. Adoption and fostering, whether in families or specialist homes, need legal sanction, and are professionalized and regulated by public bodies. Arrangements differ in different countries, as does the success of the arrangements, and their use of different culturally specific traditional expectations about the care of children deprived of parents, such as their automatically passing into the care of the mother's mother or into the care of the extended family.[1] Nevertheless, all signatories to the 1989 United Nations Convention on the Rights of the Child (UNCRC)[2] (that is, by 2007, all member states except the United States and Somalia, both of which have since signaled their intention to sign) have agreed, "A child temporarily or permanently deprived of his or her family environment, or in whose own best interests cannot be allowed to remain in that environment, shall be entitled to special protection and assistance provided by the state" (Article 20, sec. 1). It is not to minimize the momentous nature of adoption for a child, birth mother, or adopter to say that most intracountry adopted children are not significantly disadvantaged by their status except in only the most rare cases and mild senses. On the other hand, *inter*country adoption, which has burgeoned in the West in the last two decades, introduces a new spectrum of difficulties. Even though the nature versus nurture debate continues to be hotly contested; even though within it, or despite it, heredity and nurture are seen as complex systems not necessarily in binary opposition to each other as the oppositional terms themselves conjure up; and while heredity is seen as an important determiner of children's predispositions and behavior,[3] it is still assumed that adopted children will be profoundly influenced by the child-rearing practices of their adopted families. Furthermore, most adoptions occur at an early age for the child[4] so that although there may be psychological results of unconscious disruptions of attachment,[5] being adopted is a relatively "invisible" condition.

In contrast to infant adoption, when children are fostered (or adopted out of Care Homes as older children), they are usually old enough to be anxious or even reluctant entrants into new homes,[6] and are often hostile to, or unusually demanding of, new carers. They may have been damaged by their previous history of care or neglect, they may have to live alongside children who are strangers to them, and if they are fostered into a home which already has birth children, they may have to live alongside children who have been relatively advantaged in their nurture and who have a different sort of relationship to their carers. This range of fostered and adopted experiences is represented in these focus texts. While all children carry within them their unconscious and imagined histories, fostered and adopted children bring with them exaggerated and intensified versions of these in the imagined life stories they never experienced, and often in their obsessive imaginings of their distant pasts and/or their record of managing the difficulties of their recent past, and they bring with them difficulties and conflicts which are staples of these kinds of novels of abandonment.[7]

In its strongest assertion, from which Bowlby later drew back, attachment theory claimed that to be deprived of a loving mother in the first two and a half years of life would inevitably and irrecoverably lead to emotional and cognitive damage (Bowlby, *A Secure Base* 122–126). However, Bretherton points out that later summaries of Bowlby's work often disregarded the role of substitute mothers and Bowlby's emphasis on the role of social networks and economic factors in the development of well-functioning mother-child relationships (765–766). Attachment theory has been modified by studies which have suggested that deprivation can be recovered from, and new attachments can be made. For example, Gill Hodges and Barbara Tizard found that, of children taken into care in early life, those who had been placed in adoptive families fared better later in life than those restored to their parents (quoted in Clarke and Clarke 141). Michael Rutter and colleagues found that severely early-deprived Romanian orphans adopted into British homes do recover, but the speed, and presumably eventual degree, of emotional and cognitive recovery was inversely proportional to the length of time for which they had been incarcerated in orphanages (Rutter 108–133).

On discovery [in 1967] at the age of seven the twins were dwarfed in stature, lacking speech, suffering from rickets and failing to understand the meaning of pictures. The doctors who examined them confidently predicted permanent physical and mental handicap. Legally removed from their parents, they first underwent a programme of physical remediation, and initially entered a school for children with severe learning disabilities. After some time, the boys were legally adopted by exceptionally dedicated women. Scholastically, from a state of profound disability they caught up with age peers and achieved emotional and intellectual normality.... [As adults] they are said to be entirely stable, lacking abnormalities and enjoying warm relationships.

Facts revealed by J. Koluchova's study quoted in Clarke and Clarke 139)

The emotional difficulties and conflicts related to early "unattachment" are represented in Katherine Paterson's *The Great Gilly Hopkins* and in Jacqueline Wilson's *The Story of Tracy Beaker*. Gilly is an ill-mannered, insulting, defiant, cruel, threatening, racist, and dishonest eleven year old. She steals from a blind man. She is a cunning opportunist: she offers to clean other peoples' houses to give her a chance to steal, and sells her knowledge of the meaning of "adultery" to fellow Sunday school pupils who have been excited by curiosity but frustrated by the scriptural language. Nevertheless, the novel succeeds in making Gilly into a sympathetic character who wills herself to be as dislikeable as possible. Readers share in Gilly's ridicule of, and contempt for, the hypocritical and falsely cheerful way that adults deal with children like her. She describes the voice of her caseworker as "bright and fake like a laxative commercial" (Paterson 114). We see this same kind of well-developed cynicism in Tracy Beaker. She is only ten years old and even

more forthright than Gilly about her loves and hates, and she is especially good at seeing through the professional superficiality of emollient
social workers:

> They strike this special nothing-you-can-say-would-shock-me-
> sweetie pose.... "I guess you're feeling really angry and upset
> today, Tracy," they twitter, when I've wrecked my bedroom or got
> into a fight or shouted and sworn at someone, so that it's *obvious*
> I'm angry and upset. (Wilson, *Tracy Beaker* 73)

Roberta Seelinger Trites in this context raises the point about the need
for abandoned children to rebel against authority figures:

> The propensity of adolescents with neither actual nor effective sur-
> rogate parents to create imaginary parents against whom to rebel
> is a classic re-enactment of the Lacanian principle of creating the
> Name-of the-Father. After all, it would seem that the parentless
> adolescent is the most free, that being parentless is the most desir-
> able imaginable state of adolescent wish fulfilment. (61)

And she concludes that their need to do so might also be explained in
Lacanian terms:

> Because the idea of the parent is so seductive, so central to the
> subject's sense of self definition, that the process becomes inevi-
> table. (61)

Certainly this is the case for all the child figures presented in these narratives who, while rejecting and resenting the presence of the authority
figures and carers with whom they are in daily contact, continuously
entertain the self-motivating daily fantasies of and longing for their
lost parents, especially their mothers (see below). Tracy Beaker presents
herself as fearless, independent, and tough. But for all her cunning and
knowingness, in what purports to be her autobiographical diary, she is
unable entirely to conceal her "weakness" of feeling. She says that she
never cries, even though she often has attacks of runny eyes at critical
moments, which she ascribes to "hay fever" (Wilson, *Tracy Beaker* 29).
Like Gilly Hopkins, she affects to be unhurtable, and to have no need
for friends, especially in the competitive setting of the first of the books,
a residential children's care home from which newly made friends are
likely to disappear suddenly, leaving no trace. In *The Dare Game*, in
which she is fostered, Tracy does make and keep friends, both of whom
are themselves socially marginal—a school excludee and a friendless
weed. Joseph Zornado points out, "Children who have been abandoned and abused tell their story through their behavior, especially in

the ways in which they connect, and ultimately fail to connect, with other human beings in a satisfying way. Detached relationships breed detached relationships" (*Inventing* 10). Just as Gilly does, Tracy tries to protect herself by hurting others: "I had to hurt everyone to show I didn't need any of them" (Wilson, *Dare Game* 203). And, also like Gilly, she has had a number of foster homes: three in the three years leading up to the novel's events.

Gilly has learned that "it never pays to attach yourself to something that is likely to blow you away" (Paterson 124); "a person must be tough. Otherwise, you were had" (62); and "I can't go soft—not as long as I'm nobody's real kid—not while I'm just something to play musical chairs with" (71). She has developed the survival tactics of someone who thinks they are condemned to be a dispensable outsider in any family, neighborhood, or school that they are forced into. As someone who is socially and legally helpless, she also has developed all the independence and power that she can, and has a repertory of ways of extracting maximum control in her delimited spheres of power: "she could stand anything, she thought—a gross guardian, a freaky kid, an ugly dirty house—as long as she was in charge" (14). "She could tell that the child was scared silly of her. It was about the only thing in the last two hours that had given her any real satisfaction" (21).

The novels illustrate the perennial balancing act of caseworkers between the considerations of home or of institutional care that is at the center of all adoption and fostering procedures to fulfill their obligations to ensure that they are always in the best interests of the child: the sometimes impossible juggling between whether the child is best served by, on the one hand, being returned to the often socially disadvantageous position of his or her birth family, or, on the other hand, staying in care. The usual position of caseworkers in relation to placing older children in foster care or to be adopted is that these children are best served by being accorded agency in their adoptive or fostering process by being consulted about what should happen to them, and that they should have continuity and stability of placement in a family atmosphere, and continuity of schooling. All of these principles appear to be violated in *The Great Gilly Hopkins* when Gilly is returned to her grandmother. But, however eccentrically, her grandmother may give her the best chance of continuity of care and schooling. Gilly has been rejected by her birth mother and has only a very vague understanding about her early life and reasons why she is in care. She has had her early maternal attachment broken and—equally importantly, according to Bowlby—not reciprocated. But there is a suggestion that she is still capable of attracting, reciprocating, and benefiting from that close tie to an adult which Lisa Bostock says is an important enhancer of the resilience of what is now referred to in social work terminology as "the looked-after" child (2).

MISSING MOTHERS

Among the later studies in attachment were ones that tried to relate infants' subsequent adult personality and behavior (such as their responses when they became parents themselves) to types of infant attachment. For example, Cindy Hazen and Phil Shaver related ways in which adults made or failed to make romantic attachments in adult-hood to their experiences of maternal attachment in infancy (quoted in Bretherton 786). Infants who had been "detached" from their mothers tended to develop "avoidant" personalities in later life.[8] Gilly, abandoned by her mother in infancy, has an "avoidant" personality that compounds her susceptibility to be treated as an outsider. She fiercely rejects help: when her new carer overhears Gilly crying for her lost birth mother and offers sympathy, she is met with "'I don't need any help ... from anybody'" (Paterson 35) and a slammed door. She tries to annoy or frustrate well-meaning adults, as when she messes up her hair before her first day at school to try to shame her social worker (23), and when she makes plans to succeed at school up until the final test, which she will flunk to spite her teacher, and she is furious when here and else-where the understanding adults fail to rise to her bait.

Vera Fahlberg points out, "Many children in care have never learned psychologically healthy ways to connect with others" (17). Tracy Beaker, for all her smartness, is unable to understand the feelings of people who have not had their feelings as cauterized as hers have been; and Gilly Hopkins, having been treated like a portable object herself, regards other people as objects to be used. She has a manipulative charm, as with "the 300 watt smile she had designed especially for melting the hearts of foster parents" (Paterson 51). When an unfortunate, dirty, and unprepossessing girl (also with disappeared parents) tries to attach her-self to Gilly "like a louse nit," Gilly thinks, "Agnes might come in handy some day. The trick was in knowing how to dispose of people when you were through with them" (46–47). However, Gilly does have some of the resilience and self-esteem that workers with children try to develop, even though, until she is fostered by the earth mother Trotter, she seems to have had few of the experiences that promote it (Bostock viii). After all, she calls herself "The Great Gilly Hopkins." She is a proud outsider, fiercely determined to "show them" (Paterson 28), a policy that some-times ironically brings her the acceptability that she resists, as when she "shows" her teacher; and even at moments when she thinks she will not "survive," she is determined to go down fighting. She thinks of herself as "a red fox ... surrounded by snarling dogs.... She was smarter than all of them, but they were too many" (28).

> Positive relationships, at any age in the life span, can help improve poor self-image. People who take an interest, who listen, who care and love people, make others feel better. They bolster self-esteem.... Children who are not loved at home may still develop feelings of self-worth if a relative takes an interest, a teacher appears concerned and caring, or if a social worker responds with kindness and consistency.
>
> **Bostock (viii)**

Underlying the self-protective exterior hardness of these child characters, supporting their pride, and interfering with their ability to relate to those who would befriend, help, care for, and love them is their yearning for their romantically and unrealistically imagined mothers. Gilly infers from her social worker that her mother is an ex-"flower-person" who had run away from her own mother (the Virginian grandmother who takes in Gilly at the end of the novel), and she had given birth to Gilly without her own mother's knowledge. It was Gilly's birth mother who had given her the Tolkien-derived name of Galadriel (a princess) with which Gilly has a love-hate relationship. In the mode of abandoned children generally, Gilly is convinced that her mother now wants her back, and would want to rescue her from the untidy house and community of a fat uneducated carer, a "retard" fellow fosterling, and a black neighbor. Gilly believes that if her mother knew what was happening to her daughter, she would come "sweeping in like a goddess-queen, reclaiming the lost princess" (Paterson 110). Gilly's thinking is wishful, but she is also encouraged by a postcard from California on which her mother has written, "'The agency wrote to me that you had moved. I wish it were to here. I miss you. All my love, Courtney'" (34). The abandoned child thinks of her mother as "existing from before time—like a goddess in perpetual perfection" (104), and that in her photograph her mother looks like "the star of some TV show" (16). Having had no realistic account of her birth and the reason for, and circumstances of, her being taken into care, Gilly is disabled by being excluded even from the world of common sense. She replies to her mother's postcard because she wants to "stop being a 'foster-child'.... To be real without any quotation marks. To belong and to possess. To be herself.... Snow White beyond the Dwarfs—Galadriel Hopkins, come into her own" (11). In other words, she longs for an identity other than the labels that fix her in somebody else's alien, and alienating, definition of her. But by replying to her mother, she provokes an unwanted response that results in her prim grandmother, whom she had not known about and who had not known about her, rushing to her "rescue." She then has a disillusioning meeting with her reluctant mother, who is in reality frumpy and grumpy and has been persuaded to have a brief encounter with her daughter only because the grandmother has paid her to come. We can assume that the meeting with her mother might complete Gilly's grieving for her lost attachment, and assuage her unconscious guilt about her wrongly assumed contribution to the rejection. Her disillusionment helps her to move forward: she abandons her fantasies about her mother's beauty and her assumption that her mother wants her back, and she unselfishly returns to her grandmother's care and begins to call her grandmother's house "home," possibly achieving the permanence and security which she has never had, and beginning to build herself an ancestry.[9] Thus, against her will but in her own interests, Gilly is rescued from her solipsist world of defensive make-believe and taken inside the world of social reality, where she is reminded of the words of her carer Trotter about life being hard but not bad (138).

Tracy Beaker, too, knows that she was rejected by her till-then single mother when her mother lived with a "gorilla" who "beat up" Tracy (Wilson, *Tracy Beaker* 15), and is rejected again by her in the second book. She has also been rejected by two sets of foster parents, one which smacked her and objected to her scaring their little children, and a second which were foodies who denied her junk food but gave her "stews ... [which] looked like someone had already eaten them and sicked them up" (123). And there she stayed until the foster mother got pregnant and returned Tracy to the care home: "'So they're going to give the boring old baby away.... And keep me. Because they had me first, didn't they?'" Tracy remarks to her social worker with cynical irony (48). Tracy mentions her mother in 39 of the 142 pages of the metafictional autobiography we are reading, and her mother occupies a tenth of the illustrations. Of her mother's lack of interest in her, she says, "'I bet she's been trying and trying to get hold of me, but she doesn't know where to look'" (51), and she gives as a reason for not making friends, "'There's not much point, because my mum's probably coming to get me soon and then I'll be living with her so I won't need any friends here'" (56). While waiting for her imaginary rich and glamorous dream mother to visit her or even take her off to live with her in Hollywood, Tracy, movingly as well as amusingly, is working on getting herself a satisfactory foster home. For example, when Tracy meets a writer who takes an interest in her (and, in a daringly metafictional move on the part of Jacqueline Wilson, the illustrations in the book are Jacqueline Wilson look-alikes), she works on her successfully to persuade the writer to foster her. *The Dare Game* in which Tracy has been successfully fostered by the writer includes an account of how she spends a weekend with her birth mother and discovers that for all her mother's spoiling her, she is unwilling to inconvenience herself for Tracy and does not really want her. After this revelation, Tracy returns and smashes up the "home" that she and her two odd friends have made in a derelict house—her fantasy of the "home" she has never had.

NEVER COMING HOME

Being fostered or adopted by a grandmother, especially a maternal grandmother, is a common experience for children who can no longer be looked after by their mother or father. Gilly's experience in this respect makes a useful comparison with that of Dicey Tillerman, a clever thirteen year old at the center of Cynthia Voigt's Tillerman novels, *Homecoming* and *Dicey's Song*. The emphasis is on abandoned children finding and enjoying a home, hence the title of the first of the novels is a special and emphatic case of a recurrent motif of homecoming in children's and young adult fiction. Dicey has said, "Home was with Momma—and Momma was in hospital where the doctors said she'd always stay. There could be no home for the Tillermans.… Dicey would settle for a place to stay" (Voigt, *Homecoming* 212). Dicey also longs for a lost mother and is adopted by a grim, eccentric, and near-reclusive maternal grandmother who lives far away and has also lost all her family one way or another until Dicey knocks on her door. Dicey and her younger sister and two brothers had been abandoned by their incapable and mentally ill single mother, and sent away with nothing but a map and a distant address. Dicey has led them in an odyssey from Massachusetts to Maryland by foot, lifts, bus, and boat. She has fed, nursed, encouraged, soothed, defended, and lied for her "family" of little siblings—has effectively mothered them—and all through the journey has taken responsibility for finding the route, food, and campsites, conserving and sometimes earning enough money for them to survive on. In the process she has become precociously worldly-wise, cautious, cunning, and careworn, and has learned to cry only in private.

The events of the sequel, *Dicey's Song*, set at the grandmother's house, would be a recuperative return to domesticity, education, leisure, and adolescent culture for Dicey, except that she has to maintain responsibility for the upbringing of her younger siblings, albeit now with the help of the grandmother. Dicey had kept her mother unforgotten: "All the time Momma had been gone, Dicey had carried around an idea of her" (188). She has an explicit suspicion that the children may innocently have had some responsibility for her mother's breakdown, because of her inability to cope with bringing up four small children on her own, and has the kind of guilt and self-blame that many abandoned children experience.

When they come to rest, and hopefully to stay, at their frosty grandmother's house, the old lady reminds them that they are in "'My house, not yours'" (Voigt, *Dicey's Song* 375), but by the end of the narrative she can signal her acceptance of them by referring to her house when she asks Dicey, "'Ready to go home?'" (402). In *Dicey's Song*, when they are settled in the grandmother's home, Dicey can reflect comfortably, "Nothing mattered as much as sitting together around this table, in the warm yellow light, all of them together" (188). Despite the bleak realities of their grandmother's home, "home" is wherever they are together, and becomes a fantasy of light and warmth. Dicey has a special remembered and significant line of verse, found in a graveyard where they slept one night on their journey there: Robert Louis Stevenson's "Home is the hunter, home from the hill, and the sailor home from the sea" (200).

The importance of home is also apparent in the Tracy Beaker sequel *The Dare Game*. For example, Tracy is curious about other children's and people's homes; she has set up the quasi-home in the derelict house that she destroyed after visiting her mother; and she ends her story with a sampler on which it says, "HOME IS WHERE THE HEART IS." But earlier, thinking about Dorothy in *The Wizard of Oz* saying "There's no place like home," she has written:

> It gets to me. Because there's no place like home for me. No place at all. I haven't got a home. Well. I didn't have up till recently. Unless you count the Home. If a home has a capital letter at the front you can be pretty sure it isn't like a *real* [original italics] home. (Wilson, *Dare Game* 11)

She is referring, of course, to the state-run children's Home where she had lived when she was the younger child we first met in *The Story of Tracy Beaker*. Although the evidence of all she tells us about the Home suggests that it is benign and well run, it lacks privacy and personal space: the only space that belongs exclusively to her is her bedroom, but it does not have a lock on the door and so is open to anyone and everyone to walk into at any time. Even the most intimate conversations are overheard: for example, bedwetting is made common knowledge, and private possessions are constantly vulnerable to damage, revenge attacks, and the wear and tear of being shared. Tracy even has to share her birthday and a single birthday cake with another child in the home. There are few presents and treats, and no personal pets. So Tracy yearns, as well as for her mother, for a foster home. The defects and sense of powerlessness of her life in the residential Home are betrayed by her plans for an ideal, and idealized, home. In her fantasies of power and self-determination, she imagines suing for libel all the people who have made disparaging remarks about her in the confidential file in which she has sneaked a read, then of buying her own house and employing a foster parent:

> But because I'd be paying them, they'd have to do everything I said. I'd order them to make me a whole birthday cake to myself every single day of the week and they'd just have to jump to it and do so.
> I wouldn't let anybody else in to share it with me. (Wilson, *Tracy Beaker* 101)

> Recognising that the child, for the full and harmonious development of his or her personality, should grow up in a family environment, in an atmosphere of happiness, love and understanding ... [and b]earing in mind that, as indicated in the Declaration of the Rights of the Child, 'the child, by reason of his physical and mental immaturity, needs special safeguards and care, including appropriate legal protection, before as well as after birth ...'
>
> **Preamble to UNCRC**

Most policy and practice in the current care of unattached children are of getting children out of care and into families,[10] and in the wake of this policy there are high-profile advertising campaigns in local and national newspapers to attract would-be foster parents or adopters. We see the effects of the policy on individual children whom Tracy Beaker represents when she experiences the indignity of being advertised as available for fostering or adoption. Tracy is affronted that when she appears as "Child of the Week" in the local newspaper ads, her social worker describes her as

> A lively, healthy, chatty, ten-year-old [who] has a few behaviour problems and needs loving handling ... (61)

rather than, as Tracy says she would have written,

Have you a place in your hearts for dear little Tracy? Brilliant and beautiful, this little girl needs a loving home. Very rich parents preferred, as little Tracy needs lots of toys, presents and pets to make up for her tragic past. (61–62)

The statement contains many embedded issues that could be profitably unpacked in relation to children in care more generally: it is a further example of the way that they have their agency and identity eroded; about the need for reciprocal affirmation—of self and by others; and about all manner of poverty, both material and emotional. So Jacqueline Wilson makes a serious point behind this playful fantasy of her character about the one-sided nature of the power systems in which the children perceive themselves and are perceived—as "cases," as "problems," and as needing to be "handled" rather than cared for or loved. More importantly, it suggests that the children themselves might be allowed to write their own ads, rather than their being anonymized as case histories in someone else's view of them. More radically in the mode of pushing further on the issue of the children's need for self-determination, it raises the specter of the children themselves being able to choose their prospective adoptive or foster parents and the requirement that the prospective parents advertise themselves for selection by the children.

BEING AFFIRMED

Children's Society spokesman Tim Linehan said the scandals made people realise that the area of residential care had been "completely neglected"—making it fertile ground for predatory paedophiles. He said the most important change had been to open up the management of care homes and make them more transparent.

"In the 1970s and 80s residential homes, although not independent, were run like closed institutions," he said. "You didn't have the flow of people coming and going that you have today."

"You did have inspections, but if a charismatic, controlling individual was running the home he could get round inspectors."

"Children in Care: Now and Then"

The thirteen-year-old twins at the center of Sharon Creech's 2002 Carnegie Medal–winning *Ruby Holler*, "Florida" and her boy twin "Dallas," have been quite literally dumped at a residential children's home, albeit one from which the children are supposed to be fostered as soon as possible but there have already been two failed attempts at fostering. The home is in a timeless nowhere in the rural United States and is Dickensian and ramshackle, as are the Trepids, the violent, punitive, and mercenary married couple who run it. It makes the point, albeit fictionally, that the experiences of these in-care children are as if they too live in a timeless nowhere: they have no history, have no identity, are often geographically displaced, and are excluded wholly or partially, more so than most children, from knowledge about where they belong in time and place and what their identity is in relation to other people. So the fantasy element that underpins this particular novel, and distinguishes it from the others in focus here, also makes a strong social point.

The novel is a generic hybrid that has naturalistic passages and dialogue, and is intercut with fairy-tale and dream sequences, cross-cutting between scenes and with an exciting climax such as would be found in an adventure story. A potent intertextual reference is that of the quintessentially rejected orphan children Hansel and Gretel, and the recurrent bird motif that figures like something of the lost mother in the first and last of the chapters: it comes to Florida in one of her dreams and says, "Have you seen my baby? I'm missing my baby" (Creech 79), then, at the end, tells her, "You're my baby" (309).[11]

The Boxton Creek Children's Home is described as no longer inspected or supervised, and it is mad with rules such as no talking at meals that the twins constantly violate, earning themselves blows to the head and escalating punishments such as incarceration in cellars and repeated sessions of hard labor. Dallas has nursed a boy there, dying of untreated fever, whose last words were "'Who am I? Who am I?'" (Creech 9). Dallas and Florida are the oldest children in the home that is for children of six months to thirteen years. They have no knowledge of their parents because they were both left as babies on the doorstep of the home in a produce box that contained delivery notes whose destinations gave them their names. Neither do they know their correct birth dates. As children abandoned soon after birth, their only attachments are to each other, although they are surprisingly different in temperament. In their many failed fosterings they have not been separated; they have been raised together all their lives in the same environments and,

like many other twin siblings, each has an almost telepathic understanding of what the other is thinking, a capacity that comes into
play most powerfully when they are separated for the first time,
when the other is in danger. Each has been the other's only confi-
dant and consoler: Florida "hated the thought of being separated
from Dallas. She felt that the only reason they'd survived this long
without turning into cowardly wimps or juvenile delinquents was
because they'd had each other" (33). Nevertheless, as orphaned
children trying to establish and secure an identity, they too indulge
in the fantasy of the perfect mother (Chodorow and Contratto 54–
74). The dreamier Dallas tells Florida that their mother was "wispy,
like a princess, and she was extremely smart, and she could do just
about anything—she could paint and she could sing like nobody
you've ever heard in your life" (Creech 45). Florida dreams about
protecting a cardboard box as if fantasizing about her own mother
as a projection of the box in which she was abandoned; she calls,
"Hey, Mom!" when she spots a stranger with frizzy hair like her
own; and she has an intimation that she ought to know a man who
turns out to be her birth father, and who reforms his behavior when
he realizes that he is.

The twins in *Ruby Holler* typically have frequently been pushed
out of the home into the care of unsuitable foster parents and prospective adopters, where, before being rejected and returned as
"trouble," they have suffered horrors that inform their bad dreams—
forced labor, living in a rat-infested cellar, false accusations of theft,
and persecution by a birth sibling. Every time they are dumped in
an unsuitable foster home, they maintain their hope by planning to
run away, such as by hitching a ride on one of the freight trains they
hear passing nearby. They are persuaded to go with an eccentric old
couple called Tiller and Sairy, who whittle for a living and live in
a fairy-tale enchanted clearing in the wood (the "Holler") with few
modern facilities and no neighbors with children (or neighbors at
all), and in this therapeutic dreamspace, away from the pressures
and punishments, stereotypings, and expectations of themselves as
failures, they are eventually recouped into confident, self-actualizing
young people.

To go from the bucolic foster homes and the tyrannies of the Boxton Creek Children's Home to this acme of nature is the (arguably
too easy) return to a Rousseauesque ideal of the "natural" childhood, unfettered and uncorrupted by machinery and the pressures
of modern-day living, and is instead the quintessence of the natural
world ideology in which ideals of childhood flourish. Based on their

previous experience, the twins constantly expect rejection and chastisement, but it does not come because the old people actively and effectively *affirm* them in ways that the twins have not previously experienced. They are completely trusting and benevolent. They say, "Kids ought to … be able to do stuff without someone watching over their shoulders every minute" (Creech 153). When the twins misbehave, Tiller and Sairy manufacture innocent interpretations of what they have done and help them put things right. Sairy, in the best literary and child-rearing traditions, dispenses nonstop home-cooked comforts, even tempting them back from an escape attempt by cooking fragrant bacon near their hiding place.

In school, Dallas had sat at the back of the classroom. The children in front had the ideas, but Dallas believed that he was incapable of having ideas:

> If Dallas had to do a report, the teacher would say "Here, John will help you get an idea," or, "That's not what I meant. Let Bonnie show you how to do it," or, "If you can't do the assignment, just sit quietly." Dallas didn't have parents to come in and look at his work on conference days, or anyone to worry over his report card, so it had never mattered very much to him whether he did the work or not.… He daydreamed at school, imagining quiet places in the woods or how cookies were made or how trees grew. I didn't know that these things in his head were all ideas. (Creech 63)

So it comes as a revelation and a surprise to Dallas when Sairy announces that he is capable of having ideas:

> "I believe you've thought of everything, Dallas," she said. "You've got some real good ideas here, things I wouldn't have thought of."
>
> "You're kidding, right?" (Creech 63)

The way foster children are disadvantaged in education is a theme of research about them, and advocacy for them, and is indicated in numerous surveys.[12] Compared with other children, they may more frequently change schools, take their behavioral problems into a less than fully informed or sympathetic environment, be singled out for bullying, have no long-term friendships, and have no adults to interest themselves in their progress or career selection; and when they leave school, a disproportionate number of them quickly become unemployed, pregnant, or imprisoned.

[Children's charity] Barnardo's chief executive Martin Narey said: "The cycle of disadvantage that haunts these children as they grow up shows no sign of being broken as they enter adulthood.

Our report shows that many looked-after children have both academic potential and the desire to work hard and would have liked to succeed in education but the state, as a parent, fails them terribly.

Dreadful GCSE results compound the disadvantages they face and commit them to unemployment and long-term disadvantage." Barnardo's claimed multiple care home and foster care placements, repeated school changes, exclusion and insufficient support all contributed to a cycle of disadvantage. Findings of the report included: More than half reported being bullied at school as a direct result of being in care. Four out of 10 said no-one went to sports days or other school events. The number of care placements young people had lived in varied between one and 30—half had been in more than four placements. More than half were not currently in employment, training, or education. Almost half the group had attended six or more schools and 11% had attended more than 10.

"System 'Failing Children in Care'"

This year approximately 6,000 young people will emerge from the care of the state. Of these 6,000, 4,500 of them will leave with no educational qualifications whatsoever. Within two years of leaving care, 3,000 will be unemployed, 2,100 will be mothers or pregnant and 1,200 will be homeless. Out of the 6,000, just 60 will make it to university.... It is not just a tragedy for the individual. A successful system of care would transform this country. At a stroke it would empty a third of prisons and shift half of all prisoners under the age of 25 out of the criminal justice system. It would halve the number of prostitutes, and would reduce by between a third and a half the number of homeless and remove 80% of *Big Issue* sellers from our street corners.

Sergeant, *Handle with Care* (1)

MOTIVES AND MOTIVATIONS

People are motivated to become foster parents for a range of different reasons from "liking children" to "doing a job from home."[13]
The "Holler" couple seems initially to be using the children to fill
a gap in their life which has been left by their now adult birth children having left home for jobs and the world. But more specifically,
and oddly, when old Tiller and Sairy first approach the orphanage,
their explicit purpose is to collect a companion each—a girl for the
man and a boy for the woman!—to take on separate life-threatening
adventures they have planned for themselves. The plan would split
the twins from each other for the first time in their lives. Initially,
at least, the twins are brought into the family as objects to serve the
purpose of the adopters. There is an adventure in which Florida is
nearly drowned in the rapids, and a subplot of stolen money and
revenge of the Tillers. But by the end of the narrative when the children are poised to run away from the Holler again because they feel
that they may be in the way and may not be wanted any longer, they
pause and think again:

> "Who's going to chop the wood while Tiller's getting his strength
> back?" Florida said.
> "And who's going to haul the water?"
> "And," Florida said, "who's going to help Sairy with all those
> getting-over-heart-attack things she's going to have to make?
> Answer me that." (Creech 307)

And with these first altruistic thoughts in their entire lives through
which they begin for the first time to affirm their sense of self, they
decide not to run away after all, and instead they return the next day to
the familiar smell of "*Welcome home bacon*" simply because they feel
needed and because they have been affirmed.

Rachel Anderson's *The War Orphan* also raises questions about
adopters' motives in bringing abandoned children into their homes. Ha
is a severely damaged Vietnamese boy adopted by an altruistic English
couple after the Vietnam War, long before intercountry adoption was
familiar. Simon, the other young person at the center of the novel, is
scholarly, well-behaved, and domesticated—an opposite to the troubled
and unattached central characters of the other books that have been
discussed in this chapter. Simon even says he has not had the expected
"pre-pubertal hormone surges [to fill him with loathing for his parents]"
(Rachel Anderson 8), but he does find relief at his aunt's more relaxed
house, where people eat off trays in front of the TV.

David Banda's future looked set to be the same as more than a million other children in Malawian orphanages: poverty, malnutrition, HIV/AIDS, chronic disease and early death—life expectancy in the stricken African nation is just 40.

Yesterday, though, the 13-month-old boy's life took an extraordinary turn; he was taken on a private jet to South Africa, accompanied by a bodyguard and a nanny, before heading for an opulent new life in London with the singer Madonna and her family.

But even as a Malawian court granted Madonna and her husband, Guy Ritchie, an 18-month interim adoption order and the right to take David out of the country, the controversy over the boy and his newly rewritten future continued.

The issue has divided campaigners in Malawi, as well as polarizing debate internationally. For critics, Madonna is simply another example of the growing and distasteful trend of rich celebrities "shopping" for children to adopt from countries with which they have no ethnic ties, using their money and power to bend the rules without a thought for the children they do not choose.

The fact that she has pledged £1.6m to help 900,000 Malawian orphans with food, education, and shelter has only added to the belief that she has in effect bought herself a baby by flexing the muscle power of her £248m fortune.

For others, the singer is to be praised for helping at least one child out of poverty, in a country where a quarter of the population is infected with HIV and the majority of people live on less than a dollar a day, and for her financial aid to the others left behind.

Frith and Thompson (2)

So there are questions here about whether the distresses of fostered and adopted children are also a concern alongside the distresses of the birth children who have "outsiders" brought into their homes via fostering and adoption. Simon is a clever only child with no apparent friends or need for them. He attends a selective school, whose uniform he likes to wear (Rachel Anderson 45), and, when the reader first meets him, he has just addressed an audience of four at the school debating society on "Britain's diplomatic role in East–West communications"

(4). He is unfazed by, and forgiving of, the verbal and physical bullying he endures on the way home by boys who live in rougher housing and attend an unselective school, and whose disadvantages he purports to understand. He likes to "be at home listening to Vivaldi and printing wallpaper for his parents' anniversary present" (20). He lives in the loving bosom of a stereotypically white, liberal, well-meaning, theoretically and complacently antisexist, antiracist, anticlassist, and wholesome-food-loving nuclear family. How Simon comes to see his parents with an increasing exasperation (much of the book is told in his voice) provides the book's comedy. How their principles and love are tested to the limits by their intercountry adoption of the child "Ha" is one of the book's themes, and the way their subsequent difficulties are, with hindsight, presaged is one of the book's many aesthetic strengths.

Simon is therefore a quintessential insider of English liberal bourgeois society, even if he is, contentedly, an outsider with respect to youth culture. There seems little difference between his social identity and his home identity. He appears to be undisturbed and even welcoming when his parents announce that they are to foster a "rescued" Vietnam War orphan, called Ha, with the intention of eventually adopting him. They have one motive of which Simon is at first unaware, and they admit that one of their motives is guilt at the United Kingdom's support for that war: "Collective guilt. We may not actually *be* guilty. But we're all responsible," his father says (Rachel Anderson 51). He speaks guiltily, but there are often ideological "missionary motives" mixed into altruistic behavior.[14] So keenly does Simon welcome the adoption that he is atypically and amusingly rude to a social worker who tries to explore his reaction (12). But his motives are dangerously mixed, too: he betrays a suggestion that his welcome of Ha is questionably and selfishly based on a desire to enhance, pass on, and then share his interest in the technical details of warfare.

The whole family's enthusiasm is rapidly eroded, and Simon's especially so, when he realizes that Ha is what he calls (to his parents' horror) a "dum-dum" (Rachel Anderson 50). He becomes tired of Ha's incompetence, incontinence, dependence, and bouts of inexplicable violence (Ha kills the family cat), and his habit of saying everything four times. He resents the way Ha takes over and disrupts domestic routine, dominates the mother's attention, exhausts both parents, makes them uncharacteristically irritable, and drives them to what he calls, with puritanical exaggeration, "drink." Eventually, Simon develops a phobia for anything Ha has touched. He gets drunk and runs away to stay in the much more relaxed house of his aunt. Later, he seeks refuge in a church, only to find his sense of unbelonging exacerbated because he is sharing it with a congregation of people with no speech or hearing whom he also calls "dum-dums" (178–179), so he leaves and attempts suicide on a busy road.

Simon was a secure, attached child who, while not dislocated physically, has been psychologically usurped: cuckoo-ed out of the nest of his parents' uncritical and uninterrupted love. The reciprocal bond with his mother has been challenged. The contingent habits, customs, and beliefs that have outlined his selfhood have all been altered; his family history has been unexpectedly modified; and his former secure and unquestioned identity has been ruptured, so he feels an unwanted refugee in his own home. The War Orphan is about three kinds of orphaning: a child is a refugee within his own country; then that child is brought as an orphan from that colonized country to the West; and another Western child feels like he has been orphaned in his own home. Ha's experience represents some of the extremes of children being orphaned. Although this novel was written in 1984 and focuses on the Vietnam War, it is a salutary narrative of the warfare and imperialist occupation which still repeats itself. Ha has lost his original speech, his development is delayed, and he is unable to walk properly; he has inappropriate and sudden affective reactions and obsessions with routines. He has no possessions and no personal dignity. Because he has virtually no voice of his own, his experience is accessed via Simon's developing ability to read his mind. With his disabilities, he is treated almost as an object in a British orphanage, and as an object of fun in the street. Ha's nullity in both Vietnam and England is deepened by his having twice lost his originating name, the badge and prop of his sense of identity. "Ha" is a contraction that has been arbitrarily ascribed in the Vietnamese orphanage, and when he is brought to a British orphanage, the house mother calls him "Robert" because it is "more natural-sounding" (Rachel Anderson 22).[15]

Article 8

1. States parties undertake to respect the right of the child to preserve his or her identity, including nationality, name and family relations as recognised by law without unlawful interference.

UNCRC Article 8

His antecedent story, vividly told in the second and third sections of the book, explains many of the apparently irrational fears and obsessions that he exhibits, and also explains the terrifying drawings which he is described as doing. It makes it clear that before his trauma, Ha not only was articulate in Vietnamese, but also could understand and read some of the English used by U.S. soldiers. As a child he lived an increasingly destabilized life in a border village alternately taxed and educated by Vietcong forces, then reeducated, and leaflet-bombed by Southern forces. Ha sees his neighbors and family successively threatened, accused, shot, disappeared, and forced from their homes, ancestors, crops, and live-stock to a Southern "resettlement camp" (Rachel Anderson 94), where they are debauched and starved. When he and his mother escape, they are caught in a massacre reminiscent of that at My Lai in 1971. Ha crawls from under the bodies, including his mother's, in the mass grave. He survives in the jungle, is a captive for a time of U.S. forces, and finally locates his guerrilla father, who is immediately blown up by a land mine that he is trying to stop Ha from treading on. Finally Ha joins the crowds of refugees fleeing to Saigon, where he is found and put into the orphan-age where Simon's mother found him.

There is Mrs Thieu describing how, trapped beneath a pile of bodies, she was drowning in their blood.... Inevitably, there are stories of atrocities that make Abu Ghraib pale in com-parison, and a terrible casual indifference to the Vietnamese. For example, an American soldier, George Evans, describes working in an American army hospital, where he has to wash the bodies of two Vietnamese kids hit by a US army truck. "They were like little dolls lying there," he says. He found out later that the GIs had a "game going on in which, supposedly, guys were driving through town gambling over who could hit a kid. They had some disgusting name for it, something like 'gook hockey.'"

Swain (45–46)

Although Ha's ordeal takes place in his own country, if not the vil-lage that has been home, he and fellow Vietnamese are outsiders in the conflict with U.S. soldiers who, though displaced from their homes and homeland and pining for steaks and apple pie, have physical power over the indigenous people, whom they speak of as if they are objects rather than subjectivities. The invaders treat the powerless indigenes with uncomprehending contempt, recognizing no culture or cultural practices or lifestyles as legitimate except their own: "They're like animals sometimes. Eating nothing but rice. Their whole life, its food and reproduction, and if they're lucky a bit of land for growing things. That's all. No running water in their homes, no gas, no electrics, no *ambition* [original italics]" (Rachel Anderson 164).

This story of Ha's traumatization is largely told in Ha's own first person but in Standard English, the way Simon would have told it. But the novel is layered and increasingly plurivocal. The domestic comedy about the cozy family's reception of the outsider child in the first part of the story is punctuated by scenes from the Vietnam War, some of which we realize in retrospect are Ha's memories but narrated in a more sophisticated language than Ha's, and some of which seem to be Simon's telepathic dreams. Near the end, Ha's experiences in the Saigon orphanage are told in a mixture of first-person narration with Ha speaking for himself, but in Simon's language, and second-person narration, as if Simon is telling Ha what happened to Ha. It is a textual representation of the workings of a mind that is a palimpsest or kaleidoscope of unerasable but insupportable memories which put Ha outside any possibility of rational, social behavior, and an extreme example of how the memories and expectations of adopted and fostered children make it difficult for carers, especially intercountry adopters, to provide orphaned or abandoned children with the life stories that help them so much to develop a confident sense of self (Fahlberg 353–356). At a more detailed level, there are recurrent references in apparently mundane details which bind the text and resonate through it. We have read how Humpty Dumpty was seen by Simon on a poster, with a foot torn off, stuck on the Children's Home wall (Rachel Anderson 24), and Humpty Dumpty had been the toy which Ha cuddled in front of the TV after he had killed the family's cat (58); and later, we get Ha's version of Humpty Dumpty, symptomatic of his traumas, "about a man who fell down from a wall and had an accident. Soldiers arrived to make him better but they could do nothing for him, so he remained, injured, on the ground" (241). His interpretations of events, and imagery, are saturated and infected by the experience of war. The complex narration of the book is structured on the contrast then opposition between the two brothers' experiences, and leads to a final resolution into a brotherhood of two boys utterly different but mutually dependent in their respective ways.

Simon discovers accidentally that Ha has been ascribed the same birth year and birthday as his own. By sharing Ha's traumatic memories, he discovers that Ha has had a little sister who died. Then, from the aunt to whom he runs away in the night after his first discovery, Simon discovers that he too had a little sister who died. We see in this a narrative motif of doubling, familiar to children's literature, where the complexity of character is split between two lives that reflect each other, where the two protagonists become projections of each other and, with it, a recognition of "self" in "other"—a commingling of outside and inside into a new combination of oneness—from which an accompanying growth in mutual understanding between the oppositional aspects of the characters is developed. The mixing of Ha's first-person narrative, but in Simon's language, and the telling, apparently by Simon, to Ha of what Ha did, is evidence of this doubling in the narration too. At another level of interpretation, the alternation and then coalescing of their experiences and sometimes voices comprise a fitting fictional form in which to suggest their growing mutual understanding and brotherhood that radically curtail the possibility of their outsider status to each other; and that Ha's experience is sometimes expressed in Simon's language suggests how the inarticulate, like Ha, are not necessarily without thought, conceptions, and emotions, or indeed language.

With an adolescent's idealistic valuation of candor, and belief in its efficacy, Simon rejects his parents and believes that opening up Ha's past to him will cure the effects of his trauma: "At the moment he just lives in a sort of violent blur. If they tell him the truth about his past, his life can begin to make sense" (Rachel Anderson 72). The psychotherapeutic implications of this move are clearly made as both characters reconnect with their respective pasts to work out present relationships—in this case, the relationship of Simon to his own mother. In the half-happy ending, Ha's temporary removal, for Simon's sake but without Simon having been consulted, makes Simon realize how much he misses the responsibility of caring for someone else, his addiction to the Vietnam War, and his preference for "the other mother we had" (246) over his own. He persuades the social worker to bring Ha back, his former resentment of Ha is sublimated into a more practicable need for love and routine, and he achieves a new and more robust sense of self, based on an awareness of common humanity, literally brotherhood in his case.

The fictional children described in this chapter unsurprisingly exhibit common longings for a lost and idealized birth mother, a home with a small family which offers stability, a degree of privacy, and the chance to own and care for material possessions. These narratives all subscribe to the baseline assumption that families are the normal and most desirable site in which to raise children. But here we see just how diverse and disrupted and divisive so-called normal families can be, and how the experience of "family" for these unattached children—whether as a foster placement or adoption—is not always ideally located in a two-parent, two-parent and birth children, or one- or two-parent and other children family, or as part of an extended family unit. Whereas there are demonstrable benefits for very young children to be adopted or fostered into family units, it is questionable that a "family environment" is always the ideal for all children, especially older children for whom a pseudo-family is rarely an adequate substitute for the lost early attachment, and does not always provide the idealized "atmosphere of happiness, love and understanding" portrayed in the UNCRC. These narratives reveal also how the reality of the longed-for imagined family by an unattached child never quite lives up to the fantasy of family and family life dreamed of or conjectured in the mind of the outside child looking in on the image of the families presented in and by establishment images and representations. We see in these narratives that by the time these unattached fictional older children, like many of their real prototypes, have arrived in care, have languished in care for some years waiting for adoption or fostering, or have survived out of care in abusive or abandoning "families," they have already developed skills of coping that have helped them to survive outside the prescribed norms of family life, such as independence, resilience, and worldliness often overshadowed also by negative characteristics that are part of the same syndrome of survival: of being tough-skinned, aggressive, secretive, emotionally detached, cunning, deceitful, selfish, and possessive, all of which are inevitably at odds with the power structures and values that operate in most "families." They provoke the question that is a direct challenge to the received wisdom of many policy documents: that "families" as conventionally or even unconventionally understood are the most suitable settings for these abandoned, emotionally and physically deprived or abused, and "unattached" children who forever feel themselves to be, and are always inevitably regarded as being, "outsiders," despite the best- and well-intentioned psychosociological motives of the agencies and institutions that have responsibility of care. And it begs the question about the possibility of identifying alternative models of care for unattached children, such as we see in *The Story of Tracy Beaker*, that are different from, and are not already fixed in, institutionalized prescriptions of "family."

6

COLONIZED

In his critique of global capitalism, Slavoj Žižek has often described our current times as an epoch of unprecedented capitalist hegemony.[1] This chapter focuses on a selection of premillennium and new-millennium young adult (YA) fictions against this contemporary moment of globalization and the rise of an unbridled neoliberal political economy that has seen the escalation of sectarian warfare and insurgencies, fundamentalisms, nationalisms, preemptive attacks on sovereign states, and "the global war on terror."

The chapter falls into two broad sections. The first section ("Colonialism Then and Now" and "Colonized Childhoods") focuses on Malorie Blackman's *Noughts and Crosses* trilogy (2001–2005; British), Anne Provoost's *Falling* (1997; Belgian),[2] and Meg Rosoff's *How I Live Now* (2004; Anglo-American). These novels emerge from different cultural histories and have a different global distribution, but they are chosen *because* of this, and because, although many other kinds of readings are possible, when they are read against this background that I shall describe, they take on other significances that engage these questions of the potential impact of new global order politics on the lives of many young people and its consequences as levels of social and cultural fallout. Blackman's *Noughts and Crosses* trilogy and Provoost's *Falling*, for example, are arguably just other examples of YA fiction tackling the age-old problem of racial division. But, more than these immediately presented issues of race and various instantiations of alterity, these fictions lay bare the discourses and processes of, and the effects of and responses to, the power politics from which such racial divisions and alterities emerge;[3] they interrogate and expose the mechanisms of

121

power, and how it functions and sustains itself and is the agent of structural violence that gives rise not only to racism but also to all kinds and types of politically discriminatory practices. They show how power politics filter into the divisive practices of everyday lives with terrible consequences—in the case of the Blackman novels, and in the backdrop to Rosoff's *How I Live Now*—to create the conditions that breed terrorism and suicide bombers as consummate illustrations of a new global order phenomenon. And although these issues of power are not new in the historical scheme of things, they take on newly intensified resonances when they are read against such aggressive and reactionary neoliberal orthodoxies as the reinscription of "ours" that is familiar and "theirs" that is different and "other" (Burbach and Tarbell 128) and is the new imperialism.

The second section, "Imaginative Geographies," draws on four texts that feature child or young adult figures who are caught up in modern-day warfare as an epochal symptom articulating newly destabilized identities; they are two novels by Elizabeth Laird, *A Little Piece of Ground* and *Kiss the Dust*, and two biographical narratives, Zlata Filipovic's *Zlata's Diary* and Latifa's *My Forbidden Face*. My interest in these texts is two-fold: one is the particular voices and viewpoints from which the narratives emerge, and the other is their geopolitical location in what Edward Said has described as "imaginary geographies" (*Orientalism* 54), defined by Gregory as "constructions that fold distance into difference through a series of spatializations ... by multiplying partitions and enclosures that serve to demarcate 'the same' from 'the other' ... designating in one's mind a familiar space which is 'ours' and unfamiliar space beyond 'ours' which is 'theirs'" (17). My purpose here is to explore how the policies are shown in the literature to operate as a series of inclusions or exclusions either by intention or by default.

COLONIALISM THEN AND NOW

In *Against Empire*, Zilla Eisenstein describes the "West" as "a state of mind—a set of privileged cultural values," which, she says, "identifies a singular location of power across various geographic sites" (74). And in his seminal thesis on "Orientalism," Edward Said exposed the "East," in its relation to the "Orient," variously as the discursive product of the academy, an authorizing, Western style of thought: dominating, restructuring, and describing views about, and with authority over, the "Other" that was the "Orient." "The relationship between Occident and Orient," he says, "is a relationship of power, of domination, of varying degrees of complex hegemony" (*Orientalism* 5). Either way the "East"-"West" dichotomy relied for its continuing legitimacy and longevity on an imperium of nonreferential signs invested in and emanating from an assumed power structure that continually reasserted the superiority of its own position and voice while at the same time "Othering" the rest: "the West," and "the Rest." "The Rest" was constructed as alien, different, and inferior: "not us." Such extremes of alterity were unquestioningly represented in the literature of the period in, for example, Joseph Conrad's *Heart of Darkness*[4] and R. M. Ballantyne's *The Coral Island*. In more recent fiction, they have been more self-consciously reinscribed in Barbara Kingsolver's *The Poisonwood Bible* about, quite literally, the Western imperialist project to possess the heart and soul of both the individual and a nation, in this case, the Congo, against the resonant, irrepressible power of the colonizing Word (of God located in Western thought) as both language and doctrine; in Kazuo Ishiguro's *When We Were Orphans* about a fictional pre–World War II expatriate boyhood in old Shanghai against the backdrop of the opium trade foregrounding issues of national and cultural identity through the perennial self-questioning of the protagonist, Christopher Banks, for his "not behaving sufficiently like an Englishman" (73), and by his Japanese friend, Arika, for "let[ting] down his Japanese blood" (73); also in Jamaica Kincaid's biography, *A Small Place*, her scathing critique of the legacy of English colonialism on the very fabric of her identity.

Postcolonial studies have exposed that the history of Western imperialism is founded on multiple sets of dualisms invoking such oppositional frameworks as civilized/primitive, culture/nature, reason/irrationality, white/black, objective/emotional, center/margins, and masculine/feminine—a problematic of forced binaries that create and reproduce "Otherness." It will not have escaped readers' attention that the left-right prioritizing hierarchy of written, Western discourse is embedded here in this list of oppositional pairings and is itself symptomatic of the insidiously colonizing worldview. Or, indeed, for the same reasons, it will not have gone unnoticed that the narratives in focus in this chapter are those that have been written in or translated into English[5] and that, even in this small particular, it is possible to detect that the colonial project is alive and well.

It is possible to believe, or to imagine, that the postcolonial project has identified, exposed, and, therefore, put an end to such hegemonies as the repressive and imperialist systems that once saw the colonizing of "non-Western" indigenes in the name of acculturation, education, and civilization; that what we have instead are the enlightened, postcolonial fruits of hybridity, tolerance of the diaspora; that the spirit of Jacques Derrida's *différance* appropriated by Homi K. Bhabha in *The*

Location of Culture to reassert the legitimacy and voice of Spivak's silenced, subaltern subject has liberated those gray, ambiguous, indeterminate spaces of culture into an "agency of counterhegemonic resistance" (Xie 2);[6] and that the Empire has indeed written back.[7] But the evidence is that the Empire's inheritors are a generation of amnesiacs for whom the memory of Empire, imperialism, and colonization—in its many manifestations from slavery to occupation—has long since been filtered for current-day consumption through the colonizing lens of the history books and Hollywood, to such an extent that the workings of colonialism have not been perceived as mutable. "Colonialism" and colonization in the contemporary mind-set, according to Said, have been fixed in time, place, and culture as being "back there" and "over there," "confined to the fixed status of an object, frozen once and for all in time by the gaze of Western percipients" ("Orientalism Reconsidered" 130). In these senses, the colonial past is quite literally a foreign country. The referent of colonialism has thus become detached from its reference in the power structures of imperialism. Derek Gregory makes the point that "if we do not successfully contest these amnesiac histories—in particular, if we do not recover the histories of Britain and the United States in Afghanistan, Palestine, and Iraq—then, in Misra's agonizing phrase, the Heart of Smugness will be substituted for the Heart of Darkness" (10).[8] In front of this imperialist gaze that has learned and taught the art of looking backward, the *ancien régime* has mutated into a new set of signifiers out of which a new breed of colonialism, barely recognizable as the progeny of the colonial past, has emerged through the smokescreen of global capital.[9] The new breed of colonialism is premised on erased and repackaged memory and, under the auspices of its own umbrella identity, has already taken ownership of hybridized cultural identities and operates *through* them.[10] The struggle to achieve dominance is not even any longer an uncomplicated, unilateral struggle between the First World of transnational capital and the Third World of underdevelopment (though certainly these factors continue to figure significantly within it). The new colonialism, unlike its historical precursor, is deterritorialized and operates exclusively now in relation to nation-states that are "with us" and are within its ideological frame of reference. Within these neoliberal spaces, the new imperial metropolis is mapped out transnationally in a range of foreign and domestic policies. The discourses of "Westernism" are privileged and conducted not so much in relation to geographical regions or, indeed, across any recognizable "East-West" or "North-South" divides, but to a transnational capitalist class identified and accessed via the global economy, capital, and new technologies, embodied in material institutions and practices as a structuring principle of this newly unterritorialized "Western" thought. It is unterritorialized inasmuch as "Westernism" functions as a geopolitical ideology, rather than geographical prescriptions[11] that, in an unprecedentedly sophisticated age of global digitalized technology, impacts unprecedentedly globally on the minutiae of life and living.

These focus texts are uncannily prescient in their ability to intuit the impact of this neoliberal dialectic on minority groups, and on all manner of counterhegemonic subjectivities that do not easily or readily conform to the power-political paradigms, or are indifferent to them, as in Rosoff's *How I Live Now*. They show how their character inscriptions of young people negotiate their identities across the newly mapped hyperborders[12] of the contemporary political maelstrom that is the generationally exclusive frame through which macro- and micropolitics translate into their everyday lives, and to the effects of which the characters are shown to be both impervious and vulnerable. The fictions defamiliarize the meanings and motivations that lie behind the political rhetoric and interrogate its effects and consequences. Provoost's *Falling*, for example, narrates the colonization of young minds in the service of extreme nationalism embedded in "Westernism" as an identity category. Although slightly predating the new-millennium publication of the other novels mentioned here, *Falling* anticipates them by being written against the background of global economic and cultural migration that inscribes an ethnic underclass as global capital and as by-product and symptom of globalization. In its wake, many European countries such as Belgium, as well as Australia where the novel was translated into English, and elsewhere, have seen a resurgence of the kind of far-right nationalism depicted by Provoost as a reaction by the indigenous population against what is perceived to be a threat from without to an assumed status quo. Through the character of Benoît, a far-right activist, Provoost exposes how an unprecedented economy of sliding symbols, at work at every level of present-day political discourse, is exploited to resignify language and to reinvent, rewrite, and erase political and personal memory to privilege currently preferred self-interested political ends.

Žižek has adopted an overtly Marxist stance grafted onto a Lacanian model to describe the new hegemony as the "unconscious real." This seems to suggest that, in the current political economy, subjectivities are, both wittingly and unwittingly but nevertheless unconsciously, hegemonized in a system of values and behaviors that are discursively unsignified for the fact of their being unnamed and never questioned. They are the silences upon which political ideologies rely for their longevity. Žižek defines it as "the spectral subject concealed behind actual experience" (*Ticklish Subject* 276); and he goes on to suggest, "It seems easier to imagine the 'end of the world' than a far more modest change in the mode of production, as if liberal capitalism is the 'real' that will somehow survive even under conditions of a global ecological catastrophe" (*Mapping Ideology* 1). In Meg Rosoff's *How I Live Now*,[13] we see how such an imagined scenario of global capital disintegration is played out; and the fragility of the capitalist infrastructure is exposed when it collapses against the ravages of not just ecological but also economic and global catastrophe in the grip of transnational terrorism. The novel depicts the future potentially corrosive effects on a generation of such a globally catastrophic eventuality, and how its seemingly unwitting subjects fall victim to the devastating consequences that ensue.

Two of these focus texts are set at a once-remove from present-day "reality" as dystopian projections. They suggest the emergence of a generic strain of political dystopias in YA fiction that narrates with unusual candor the underbelly of capitalist imperialism, but, in so doing, they perform a paradoxical function. By definition of their very existence as a counterhegemonic phenomenon, these fictions function as agents of resistance. However, by setting themselves up as antithetical, they unwittingly act as one of the desirable side effects that all quasi-totalizing and totalizing systems rely upon, that is, some form of counterinsurgency, or alien "Other," to promote or sustain themselves as fully functioning systems. They therefore work both intratextually and extratextually as a mode of antagonism to the prevailing political climate—even while narrating characters for whom the outcome is always and depressingly tragic, and who thus appear to be seemingly impotent to act as counterhegemonic agencies. This latter point raises a series of wider questions relating to the intransigence of imperial rule. Žižek points out that counterinsurgency is global capitalism's "symptom," that capitalism *as* a world system is conceivable only against the background of constitutive antagonism (*Tarrying* 224–225). We might call it a symbiotic reliance on the "reality" of "the enemy without," and regard it as a necessary counterpart to the power project. In other words, while the new imperialism exercises a *rhetoric* of plurality, because these are recognized to be profoundly necessary to the relativism through which it sustains its internal integrity and supremacy, at the same time, and at another level of hegemonic power, it has an apparent ambition to homogenize difference, to "democratize" in its own image through tyrannical means if necessary, premised on a simple binary logic that essentializes through its own, exclusivist set of signifiers refined into the simplistic maxim of those who are either "in" or "out" of the camp.[14] In these ways, then, the new imperialism of neoliberal capital has destabilized and redefined determinable borders that structure various and multiple notions of identity, to effect not new pluralisms but a new set of binaries and new instantiations of "us" and "them," "ours" and "theirs," on an axis of the "civilized world" and "the Rest" that has been defined as "barbaric" or, at the very least, "primitive."[15] We see this kind of duplicitous and deeply divisive rhetoric operating at structural and subjective levels in the politics of Blackman's *Noughts and Crosses*, and in the character of Benoît in Provoost's *Falling*. The quasi-assimilationist policies of political rhetoric that we see at work through these character inscriptions are grounded in a rhetoric of conformity that echoes, in nearly so many words, Renato Rosaldo's "'Come in sit down, shut up. You're welcome here as long as you conform to our norms'" (reference and source to be located). Such power policies are ostensibly designed to neutralize the counterhegemonic voice, but, as these narratives demonstrate, they effectively always and only ever serve to provoke it by an insidious process of exclusion that breeds the types of resistance it desires and requires and depends upon.

Participation in or exclusion from both macro and microsystems of power, then, is seen through these fictions to be determined and defined for the subjects of the neoliberal dispensation not only by the constituent elements of monocultural materialism, identified by Jean-François Lyotard (1984) as symptomatic of late capitalism's postmodern identity in a ubiquity of blue jeans and McDonald's. They also are required to buy into an economy of globally articulated sets of abstractions that are unprescribed by national or geographic borders and are expressed as a packaged and codified transnational neoliberal inscription of "freedom" and "democracy," gift-wrapped with the promise of an unadulterated pursuit of pleasure and the pledge of unlimited protection from a malign outside threat of pain at the cost of curtailed civil liberties. In Rosoff's *How I Live Now*, we see how such promises of protection from malign, political, and military insurgency are exposed as sham when its characters become victims of the effects against which the policies are supposedly designed to protect them, and we see that political naïveté or indifference is simply not an option as the escalating global war of terror impinges on their private lives. In this political backdrop, in the punitive and corrupt state bureaucracy and petty politics at work in Blackman's *Noughts and Crosses* trilogy, and in the colonization of young minds in the racist rhetoric of the far right of Provoost's *Falling*, we see how the institutionalized modes of violence of the kinds that are structurally inherent in neoliberalism produce their effects. The literature responds to the colonizing processes at work in corporate identity politics, and to the question of its subjects simply *knowing how to be* in an epoch where meanings are shown to be a shifting and destabilized phenomenon and the "past" is neutralized and fused into collective or individual responses to the prevailing political hegemony of "in-group" and "out-group" definitions. In these ways, it deconstructs the normative, homogenizing forces of capitalist structures.

COLONIZED CHILDHOODS

The apportioning of "us" and "them" is one of the issues behind Malorie Blackman's *Noughts and Crosses* trilogy that I am reading here as a metonymic instantiation of the global. The narrative is set in a supposedly British, but effectively it could be an "anywhere" semifuturistic Western inner-city landscape. In a simple, arguably simplistic, act of inversion, Blackman locates power in the majority black community of her novels who are the "Crosses," and inscribes the white "noughts" as a disempowered minority—a fact that does not become clear in the narrative until fifty pages in. She thus brings into sharp relief the taken-for-granted, internalized, and unexamined assumptions of any of her white, middle-class readers about the way that power and privilege may be located in them.[16] By displacing the white and black characters of her novels in a number of culturally contradictory and discursively estranged locations in this way, Blackman, in the words of Bhabha, "distantiates" them; she makes them "uncanny" by defamiliarizing a set of naturalized assumptions (*Location of Culture* 168), and in this seemingly simple act of displacement she not only effects a profoundly shocking experience for any of her self-defined, liberal-minded, educated, white, middle-class readers who believed themselves to know better. She also lays bare the binary structuring of power that inscribes identity and agency, and exposes how it operates arbitrarily to exclude and discriminate against certain groups that become, then, by default or intention of the power elite, silenced, marginalized, excluded, disempowered, and nonconformist through the very fact of their exclusion from mainstream systems of privilege.

Like a number of other examples of YA fiction, the first-person narration is in multiple voices, with different chapters adopting the voice and viewpoint of the various characters.[17] The shifting viewpoint gives the reader multiple perspectives on any given narrative event that unsettles their sympathies and frustrates their desire for a unified, stable vantage point from which to spectate, or vicariously partake in the fiction. The effect is to provoke an estranged and hybridized reading experience as the reader juggles the multiple and conflicting values that the narrative throws up and struggles with the cerebral inconsistencies of emotional engagement and intellectual censure: they may not necessarily condone but they might sympathize with the variant (often for some, dissident) voices and viewpoints. In provoking these kinds of hybrid positionalities in her readers, Blackman both disturbs and exposes the limitations of the binarities in which both the novel itself and the power systems it narrates are structured. By so doing, she implicitly suggests the possibility of alternative, more pluralist, polyvocal frameworks in and through which systems and subjects might accommodate difference. She also displaces the old-style binary myth of liberal fantasy that holds that somehow things would be better if positions were reversed and those currently marginalized, be they blacks or women, were in charge; that the marginalized class would somehow know and do better than the bellicose and oppressive white, Western-defined, male power structure. Equally, the strategy effects an intimate insight into the duplicity and motivation of characters by narrating the slippage between inner resolve and outward behavior, and the gulf between intentions and consequences and between rhetoric and action. The first book of the trilogy, *Noughts and Crosses* (2001), and its sequels, *Knife Edge* (2004) and *Checkmate* (2005), suggest a political landscape in which current-day domestic and foreign policies have reached their logical operational conclusions: for example, ID cards that were prospectively introduced to protect individual identity and national interests function in practice to curtail individual liberties, in this case to give or deny access to state services that operate as malfunctioning institutions for the underclasses, such as we see when Callum and his brother Lewis take their mum for hospital treatment:

> "Before we can administer any kind of medical care, I'll need to see your ID cards."
> "Sorry?" Mum frowned.
> "It's the new government ruling. All patient IDs have to be checked and registered. I think it's their way of trying to stop benefit swindles."
> "I beg your pardon?" Mum's frown deepened. "I'm not even on benefits."
> "It doesn't matter. This hospital and every other nought hospital in the country gets a certain amount of money per patient we treat. So, the government's foolproof plan … is to check each patient's ID card photo and fingerprint, so that patients can't hop around from hospital to hospital getting sickness certificates and hospitals can't lie about the numbers of patients they treat. That's the theory anyway." (Blackman, *Noughts* 215)

As metonyms of the global, the communities of these narratives are deeply ghettoized into rich and poor zones divided along racial lines and signify the hegemony of a racially inscribed global underclass as the necessary by-product in the advancement of corporate capitalism. A radical, militant, white minority group, "The Liberation Militia," wreaks terror on the urban infrastructure in a wave of bombings, insurgencies, and political murders, and capital punishment is a state-sanctioned judicial solution to terrorism, intoned through the media pronouncements of Cross politicians:

> The Liberation Militia are misguided terrorists and we will leave no stone unturned in our efforts to bring them to justice.... I can tell you that our highest priority is to find those responsible and bring them to swift and irrevocable justice. Political terrorism which results in the death or serious injury of even one Cross always has been and always will be a capital crime. (Blackman, *Noughts* 67–68)

There are sharp social divisions between the privileged, black "Cross" (uppercase) elite and the disempowered, white "nought" (lowercase) underclass; "plasters" (Band-Aids) come in only one color, dark brown (76); and Christmas has been renamed "Crossmas" in recognition of the Cross's status as "God's chosen" (81). These are the examples of racialized, patriarchal privilege that has been normalized and reproduced in Western capitalist power systems through which minorities are "Othered" and their citizenship and rights denied, and that, typically, as we see through the narratives, is the recruiting ground for political insurrection and unrest.

> In October/November 2005, thirteen successive days of rioting in the Paris suburbs by non-white youth exposed a practice of non-integration that was interpreted as a consequence of the inherent flaws in the integrationist principles of the Constitution. Under the banner-headline: "Liberté? Égalité? Fraternité?" *The Independent* reported "France's non-whites [are] twice as likely to be unemployed. French government admits integration policies have failed.... The violence is a statement of violence and rejection against main-stream French society.... The youths setting fire to their own brothers' and sisters' schools or their neighbours' cars are part of a multi-racial under-class of 15-22 year olds whose only currencies are drugs and violence. The wider significance is therefore not politico-religious but a warning of what happens if problems of deprivation and violence fester" (The newspaper article carried a picture bearing the caption: "A burnt-out McDonald's in Corbeil-Essonnes.")
>
> **Litchfield (1–2)**

Through the three books of the trilogy, we observe how the main characters on either side of the political divide become radicalized into their extremist positions. The "nought" Callum McGregor is intelligent, ambitious for his future success, and in every sense idealistic. He has a love relationship with a black "Cross" politician's daughter, Sephie Hadley, who has dared to cross the black-white power divide. Sephie eventually bears Callum's child, Callie Rose, who becomes a key character in the two sequel novels. The noughts are collectively referred to as "blankers" by the Crosses, by which label the Crosses signal the nonstatus of the noughts upon whom they openly enact their racially motivated contempt. Such attitudes and actions fix the noughts in their marginality and ensure that they are othered in the regimes and discourses of representation: "'Nothing. Nil. Zero. Nonentities'" (Blackman, *Noughts* 81); "'They're blank by name and blank by nature'" (87); "'They smell funny and they eat peculiar foods and everyone knows that none of them are keen to make friends with soap and water'" (85). Only the most intelligent of them, like Callum, is allowed entry by scholarship to the privileged, black, Cross schools on the basis of a presented political rhetoric of inclusion and assimilation, such as in the media interview with black politician Kamal Hadley:

> Our decision to allow the crème-de-la crème of nought youth to join our educational institutions makes sound social and economic sense. In a civilized society, equality of education for those noughts with sufficient aptitude. (67)[18]

Blackman evidently has done her homework by minutely observing the duplicity and hypocrisies that typically lie behind the rhetoric of democratically elected politicians. The Hadley psuedo-assimilationist-by-conformity speech resonates with the policy of inclusion and relates back to Rosaldo's comments, above, grounded on a fundamental and necessary exclusion and silencing of the counterhegemonic voice: "an exclusion so thoroughly buried it goes virtually unnoticed, almost unread" (Johnson and Michaelsen 23). Here, too, Blackman narrates the gap between political pretension to racial, cultural, and class integration and the lived experiences of disempowered groups by reproducing in the mouths of her black political elite the clichéd, vacuous platitudes of power polemics of the kind that saturates present-day media reports.

On his first day at the Cross school, Callum is confronted by a mob of Crosses at the school gate chanting, "'NO BLANKERS IN OUR SCHOOL … BLANKERS OUT'" (Blackman, *Noughts* 56–57). It is tempting to compare this incident with the actual, lived experience of the first black children in the southern U.S. to attend newly integrated schools in the 1950s, and with that of critic Frantz Fanon, who writes in "The Fact of Blackness" of his encountering just such an enactment of racial exclusion as we see being played out in the fictional account:

> I was expected to behave like a black man—or at least like a nigger. I shouted a greeting to the world and the world slashed away my joy. I was told to stay within bounds, to go back where I belonged. (324)

Once inside the school, Callum quickly relearns his marginal and subordinate status in the black power system that is built on a series of erasures. He is a figure of the new imperialism, and the reader is reminded how the rights of colonized people to make their own history have been subjugated by the colonizer's own stories of self-production: Callum learns, for example, that his voice and views in the classroom are silenced, just like the voice and experiences and achievements of whites in history have been silenced and erased from his school history books that have rewritten and skewed history to privilege black successes:

> "Because all the history books are written by Crosses and you never write about anyone else except your own. Noughts have done lots of significant things, but I bet no one in this class knows...."
> "That's quite enough." Mr. Jason cut me off in mid-tirade. (139)

It is an example of old-style colonialism displaced in the contemporary setting, all the more problematic for being unnamed, through which process the margins in general are formulated historically. Through an orchestration of daily petty injustices, exclusions, discriminations, psychological and physical abuses, racial insults, and, worst of all, being ignored by the teachers despite the fact that he is one of the brightest students, Callum continually finds himself in trouble with the teachers, the head (principal), and the other kids. "'If the blankers are finding it tough here, maybe they should go elsewhere,' came Mr. Costa's reply" (Blackman, *Noughts* 141). Predictably, he becomes disillusioned, dispirited, angry, and resentful, "pushing the knot of loathing deeper inside me. Deeper and deeper the way I always did" (113–114), and he drops out of school.

In his essay "Local and Global," Stuart Hall has identified what may happen when the margins are so profoundly threatened:

> They can themselves retreat into their own exclusivist and defensive enclaves. And at that point, local ethnicities become as dangerous as national ones. We have seen that happen: the refusal of modernity that takes the form of a return, a rediscovery of identity that constitutes a form of fundamentalism. (184)

Hall's simplistic formula that pitches modernity against fundamentalism and reinscribes the old binarities that are being exploited with impunity in the political discourses of Western hegemony should be challenged. Equally, Blackman might also be challenged for reconfirming the stereotyped status quo of minorities by orchestrating the retreat of her character Callum into just such a defensive enclave as Hall has described. But her decision to do so may be explained by her mission to "tell it how it is," and to provoke discussion around the genesis of modern-day radical fundamentalist groups—that despite what politicians would have us believe (i.e., that they exist in a vacuum unhinged and psychotic), there is a history in which something causes the switch to flip, when everything becomes political and everything is perceived as politicized now.[19] Callum joins his already disillusioned father and elder brother, Jude, in the Liberation Militia, and asserts a revised sense of his identity. Through the remaining books of the trilogy, Blackman goes right to the heart of terrorist motivation: we observe how the process of radicalization intensifies through successive generations as these characters struggle to find spaces in which to act to reassert their own voices and agency, culminating in Callum and Sephie's illegitimate daughter, Callie Rose, becoming a suicide bomber with insight into her perverse sense of her share in generations of power denied: "I held death in my hands. It was a strange feeling. A kind of calm, deliberate disquiet" (Blackman, *Checkmate* 468). Callum has been publicly hanged for being wrongly convicted of bombing a local shopping mall on the basis of fabricated police evidence and guilt-by-association for his part in the Liberation Militia.

Racially marginalized underclass kids dropping out and turning radical is arguably a too easy cliché for Blackman to adopt through her novels, and the issues she raises also are arguably too schematically drawn. But, as a form of political critique in an era in which suicide bombers and global terrorism as reactions against imperial dominance have become a daily fact of life, they carry a particularly timely reverberation. In *Against Empire*, American critic Zilla Eisenstein points out how she believes that there are all kinds of "terrors":

> Homelessness, starvation, disease, bombs, US prisons are filled, public schools are crumbling, millions of people have lost jobs, over forty-two million people do not have health insurance. All this is also terrifying.... Security for the wealthy few is not the answer. (11)

In the *Noughts and Crosses* trilogy, the conflict is more than an analogy or instance of global conflict; it is a product of it. The narratives develop around and move between the political system's will to mete out justice to members of the Liberation Militia who pose a terrorist threat and the latter's determination to resist it. It shows the black power elite's resolve to keep power in its own hands at all costs through the ruthless pursuit of regressive law-and-order policies that define the "out-group" conditions for an excluded and dispensable minority, which, like so many of the other points made here, we might read for its ramifications for the drive for "Western interest" domination on the world stage. Though Blackman's trilogy is structured in a series of binaries, it in fact cracks open the binary logic of the kind that drives present-day neoliberal policies, and is an effect of corporate globalism, to deconstruct the premises on which a set of its unexamined, imperialist assumptions have rested: of ethnic divisions, of the "West" versus "the Rest," and, residually, in relation to the novel's immediate focus in this context, of the individual citizen versus the state. It raises an uncomfortable question of identity politics and interrogates the relativism embedded in the rhetorical devices of political argument: the question is not simply whether Callum's family, the McGregors, and their role in the Liberation Militia should be identified and named through the eyes of the power elite as "terrorists" or through their own view of themselves as part of a resistance movement against what they perceive to be the evils of imperial domination. It is also about unclothing discursive rhetoric that produces and maintains these kinds of diametric oppositions as a political expedient; and it is about how to deal differently, through means other than binary inscription and exclusion, with categories of ambivalence, ambiguity, and difference. The multiperspectivity and first-person narrations that these novels adopt appear to have gone some way to dissolving the binarity of narrator and narrated, and between narrative and narratee, leaving the latter ambivalently positioned in relation to both sides of the political divide that the novels themselves set up, but better positioned, then, to interrogate its deficiencies *as* a system. Perhaps this is the intention because it pushes the reader to advance the limits of the divisive political rhetoric and the crude cultural schisms in and by which they would be duped, and through which morass of coded and euphemized language they negotiate their identities. In the words of Eisenstein, we need now to "try to see what is not easily visible. Rethink invisibility; rethink as overt the covert realms of power that are not being named" (150).

Anne Provoost's *Falling* is another novel about racism and racial unrest set in present-day Europe. It addresses the specific issue of migrant labor as economic capital that is the local manifestation of the practices of production of globalization: the erosion of state sovereignty under globalization means increasingly that the state serves interests other and wider than those of its indigenous citizens; and this produces the displacement and mass movement of peoples across national and international borders as labor migration, technology transfer, the unequal distribution and flow of capital in the global system, economic exploitation, and the resurgence, in these hegemonic economies, of political extremism in the form of far-right nationalist political activism as a politico-ideological reaction.[20] Globalization has a particular resonance for Belgium, a small European country with land and sea borders, a colonial past, a recent history of occupation, two official languages, and a 10 percent nonnative population. Belgium is a microcosm of globalization, and the issues that the novel addresses reflect an international pattern about the rise of fundamental extremism in the face of a perceived erosion of national unity, identity, and attitudes toward sociodemographic change. The novel also explores the complex issue of national, cultural, and personal memory as a political project: the idea of the past repeating itself as a negative continuum in successive generations, and the place of revisionist memory in hegemonic and counterhegemonic discourses. In this connection, Edric Caldicott and Anne Fuchs describe memories as "advancing stories," located in between the present and the past, that "change to meet emerging needs" (12). This is important because *Falling* hinges on the idea of the fluidity of memory and generational identity, and the ease with which memory can be manipulated or erased and the past rewritten to suit present political or ideological biases of individuals, or groups, to harness allegiance to a preferred persuasion.

> If one thing unites these books on childhood in the camps, however, it is an absence of sentimentality. It is as if the authors could not afford self-pity, as if they needed to protect their experiences in ironic detachment, whether through detailed description or with the qualification of a theoretical framework. Thus, there may be personal as well as narratological reasons for the survivor-narrator to adopt a defamiliarizing mode of representation.
>
> **Reiter, "Holocaust" (237)**

The first-person narration is the flashback of Lucas Beigne, who is spending another summer with his mother at the house of his recently dead grandfather. It tracks Lucas's slow process of coming to know how memories of his grandfather's past actions impinge on his present-day relations with Caitlin, a young American dancer who spends her summers at the convent adjoining the grandfather's land. By piecing together the bits and pieces of information that have been hitherto withheld from him, Lucas gradually but reluctantly learns how during the World War II occupation, his grandfather had informed the Nazis that the nuns at the convent were hiding fifteen Jewish children, who were subsequently removed to concentration camps or shot, along with five of the nuns. It transpires that Caitlin's mother, Ruth, was one of those children, and that "Soeur," who continues to live in the convent, was the only nun to escape the massacre because, it is rumored, the grandfather, who had been Soeur's former lover, arranged for her to be away from the convent that afternoon to have her papers checked by the Nazis. By replicating the processes of memory as fragmented and partial, Provoost shows how the pattern of the grandfather's past behavior emerges through the various fragments of documentation, through past newspaper cuttings, through the disparate items of evidence that Lucas finds in and around the house, and from the snippets of gossip he has gleaned from the townspeople that his grandfather had been a Nazi sympathizer who had been ostracized by the townspeople and had remained so until his death.

Unlike the *Noughts and Crosses* trilogy, in *Falling* the viewpoint is singular. Nevertheless, it carries the polyvocal elements of the *Noughts and Crosses* trilogy through its characterization; it juxtaposes individual and public memories and the historiography of Nazism by narrating the grandfather's action as a fact in its own right but one which bears down inexorably on the lives of successive generations. It exposes the difficulties of the inherently elusive nature of what Sabine Egger has described as "true" memory (106) by showing how subsequent generations—in this case, Lucas, Caitlin, both their mothers, and Benoît, the louche, smooth-talking, Aryan, fascistic revisionist leader of a local neo-Nazi group—interpret the historical fact. They each have an understanding of the grandfather's actions arrived at through a process of remembering events that they would prefer to forget by elisions and silences, or to reinvent through self-deception. For example, Lucas's mother tries to justify her father's action by saying he acted out of grief for the death of one of his daughters, who had died from pneumonia while underfed, because he had believed that the nuns who distributed the scarce rations were siphoning them for the Jewish children (Provoost 129). She tries to erase the memory of her father's past deeds by burning all of his papers and photographs, and, by her actions, potentially to erase what she may believe to be her share in the collective burden of guilt even before Lucas has learned any of its details: "It's a relief that it's all gone.... It's so clean" (130). And after Lucas has unwillingly acknowledged the bare fact of his grandfather's action, Benoît performs the agency of national and nationalist memory by resorting to the type of the master discourse; he rationalizes his grandfather's actions to Lucas, thus reducing the possibility for any degree of ambiguity in Lucas's interpretation by performing his own, monosemic interpretation, and by recourse to a partial fact: that his grandfather had acted altruistically for the good of the community. "He reported those Jews because he thought that was the right thing to do. The kids in the school in town weren't getting enough to eat because the food was going to those Jews. Illegal Jews, that is!" (118). Against this piece of information, Lucas deduces from the imprint of an old print roller that his grandfather had been a postwar revisionist involved in distributing revisionist literature; but, even now while the facts are all but staring him in the face, or at any moment immediately subsequently, he is either unable or unwilling to fathom them for himself: "The large letters were clearest: *Auschwitz greatly exaggerated* ... as far as I could see the text dealt with the return of a group of Jewish children from the concentration camps. I could see the word '*Sainte-Antoine*' and a date in 1945" (145), all of which raises the question of Lucas's being naïvely or willfully ignorant of the facts. It is one of the most profoundly political comments that the novel engages: an apparent framework of generational amnesia in which displaced memory breeds the conditions in which the repetition of the racist fundamentalism of the past flourishes. Through such narrative incidents as these, Provoost illustrates what Jeffrey Prager has pointed out: how the historical past is a process of misremembering because the generational memories, though "embodied," are also always embedded and interpreted through social and cultural frameworks (*Presenting* 70). Provoost thus reveals the premises on which power groups, including the new global hegemony, operate by systematically disconnecting past from the present, and by the slippage and manipulation of language to instate new "truths" upon which to base and justify a set of preferred actions, behaviors, and beliefs.

Lucas is a loner and an outsider, and the narrative tracks how the fact of his supposed political naïveté and unquestioning belief in others makes him infinitely exploitable by those less well intentioned than himself, and in these senses the narrative inscribes him as the average young guy on the street. He becomes the perfect target for the manipulative and persuasive influences of Benoît, who sucks Lucas into his neo-Nazi activism by mercilessly exploiting his weaknesses and fears with a mixture of menacing threats, flattery, and emotional blackmail, and through the systematic manipulation of language and meanings. Benoît plays on the idea that Lucas is his grandfather's progeny, so much so that Lucas begins to doubt that he has an individual identity that is separate from his genetic inheritance, and to half-believe—as the subsequent narrative events bear witness—that there is an inevitability, an inexorability, about who he is or will become, and what he will do. "Don't become like your grandfather," his mother warns (Provoost 128). He symptomatizes the second- and third-generation children discussed by Caldicott and Fuchs (31), who struggle to negotiate their fragmented sense of identity through the interplay of silences that surround such past actions as those of his grandfather and their own inner rage that are the generational reverberations of the trauma. "You're a man of character, Lucas, a proper grandson of Felix Stockx" (Provoost 124). "Our ideals are the same as your grandfather's. We want to act the way he acted, for the good of our country. People like him have taught us about obedience and loyalty" (74). So, when Lucas's grandfather's house is burgled for a second time, he listens to his mother's complaints that holidays in the small town of Montourin are not what they used to be: "The shops were too crowded; there were beggars in the streets; bags, bicycles and prams got stolen" (50), and she names "the Arabs" (58) as the invisible threat to their security. He listens to the locals who cannot find work: "'No jobs to be had here these days.... 'Every one of them has been taken. By illegals. They're cheap, and they've got strong backs'" (76). He listens to Benoît's ironic but persuasively divisive "us and them" scaremongering rhetoric: "'Think of the consequences for the Cercle [a district of the town where people congregate as if it is a 'gigantic evening market' (107)]. Ghanaians, Chinese, Brazilians, all together, all in the one place. Now there is an explosive mixture for you. They've got no money. They don't speak the language. Just what the neighborhood needs'" (203–204); "'We are fighting a noble cause. We are not doing this for ourselves. The people of this country are asking for it'" (169). And he stores up what he has heard to rationalize his inertia at being recruited as front-line fodder in the violence provoked by Benoît's extreme nationalist views.

Benoît is sketched as the paradigm of a pathologically motivated nationalist exploiting people's fears. Like Blackman, Provoost has tapped into the microdiscourses that mobilize the behavior of such individuals and groups: in the ways in which they euphemize acts of violence into acts of patriotism uttered in messianic tones, and in the language of valor, heroism, and comradeship conducted along binary lines and valorized on the basis of nationalism, such as "'Our people and our country are threatened with being overrun'" (204), "'They must assimilate and the boat is full'" (211), and "'It's no coincidence that we are the first generation who have to share everything with the Muslim brethren'" (211–212). And they pitch their argument in the "civilized" versus "barbarism" debate, on which logic the supremacy of "Westernism" flourishes: "'We are regressing to barbarism'" (118). In Benoît's brave new, all-white, Westernized, Aryan world utopia, the present-day "Muslim brethren" as the negative stereotype of the "enemy without" have replaced the Jews of the historical past as the real and present danger. They "land here like a swarm of flies" (158). Provoost exposes how easily the language of national identity, patriotism, "democracy" (154), and "human rights" (153) and the appeal to "tradition" are narrowed into acts of xenophobic cruelty,[21] and how, equally easily, seemingly rational arguments are distorted into ideologically motivated justifications for in-group–out-group antagonisms and repudiation. Benoît says,

> Other cultures fascinate me. I have tremendous respect for them. But their different character cannot be fully developed here.... We must protect them from Western influences and send them back to the land of their birth.... In order to integrate, they'd have to give up their own individuality. Farewell customs, farewell tradition. Surely that would be a terrible shame? (204–205)

With an absent, mostly silent mother who is in denial of the historical facts and a right-wing revisionist extremist whose voice and views Lucas begins to internalize and reproduce, Caitlin's is the counterhegemonic voice in this narrative. She identifies the voice of political fanaticism by recognizing the seductive power of Benoît's persuasive logic and its inherent dangers: "'I have the feeling I could fall violently in love with him.... But he's dangerous too'" (Provoost 197–198). But, most significantly, she recognizes its potential for the radicalization of an already alienated underclass and expresses just how easily people like Benoît can sway the popular mind:

> Just look for a disaffected young man who's unemployed.... He has no political convictions. You persuade him that the guest workers have robbed him of his birthright, his flat, his job and even the most beautiful of white girls. Once he swallows that, you tell him the latest myth, the one about the Jewish plot. All our problems stem from the Jewish plot to dominate the whole world. It's easy. There's nothing to it. (202)

However, as with all the other resistant voices in these narratives, Caitlin pays the personal cost of her resistance: Lucas severs her foot with his grandfather's chainsaw to free her from the wreckage of a car crash that the narrative hints has been orchestrated by Benoît because he has discovered her Jewish roots. The chainsaw has been a recurrent motif of fascination for Lucas and a source of power and destructiveness throughout, and it is now poised as the ultimate power statement: of the power elite's capacity to destroy the resistant voices, even while professing its benevolent, well-intentioned motivations, as Lucas has done about his severing of Caitlin's foot. Because Caitlin is a dancer, the action destroys not only her future career and livelihood, but also her reason to exist.

In this novel, Provoost captures how cultural memory and political ideologies are discursively generated, and how the narratives that ensue are the power tool through which individuals and groups construct their identities not as authenticity but, as Caldicott and Fuchs (15) and Benedict Anderson (6) have shown, by process of change, assimilation, and redefinition through acts of imagination. The mutated narratives may be objectively or subjectively benign or malign, and/or the result of a deliberate strategy of national or individual manipulation; but, in all cases, it is shown how they are used to forge viewpoints that variously interrogate, distort, or reproduce a "normative" position, or are complicit with it. Provoost juxtaposes revisionist rhetoric of the Nazi past and the question of national and personal identity in an age when discrete national identities are perceived simultaneously as discursive productions and as stable phenomena under threat from escalating global economic instability and labor and capital migration. She dramatizes the power of language, particularly political language, to mobilize opinion, and exposes how acts of aggression are resignified and rationalized through those same discursive manipulations into acts of liberation and valor, not domination. We recognize such moves in the language of neoimperialist ideology and its struggle to expand its power base in what effectively has become the "Project for the New (Western) Century."[22] As in the *Noughts and Crosses* trilogy and in Rosoff's *How I Live Now* that follows, the small, daily, domestic occurrences reflect the wider global picture in which power-hungry regimes and groups—be they ("Cross") politicians, corporate capitalists, or a nationalist majority—exercise forms of authority that wreak devastation on certain individuals and groups. Lucas is inscribed in this reading as the locus of the type of pliable, gullible, sycophantic political institution upon which power regimes rely and on the existence of which they flourish. As in the reading of the *Noughts and Crosses* trilogy, the reader

in this text is again suspended in a state of ambivalence—recognizing
the complexities of moral and political choices and recognizing, too,
that the action-reaction and "us" versus "them" politics that the novels
exemplify are not a viable solution to the problems of global and local
narratives of inequality; that current conditions of unequal distribution
of resources and an asymmetrical world economy under corporate capitalism will forever be the source of antagonism and bipartisanship in
which the political hegemony of elites delegitimizes notions of popular
democracy and socioeconomic equity; that they construct minorities
designed to protect their dominant interests, to secure dominance, and
to determine political outcomes; and that at every turn, as these two
narratives depressingly demonstrate, popular resistance is defeated in
the face of excessive might.

The tragedy that besets those who set themselves to resist hegemonic
power in the Blackman and Provoost novels (the McGregors and Caitlin, for example) is, depressingly, not dissimilar from the fate of the
politically indifferent generation depicted in Meg Rosoff's *How I Live
Now*. Among other possible readings relating familial breakdown and
the intersubjective relationships of its young adult characters, the narrative distinguishes itself for its postmillennium inscription of these
essentially apolitical subjectivities against their powerlessness to protect their private selves from the ravages of transnational terrorism as a
key indicator of the twenty-first-century global political economy. New
Yorker Daisy has taken summer refuge with her family of eccentric
English cousins to escape the emotional stress of her divorced father's
second family, and comes to realize that political indifference is not
an option. Set in a future but recognizably English landscape, Daisy's
story emerges from a quasi-autobiographical space as memoir written
in stream-of-consciousness style, reminiscent of a latter-day Holden
Caulfield, that has dispensed with quotation marks as conventional
markers of speech and focalization to effect something of a dramatic
monologue. So Daisy's voice is the vehicle and motif of this narrative;
hers is the only voice we hear, and the voices of all the other characters
who speak are embedded in hers: in this sense, she speaks for her postmillennium generation. She is written into this narrative as one of the
unsignified casualties of neoliberal capitalism, not as a victim of poverty or as politically marginalized, but caught up in its hierarchies of
violence and structures of deprivation that are the postmillenium poverty of feeling of the materially wealthy but emotionally impoverished
new middle classes and that resonate with those suggested by Eisenstein (above), manifested as emotional poverty, not material perturba-
tions, and expressed as a series of refusals, not least Daisy's refusal of

food, hinted through the narrative, that is the simultaneous expression of a failure of self-love. When she arrives in England, she bears these burdens of her own private, generational terrors: she has been metaphorically erased psychologically, and quite literally erased physically from her family home, where she had become the mere by-product of a fragmented, unlistening, uninterested, too busy, overworked, working stepfamily with a new baby half-sibling on the way. In this context, anorexia becomes the generational expression of her desperate attempt to erase her own body and to attempt to exert some control in at least one area of her life. In addition, she has the burden of guilt of her mother's death in giving her birth, and a history of being in therapy as a first-line solution for the ills inflicted by just such manifestations of twenty-first-century living and lifestyles. It is in these senses that Stuart Hall is able to locate the instabilities of contemporary institutions as political: "The great social collectivities that used to stabilize our identities (family, community) … have been in our times deeply undermined by social and political developments" (Hall, "Ethnicity" 73).

Territory becomes an intrinsically important motif, too, because the narratives of place instantiate the narratives of self. When Daisy arrives in England, she is not only in exile from her immediate family but also and unsurprisingly in exile from herself. Thus the home and family that were traditionally supposed to be spaces of refuge have become spaces of endangerment and exile, and the house to which she has been exiled turns out subsequently to be a space of sanctuary that she comes to regard as her home. The idea of "homeland" and "another country" have been ironically inversed (Said, "Mind in Winter" 25), the former being a space of disconnection and alienation and the latter becoming operational as a liminal space in which Daisy negotiates between her past and her present and through which she reconnects with her bodily and emotional self.

Through her ironic voice and sardonic humor, the events of that English summer unfold around the cousins' initial determination to cocoon themselves in their country house pastoral idyll and love nest, and their resolution to ignore what becomes in the course of the narrative a devastatingly destructive terrorist "War." It begins with a bombing of a London train station and rapidly escalates into a terrorist takeover of major Western cities. Daisy's comments reflect her generational ennui and political indifference toward such an event:

> And something like seven or seventy thousand people got killed.
> (Rosoff 25)

No matter how much you put on a sad expression and talked
about how awful it was that all those people were killed and what
about Democracy and the Future Of Our Great Nation the fact
that none of us kids said out loud was that WE DIDN'T REALLY
CARE. (41)

Just at the point where she feels that she has found a place of refuge and
begins the process of reengaging her emotions, it is snatched from her
when the house is sequestrated by the army and she and the rest of her
cousins are dispersed: her private space that she believed to be invio-
lable to the privations of society is transmuted into a place of political
contestation into which both local and foreign occupations erupt. Thus,
the house that functions as a quasi-sovereign nation-state in which
local identities are forged has its boundaries "besieged," and the location of private politics becomes politicized into what Stuart Hall might
describe as a space of "*dis*location" ("Ethnicity" 13); it is a dramatization of late modernity's fracturing of lived personal space and the vulnerability of even the most remote and private refuges to the disruption
of the instabilities of an aggressive global politics and the violence of
internal and external resistances to it.

By the end of "the Occupation," the army has wrecked their country house and Daisy's Aunt Penn (her cousins' mother), who had got
stranded in Oslo airport while attempting to return home from a peace
rally at the outbreak of hostilities, has been shot dead as a security threat.
The cousins have witnessed the devastation of the terrorist insurgents'
massacre of the inhabitants of the farm to which Edmund had been
evacuated at the outbreak of hostilities; Daisy and her youngest cousin,
Piper, have survived in the wild on a diet of berries, hazelnuts, and wild
mushrooms while trying to get back to the house from the place to which
they had been evacuated—and it is the wild, uncultured places that
have paradoxically restored Daisy's appetite; and Cousin Edmund, who
had become the love and life and salvation of Daisy during their short
sojourn together at the country house, has become deranged. Edmund
is the embodied expression of generational rage against the political
and economic violence of the age that has effectively stolen their bodies
and their minds from them. But instead of projecting his rage, he turns
it back on himself: "He didn't know how to turn off the noise, or turn
the hate back out on the world like the rest of us. He turned it on himself. You can see that from the scars on him" (Rosoff 185).

The fictional account of the latter days of the Occupation reads
uncannily like the events taking place in contemporary power struggle zones around the globe—in Ramallah, Jerusalem, or Baghdad—or

indeed what we might well come to recognize as the fabric and circumstances of a not-too-future London, New York, or Melbourne, or any other Western metropolis, and the narrative is dystopian in these respects. Urban spaces have gone moribund, communications have collapsed, and the people have migrated to the countryside for the best chance of sustenance and survival from the land. The speed with which the material infrastructure has been dismantled is a marker of the system's overreliance on an all too obviously fragile edifice of economic capital and global communications, the irony, and no doubt *the point*, being that the only remaining line of communication is the capacity for telepathic communication between Edmund and Daisy that has sustained their relationship, even throughout their period of separation.

> There were snipers and small groups of rebels everywhere, disorganized bands of covert fighters and half the time you couldn't tell the Good Guys from the Bad Guys and neither could they. Buses blew up, and occasionally an office building or a post office or school, and bombs were found in shopping malls and packages. You could ask a thousand people on seven continents what it was all about and you wouldn't get the same answer twice ... you could bet one or more of the following would come up: oil, money, land sanctions, democracy. (Rosoff 168)

So the personal cost of hostilities on a group who believed themselves to be immune has been huge. The novel ends with the damaged survivors cultivating a garden, removed once again from the outside world but with the violence it has inflicted on them inscribed in their seemingly seriously curtailed subjectivities and emblematized in the eponymous way they live now. The garden is a clichéd image of revival and restoration in literature, especially children's literature, but here it is no Romantic iconography: it marks the return to what might remain when the imperialism of global capital has been laid bare and the people have returned to the land, not as aesthetic pleasure, but for the grim business of simply "staying alive in a country deformed and misshapen by war" (Rosoff 185).

"IMAGINATIVE GEOGRAPHIES"

All four narratives in this next section are set in contemporary towns and cities and record the experiences of young people caught up in modern-day warfare: in Ramallah (*A Little Piece of Ground*); in Sulaimaniya, a Kurdish town in northern Iraq (*Kiss the Dust*); in Sarajevo (*Zlata's Diary*); and in Kabul (*My Forbidden Face*). *A Little Piece of*

Ground and *Kiss the Dust* are fictional accounts of historical events; *Zlata's Diary* and *My Forbidden Face* are autobiographical, which means that these narratives quite literally straddle the boundaries between art and life. Because of it, they provoke all manner of interesting questions and responses in relation to, for example, voice and viewpoint: who is speaking, what are the ideological spaces from which these narrative voices emerge, and to whom are they addressed? There are several sources of interest in these narratives, therefore: one is their genesis as either fictional or autobiographical accounts of actual historical events that in itself poses a number of complex narratological considerations. Another is how the events they narrate are themselves already the products of certain nuanced discourses, and, in these senses, I am interested in how the narratives emerge from particular sociopolitical and ideological spaces to enact and produce particular effects. The narratological questions are therefore further complicated by the fact that the geographical locations of their setting are themselves already entangled in hugely partisan histories of which the wars they narrate are an effect. More particularly, they are located in the geopolitical spaces of the kind that Said has described as "imaginative geographies" (*Orientalism* 49–73): they each inhabit identities that have been discursively generated *by* their entanglement in complex networks of bipartisan histories and geopolitical configurations. Said believes that geographical spaces such as these are "fabrications" and are no more or less than the "effects" of certain practices of representation in which the ascribed geographic boundaries accompany also "social, ethnic and cultural ones" that have been ascribed as familiar or distant (*Orientalism* 54). He goes on to describe how these geographical distinctions can be entirely arbitrary and a product of a particular mind-set: "It is enough for 'us' to set up these boundaries in our own minds; 'they' become 'they' accordingly and both their territories and their mentalities are designated as different from 'ours'" (*Orientalism* 54).

Such insights as these from Said may help to explain why reactions to, for example, Elizabeth Laird's *A Little Piece of Ground*—the story of the daily experiences of Israeli occupation in Ramallah for a Palestinian boy, Karim—have been so virulent, as voices from each side of the political divide attempt to counter the discursive configurations the narrative is perceived to have set up.[23] Laird has been accused of bias for the singular viewpoint that her narrative adopts.[24] More interestingly, Laird's *Kiss the Dust*—focusing on the plight of Iraqi Kurds under the rule of Saddam Hussein—has not attracted any of *A Little Piece of Ground*'s negative criticism, and neither have either of the two autobiographical accounts cited here, even though *Kiss the Dust* adopts the same, singular third-person voice and child's-eye viewpoint as *A Little Piece of Ground*, and the voices and viewpoints of the *Zlata's Diary* entries of the 1990s Balkan War siege of Sarajevo, and Latifa's account of the Taliban takeover of Kabul, are arguably equally as singular and partisan, and equally as biased, as the fictional Karim's. Clearly there is political partisanship at work in the critical responses to Laird's *A Little Piece of Ground* that is not so mobilized in relation to young Afghan women, displaced Kurds, and besieged Bosnians. Another explanation might lie in the fact that the fictional narrative is more easily accused of "bias" because it is filtered through its author, while the autobiographical narratives are perceived to be the unmediated voice of the "subaltern" speaking on behalf of him or herself. It is also the case that the various geographical settings of these conflicts have themselves lost their rootedness in their various histories of conflict and colonization and that their geopolitical situations are arguably now inhabited by a contemporary mind-set that is, in Said's definition, the "effect" and "fabrication" of particular modes of representation and practices. At the heart of these considerations, then, are the two discursive and dialogic components of voice and viewpoint that are diachronically and synchronically situated, and are multiple and complex. The question is, then, how do they behave to mediate the production and reception of their respective stories in the performative sense that Judith Butler has suggested?[25] That is, how are the historical events they narrate themselves a performance of certain classifications of reality in which the narrating child figures are sited, positioned, caught up, and produced, either as themselves or as the creation and effect of their authors' mediation?

James Der Derian observes, "More than a rational calculation of interests takes us to war. People go to war because of how they *see, perceive, picture, imagine and speak of* (emphasis in original) others: that is, how they construct the difference of others as well as the sameness of themselves through representation" (quoted in Gregory 20). This is another important observation in this context of Said's "imaginative geographies" because it explicates the pervasive role of the gaze that is the very premise of his thesis and is also the basis on which colonial modernity—that is, the new imperialism—encodes the effects that it gazes upon, names, and thereby produces. The idea of the colonial gaze is important too because, as Gregory points out, it implies other fundamental questions such as the following: who owns the privilege to gaze on "the Other" and to practice the meanings of "Self" and "Other"? Who owns the power to narrate "the Other's" histories (Gregory 24)? But, in this context, we might also ask, who owns the power to narrate the "Other's" histories, and to invest them with a repertoire of meanings that effectively produces this phenomenon that Said has named "imaginative geographies"? More particularly, we might raise the question of what happens when the one-way gaze of the imperialist eye is unaccustomedly confronted by the return gaze of "the Other"? What happens when its asymmetry is disturbed as when, for example, the hegemony of the Westernized gaze of the world's media is destabilized by the emergence on the world stage of the voice of the Al Jazeera network? In literature, the return gaze has emerged through postcolonial criticism that effectively has turned the newly critical eye of the gazed-upon subaltern subject back upon the metropolis and interrogated the latter's "customary privilege to inspect the rest of the world" (Gregory 24). The voice of this criticism is also, in Gayatri Spivak's terms, a demonstration that the subaltern is indeed able to talk back ("Can the Subaltern Speak?") and is thus better placed to threaten to disrupt the status quo of hierarchical privilege, power, and knowledge that historically has been believed to be exclusively located in the Westernized eye of the beholder. These are the little pockets of power and resistances that Michel Foucault speaks about in his theses on power and knowledge,[26] and are examples of Butler's everyday little speech acts[27] through which "the other" enacts its alternative reality that destabilizes the certainties embedded in the imperialist grand narrative, even as it utters them.

What we see in these four narratives, irrespective of their fictional or actual status, is the little histories: the speech acts of the everyday lives of "ordinary"[28] children in differently extraordinary circumstances set against the backdrop of the big histories that are the ethnic, territorial, religious, and demographic entanglements in which they are caught up—the virulent unrest of nationalism and ethnonationalism, and of state versus nation. These big histories are alluded to through each of the books, but they are never fully narrated. In *My Forbidden Face*, a good deal of factual historical detail is reported by Latifa, and the book itself is prefaced with a short chronology of the political events leading up to the start of her story detailing her life of entrapment in her Kabul apartment after the Taliban takeover of the city. The event signals the bigger history that bears down on her everyday life through the enforcement of Sharia law; the end of any residually pro-Western-leaning lifestyles in that country; the suspension of female aspirations, independence, and education; and the beginnings of a "fully Islamicised" media (Latifa 27):

> "The Taliban are more monstrous than I ever imagined.... It's all over for us Latifa, my career is up the spout. I'll never fly again.... No woman will be allowed to work again." (19)

This time they're really murdering us—girls and women.... No more work for women means the total disintegration of the medical services and the administration. Her mother runs a secret school in her home. No more school for girls, no more health care for women, and no fresh air to be breathed anywhere. Back to the home, women! Or bury yourselves beneath your burqa. Far from the eyes of men. (33)

This little real-life fact of life under Taliban rule parallels the fictional account of Gleitzman's *Boy Overboard* (chapter 2) of Jamal's mother whose family flees for its life after she has been discovered by the Taliban to be running a secret school in her home, and of his sister Bibi's confinement to the house because she is a girl when what she really wants to do is to play in the streets with the boys in their game of football.

The veiling of women has become a political statement from whichever position it is adopted and viewed—either as a symbol of defiance against Western rule and values, or of oppression. According to Eisenstein's unquestionably pro-Western view, the enforced veiling of the female body is a symbol of what she describes as "global misogyny" in which "gender is connected to multiple systems of power" (151). In relation to the oppression specifically of Afghan women under the Taliban, she points out,

Veils and veiling bespeak the crucial site of female bodies in and for expressing relations of power.... Veils, like any piece of clothing or drapery, cover over; they create both fantasy and fetish at the same time. All clothing is used to cover over desire.... The veil covers over, and porn uncovers, exactly what the West wishes to dominate. (170–171)

And in relation to her concept of global misogyny in this connection, she says, "Fundamentalist misogyny has no one singular site or home. Women across the globe continue to resist gender apartheid and sexual terrorism in the diverse war sites where they continually reappear: Bosnia, Chechnya, Rwanda, Algeria, Nigeria and Palestine" (151).

In *A Little Piece of Ground*, Karim's little history of his life as a Muslim boy locked down with his family by Israeli curfews in a central Ramallah apartment block can be matched with the big history of Western colonization and partition that is the cause of their everyday oppression. When Karim's family travels to the village to visit the grandparents, the story is of traffic queues, checkpoints, and searches:

They were round the corner now. Ahead of them instead of the emptiness of the country road which they were expecting, was a queue of cars and minibuses. Beyond it was a khaki armoured vehicle, with a yellow light flashing on its roof.... A sudden violent hammering on the roof of the car made everyone inside jump with fright. Through the square of the car window he could see only the chest of a soldier who was standing beside it, the body armour which covered his upper half and the rifle he was gripping in his arms. "Move up," he said in thickly accented Arabic, pointing to the queue of cars in front.... He's terrified, he thought, with surprise. He thinks we're going to attack him. He could almost smell the soldier's fear. (39–41)

> At the Qalandya checkpoint, there was a massive traffic jam of taxis, cars, buses, minivans and trucks. Some were trying to find a place to park; others to get out of the parking spaces they had been wedged into. Hundreds of people were milling about, women, children, men carrying boxes and suitcases, farmers carrying crates, merchants carrying loads of material, all hoping to find cars or buses or trucks to their final destination, or, more likely than not, just to the next checkpoint.
>
> **Makdisi, "Diary: Living with the Wall"**

> Obviously the minute you put on a uniform you're no longer an individual as far as the other people are concerned. You represent the Israeli army, the one that confronts the Palestinians every day ... whatever your own feelings and convictions may be. That's the way it is, but it shouldn't stop you thinking.
>
> **Zenatti, *When I Was a Soldier* (131)**

And of the sequestration of his family's farmland:

"Didn't you know that this had happened? Didn't you hear us talking about the new settlement here?"

… From further along the terrace, he heard his father call back, "We don't have weapons. No arms. We come only to pick our olives."

"*Your* olives? Forget it. This is part of the settlement now. You won't ever pick olives here again. You want to get shot? No? then get out now."

"This place," he called out bravely, "it is ours. We have the papers. My grandfather—" (47–48)

> If there are errors in the original registration of the land, or if the original owner has died or moved overseas, or if there are questions about inheritance or the reallocation of land among or between families, or any questions about bills of sale or titles—that is, if there are any of the legal problems associated not merely with land ownership in general but, in particular, with ownership of land whose legal documentation has passed through countless municipal offices under four different administrations (the Ottoman Empire, Britain, Jordan, Israel)—then the application for permit will be suspended.
>
> **Makdisi, "Diary: Living with the Wall"**

> There are a thousand ways to describe Jerusalem … which is what I do: endlessly walking from the Arab quarter to the Jewish quarter, from the Armenian quarter to the Christian quarter, from the ramparts of the Old Town to the cafes of the new town.
>
> **Zenatti, *When I Was a Soldier* (217)**

With his best friends Joni, a Christian, and Hopper, another Muslim from the refugee camp, who together represent the factions of their collective historical displacement, they clear a piece of waste ground to make a football pitch that metaphorically invokes the big history of Palestinian entrapment in the occupied territories against the nationalist quest for sovereignty and self-determination: "the place, this space that was their own creation" (Laird, *Little Piece* 153); "It'd be their own place. They'd be in charge of it themselves" (118); "That would be good. We'd have a place to do. A place of our own" (93). The story centers round their struggle to take ownership of the football pitch and their attempts to outwit the soldiers of the Israeli tank that has settled at the edge of the pitch.

> Like Gali and like me, everyone here thinks there needs to be a revolution, and we sometimes go and demonstrate with the "women in black" calling for Israel's withdrawal from the Palestinian territories. They wear black as a sign of mourning and they're treated to torrents of abuse from the right-wing counter-demonstrators every Friday.
>
> **Zenatti, *When I Was a Soldier* (217)**

> We also talk about the political situation. He says we'll have to give everything back, give it all to the Palestinians, including the bit of Jerusalem they want from us. He thinks that there's no price on life, and that's the only worthwhile slogan.
>
> **Zenatti, *When I Was a Soldier* (214)**

> At the other, northern end of Gaza, close to [the] al-Nada apartment blocks between Beit Hanoun and Beit Lahiya, Aref Abu Qaida, 16, was killed by an artillery shell on 1 August. Sharif Harafi, 15, said: "We had been playing football and we had just finished. I was carrying the ball. I was going to my home, and [Aref] was going to his home. I heard a loud boom and then I saw him cut to pieces."... The IDF says that on 1 August it had fired and hit "a number of Palestinians" in "the area of Beit Lahiy" who had "approached a number of rocket launchers placed in the area."
>
> **Macintyre (2)**

Similarly, when Kurdish Tara (*Kiss the dust*) flees across the mountains to Iran to escape the Iraqi militia, it is played out against the big history of the Iraqi government's suppression of the Kurdish struggle for independence, and in front of her own eyes when a Kurdish boy is shot dead in the street:

"Enemies of the state! Spies! Shoot them!"

"You know why," she said. "That boy was a Kurd, like me."

"He must have been in league with the rebels, I suppose," said Leila doubtfully.

"They didn't bother to stop and ask before they shot him, did they?" Tara said furiously. "And anyway, the pesh murgas aren't rebels. They're freedom fighters!" (5–7)

> Let's just take the Kurds. What was Britain doing about the Kurds? Here is a little lesson in history that they don't teach in the schools in England. But we know it from declassified documents.... They figured that [air power] would be a good way to reduce [the] cost of crushing the barbarians. Winston Churchill, who was then the colonial secretary, didn't think that was enough.... So the question was, Should we use poison gas?... Well the document was circulated around the British empire. The India office was resistant. They said, if you use poison *gas* against Kurds and Afghans, it is going to cause us problems in India. Churchill was outraged by this, and he said: 'I do not understand this squeamishness about the use of gas.... I am strongly in favour of using poisoned gas against uncivilised tribes.... It will save British lives. We will use every means that science permits us.'
>
> **Chomsky (119–121)**

Their voices and viewpoints are in these respects partial even when, as in Zlata's case, her apparent naïveté studiously avoids any suggestion of political allegiance or partisanship. Each emerges from these complex histories of struggle and human atrocities that provide an apt metaphor for Žižek's "the Real" when it is understood, in the Lacanian definition, to mean the inexpressible, unsignifiable dimension of human experience that exists in the folds of the Möbius strip between the symbolic and the semiotic. This notion is even more interestingly metaphoricized when it is appropriated in its wider application to the unspeakableness of the atrocities to which these narratives allude—from whichever side of the political divide they are narrated and observed—and that continue to work themselves out in front of the gaze of the world media. In the extent to which these atrocities fall outside the realm of signification, the child figures on whom they are perpetrated are also themselves rendered beyond the margins of signification: they occupy the "space of exception" (Gregory 62),[29] which means not only or simply that they are the marginalized of a sovereign or (in these cases, and from the viewpoint of their narrators) invading power. More than this, they lie *beyond* the margins in a zone of not merely exclusion but also abandonment. In this space their lives and their deaths are of no consequence,[30] and these narratives go some way to countering the silence that has been otherwise imposed upon them by the imbalance of power from which they suffer.

All of these wars are being waged along ethnopolitical lines; but, at the same time as the narrative voices virulently condemn the respective and unquestionably intolerably oppressive effects of these invading alien forces, the inevitable (or intentional) naïveté of the child's-eye view through which they are reported (though Latifa is undeniably more politically aware even if equally implicated) unwittingly absolves the historical Western and pro-Western politicoeconomic contribution toward the events they now narrate.[31]

Every one of these child figures has been displaced at least historically, and in some cases contemporaneously, quite literally, by an arbitrary colonial partitioning of his or her homeland. Each of the struggles carries its own historical characteristic as a struggle for land and/or national identity. However, whatever the declared or undeclared, partisan, or apparently nonpartisan stance that their narrating voices adopt, and while none would condone the acts of violence they record, the viewpoint of each of them is either unwittingly or complicitly pro-Western, narrating from a pro-Western stance (that it knowingly shares with its target, Western, or at least Westernized audience) that has been besieged and violated by a belligerently "Other" and alien outside agency. In Ramallah, it is the Israeli military; in Kabul, the Taliban; in Kurdish Iraq, the pro-Saddam Iraqi military; and in Bosnia-Herzegovina, it is (presumably, though it is never actually named by Zlata) the Bosnian Serb militia's siege of Sarajevo. And this is the point and also the complexity of the struggle: that modernity has been colonized by and has become synonymized with the West, and that part of what is seemingly at stake in these struggles is a complex set of attitudes that seeks to wrest modernity from its exclusive and exclusionary definition in or by Western values and commodity effects, in ways that are not simply defined and dismissed as "primitive" or "a failure to modernize."

> [The] United States decided to pick Bosnia as its piece in the chess game. It blocked a peace settlement that might have worked, the Vance-Owen plan. It had plenty of problems, but if you take a look at the plan, it is not very different from the way things ended up after years of slaughter.... Finally the United States stepped in and—you know the rest of the story—imposed the Dayton agreement in 1995.
>
> **Chomsky (133)**

The point to make from this latter observation is both specific and general: that for the child in this narrative, "normality" is implicitly encoded in a pro-Western modernity and lifestyle, typically city based and infused with the commodity affects of global capitalism. For Palestinian Karim Aboudi of *A Little Piece of Ground*, it is a Ramallah apartment block where everyday life is bound up with PlayStation games, mobile phones, his sister's playing with her Barbie dolls, and watching *Tom and Jerry* cartoons on TV (Laird 130–131). In her Sarajevo apartment, Zlata enjoys "MTV, RTL, Sky" (Filipovic 8), Michael Jackson, and Madonna (13); playing the *Monopoly* board game; and watching *Murphy Brown*, *The Witches of Eastwick*, and *Bugs Bunny* cartoons on TV (15, 19). And in her pre-Taliban life in Kabul, Latifa and her sister relaxed in jogging trousers and trainers (Latifa 8); the walls of their shared bedroom displayed wall posters of Brooke Shields and Elvis; she says, "I love rock music. I have stacks of cassettes" (18); and they watched Bollywood films on TV (18), owned radios (before they became banned by the Taliban), and listened to "the BBC and 'The Voice of America'" (16). Kurdish Tara, after fleeing her town and arriving safely to lodge temporarily in the safety of her cousin's house in Iran, rejoices in shopping: "browsing through racks of clothes, picking out shoes and sweaters" (Laird, *Kiss the Dust* 216). When she and her family eventually escape from their short but harsh exile in Iran—during which time Tara has been forced by her male Iranian keepers to cover herself completely in strict Islamic dress—and arrives to seek asylum in England, we are told, "She'd forgotten how bright and different women looked without the scarves and dull, long, button-through dresses and chadors that covered them from head to foot in Iran" (237). Both Latifa and Tara locate their identities in their code of dress (Tara also longs for the color and flamboyance of her traditional Kurdish dress). Dress and lifestyle, nationhood and identity, are important indicators of selfhood. Eisenstein observes,

> Women remain the symbolic of nationhood.... Women's bodies are clothed to represent the status of the nation: chadors, burqas, saris, miniskirts, spiked heels, eye make-up, facelifts, and so on. Non-modern dress, read as non-Western, is seen as a sign of backwardness or underdevelopment. Modernity exposes the woman's body; the more the body is revealed the more modern the nation. (191)

The "normal" life these young people long for and return to is a localized version of Western modernity regarded as familiar, and is paradoxically at the heart of the ideologically and ethnically motivated conflicts in which they are caught up. In their war-torn minds, the peace and freedom from which they are excluded are synonymized with "Westernism" that is paradoxically the source of their oppression. These are the senses in which they are colonized.

These narratives interrogate the instantiations of "Otherness" amid a virulent political economy that would have us believe the imperialism of colonization to be "out there," "back there," and "over there." They expose how the imperialist gaze continues to operate, unsignified and therefore unrecognized, in the sight and sound of a new generation caught up in its hegemony, and is the colonial present. The argument throughout has been that globalization *is* the new imperialism. These novels powerfully instantiate the familiar themes of racism, the discovery of uncomfortable family history, and young love amid social disruption. But they also show how their settings, the subjectivities of the child or young adults caught up in them, and the forms that those familiar phenomena take are shaped by the violence newly inherent in a contemporary climate dominated by the unavoidable effects of globalization, deterritorialization, and neoliberal politics. These effects resonate through and beyond the particular settings of Blackman's dystopic city, Provoost's European town, and Rosoff's English countryside; Laird's Ramallah and Iraq, Zlata's Sarajevo, and Latifa's Kabul. In Blackman, the theme is not just racism, but also the way dominant power necessarily generates self-assertive and derogated minorities and drives them to terrorism; in Provoost, it is not just the legacy of Nazism, but also present-day manipulations of fear of the exploited and imported "'Other' World" that inform resurgent neofascism; and in Rosoff, what overtakes the young adults is the imminent collapse of the fragile capitalist system into worldwide terrorism and the destruction of the very possibility of home and refuge in a world where actual lived space replicates the fluidity of homogenized spaces of globalization. Globalization necessarily generates violent challenges to its hegemony, but it also generates artistic exposures of its existence, effects, and false binaries in the art form whose purpose and achievement have always been the assertion and celebration of human worth, individuality, and resilience. In these ways, these texts enunciate powerful modes of resistance to the prevailing interpellations of neoliberal subjectivities in globalization, but with little hint or hope of creating something better.

BIBLIOGRAPHY

Achebe, Chinua. "An Image of Africa: Racism in Conrad's *Heart of Darkness*." *Postcolonial Criticism*. Ed. Bart Moore-Gilbert, Gareth Stanton, and Willy Maley. London: Longman, 1997. 112–125.

Agamben, Giorgio. *Homo Sacer: Sovereign Power and Bare Life*. Trans. Daniel Heller-Roaxen. Stanford, CA: Stanford University Press, 1998.

Ahmad, Aijaz. "From *In Theory: Classes, Nations, Literatures*." *Postcolonial Criticism*. Ed. Bart Moore-Gilbert, Gareth Stanton, and Willy Maley. London: Longman, 1997. 248–272.

The American Declaration of the Rights and Duties of Man ("Persons" since 1998). www.cidh.oas.org.

Althusser, Louis. "The Ideological State Apparatuses." *Essays on Ideology*. By Louis Althusser. London and New York: Verso, 1984. 1–60.

Alvarez, Julia. *How the Garcia Girls Lost Their Accents*. Chapel Hill, NC: Algonquin Books of Chapel Hill, 1991.

Anderson, Benedict. *Imagined Communities: Reflections on the Origin and Spread of Nationalism*. 7th ed. London and New York: Verso, 1996.

Anderson, Rachel. *The War Orphan*. Oxford: Oxford University Press, 1984.

Armstrong, Judith, and David Rudd. "Sonya Hartnett's *Thursday's Child*: Readings." *Children's Literature in Education* 35.2 (2004): 115–170.

Ashcroft, Bill, Gareth Griffiths, and Helen Tiffin, eds. *The Empire Writes Back: Theory and Practice in Post-colonial Literatures*. London: Routledge, 1989.

Australasian Society for Traumatic Stress Studies. "Submissions on the Psychological Health of Child Asylum Seekers to National Inquiry into Children in Immigration Detention." 14 Oct. 2006 <http://www.hreoc.gov.au/human_rights/children_detention/submissions/astss.html>.

Australia. *A Last Resort? National Inquiry into Children Immigration in Detention*. Sydney: Human Rights and Equal Opportunities Commission, 2004.

Backett-Milburn, Kathryn. "Parents, Children and the Construction of the Healthy Body in Middle-Class Families." *The Body, Childhood and Society*. Ed. Alan Prout. Houndsmills, UK: Macmillan, 2000. 79–100.

Bakhtin, Mikhail. *Rabelais and His World*. Trans. Helene Iswolsky. Bloomington: Indiana University Press, 1984.

Baleswaran, Darshika. An Entry of Reader's Comment on Zephaniah's *Face* on 20th July 2005." *Reading Matters.* 7 Nov. 2006 <http://www.reading-matters.co.uk/book2.php?id=97>.

Ballantyne, R. M. *The Coral Island: A Tale of the Pacific Ocean.* 1857. London: Puffin, 1994.

Baudrillard, Jean. "Simulacra and Simulations." *Jean Baudrillard Selected Writings.* Ed. Mark Poster. Stanford, CA: Stanford University Press, 1988. 166–184.

Bauman, Zygmunt. *Legislators and Interpreters: On Modernity, Postmodernity and Intellectuals.* Cambridge: Polity Press, 1987.

Bawden, Nina. *Carrie's War.* London: Chivers, 1985.

———. *The Finding.* Oxford: Heinemann, 1988.

———. *The Outside Child.* London: Puffin, 1991.

———. *Squib.* Harmondsworth, UK: Puffin, 1973.

Becker, Anne E. "Nurturing and Negligence: Working on Others' Bodies in Fiji." *Embodiment and Experience: The Existential Ground of Culture and the Self.* Ed. Thomas J. Csordas. Cambridge: Cambridge University Press, 1994. 100–115.

Bell, Rachel. "Point Blank. Amy Fisher: The Long Island Lolita." *Crime Library.* 4 Oct. 2006 <http://www.crimelibrary.com/notorious_murders/young/amy_fisher/>.

Berlant, Lauren, and Michael Warner. "What Does Queer Theory Teach Us about X?" *PMLA* 110 (1995): 343–349.

Bhabha, Homi K. *The Location of Culture.* London: Routledge, 1994.

———. "'Race,' Time and the Revision of Modernity." *Postcolonial Criticism.* Eds. Bart Moore-Gilbert, Gareth Stanton, and Willy Maley. London: Longman, 1997. 166–190.

Blackman, Malorie. *Checkmate.* London: Doubleday, 2005.

———. *Knife Edge.* London: Doubleday, 2004.

———. *Noughts and Crosses.* London: Doubleday, 2001.

Boaz, George. *The Cult of Childhood.* London: The Warburg Institute, University of London, 1966.

Bosmajian, Hamida. *Sparing the Child: Grief and the Unspeakable in Youth Literature about Nazism and the Holocaust.* New York: Routledge, 2002.

Bostock, Lisa. "Promoting Resilience in Fostered Children and Young People." London: Social Care Institute for Excellence, 2004. 19 Nov. 2006 <http://www.scie.org.uk/publications/resourceguides/rg04/index.asp>.

Bowlby, John. *Attachment and Loss.* 3 vols. London: The Hogarth Press and The Institute of Psycho-analysis, 1982.

———. *A Secure Base: Clinical Applications of Attachment Theory.* London: Routledge, 1988.

Bradford, Clare. *Reading Race: Aboriginality in Australian Children's Literature.* Melbourne: Melbourne University Press, 2001.

Brand, Madeleine. Interview with Elizabeth Laird. "Profile: Controversy over Children's Book *A Little Piece of Ground.*" *Day to Day.* NPR 30 Sept. 2003. 4 Oct. 2006 <http://www.npr.org/programs/day/transcripts/2003/sep/030930.brand.html>.

Bretherton, Inge. "The Origins of Attachment Theory: John Bowlby and Mary Ainsworth." *Developmental Psychology* 28 (1992): 759–775. 19 Nov. 2006 <http://www.psychology.sunysb.edu/attachment/online/inge_origins.pdf>.

Briemberg, Mordecai. "A Response to the Campaign to Suppress the Publication and Distribution of *A Little Piece of Ground.*" *canpalnet: Canada-Palestine Support Network.* 20 Nov. 2006 <http://www.canpalnet.ca/archive/vkbs.html>.

British Association for Adoption and Fostering. "Summary Statistic." 19 Nov. 2006 <http://www.baaf.org.uk/info/stats/england.shtml>.

Brown, Colin, Nigel Morris, and Marie Woolf. "Are You Thinking What They're Thinking?" *The Independent.* 22 Apr. 2005: 1.

Burbach, Roger, and Jim Tarbell. *Imperial Overstretch: George Bush and the Hubris of Empire.* London and New York: Zed Books, 2004.

Burgess, Melvin. *Bloodtide.* London: Penguin, 2000.

———. *Junk.* London: Andersen Press, 1996.

Butler, Judith. *Antigone's Claim: Kinship between Life and Death.* New York: Columbia University Press, 2000.

———. *Bodies That Matter: On the Discursive Limits of "Sex."* New York and London: Routledge, 1993.

———. "Bodily Inscriptions, Performative Subversions (1990)." *The Judith Butler Reader.* Ed. Sara Salih. Oxford: Blackwell, 2004. 90–118.

———. "Competing Universalities." *The Judith Butler Reader.* Ed. Sara Salih. Oxford: Blackwell, 2004. 258–277.

———. "Foucault and the Paradox of Bodily Inscriptions." *The Journal of Philosophy* 86 (1989): 601–607.

———. *Gender Trouble: Feminism and the Subversion of Identity.* New York and London: Routledge, 1991.

———. "Introduction: Acting in Concert." *Undoing Gender.* By Judith Butler. New York: Routledge, 2004. 1–16.

———. "Performative Acts and Gender Constitution: An Essay in Phenomenology and Feminist Theory." *Performing Feminism: Feminist Critical Theory and Theatre.* Ed. Sue-Ellen Case. Baltimore: Johns Hopkins University Press, 1990. 270–282.

———. *The Psychic Life of Power: Theories in Subjection.* Stanford, CA: Stanford University Press, 1997.

———. "Subversive Bodily Acts." *Gender Trouble: Feminism and the Subversion of Identity.* By Judith Butler. New York and London: Routledge, 1990. 79–141.

———. *Undoing Gender.* New York: Routledge, 2004.

Butler, Judith, Ernesto Laclau, and Slavoj Žižek. *Contingency, Hegemony, Universality: Contemporary Dialogues on the Left.* London: Verso, 2000.

Caldicott, Edric, and Anne Fuchs. *Cultural Memory: Essays on European Literature and History.* Bern: Peter Lang AG, European Academic Publishers, 2003.

Carey, John. *What Good Are the Arts?* London: Faber, 2005.

Case, Sue Ellen. "Tracking the Vampire." *differences* 3.2 (1991): 1–20.

Ceci, Stephen J., and Wendy M. Williams. "Born vs. Made: Nature-Nurture in the New Millennium." *The Nature-Nurture Debate: The Essential Readings.* Ed. Stephen J. Ceci and Wendy M. Williams. Malden, MA: Blackwell, 1999. 1–9.

———. *The Nature-Nurture Debate: The Essential Readings.* Malden, MA: Blackwell, 1999.

Chanter, Tina. "Abjection, Death and Difficult Reasoning: The Impossibility of Naming Chora in Kristeva and Derrida." *Tympanum.* 20 Nov. 2006 <http://www.usc.edu/dept/comp-lit/tympanum/4/chanter.html>.

"Children Are Being Poisoned by Modern Life." *Times On-Line.* 12 Sept. 2006. 7 Nov. 2006 <http://www.timesonline.co.uk/article/0,,2-2353701.html>.

"Children in Care: Now and Then." *BBC News* 15 Feb. 2000. 19 Nov. 2006 <http://news.bbc.co.uk/1/hi/uk/642288.stm>.

Child Rights Information Network. "Human Rights-Based Approaches to Programming." 14 Oct. 2006 <http://www.crin.org/hrbap/index.asp?action=theme.subtheme&subtheme=14>.

"Chirac Upset by English Address." *BBC News* 24 Mar. 2006. <http://news.bbc.co.uk/1/hi/world/europe/4840160.stm>.

Chodorow, Nancy, and Suan Contratto. "The Fantasy of the Perfect Mother." *Rethinking the Family: Some Feminist Questions.* Ed. Barrie Thorne with Marilyn Yalom. New York: Longman, 1982. 54–75.

Chomsky, Noam. *Power and Terror: Post-9/11 Talks and Interviews.* Ed. John Junkerman and Takei Masakazu. London: Turnaround, 2003.

Christensen, Pia, Allison James, and Chris Jenks. "All We Needed to Do Was Blow the Whistle: Children's Embodiment of Time." *Exploring the Body.* Ed. Sarah Cunningham-Burley and Kathryn Backett-Milburn. New York: Palgrave. 201–222.

Clarke, Ann, and Alan Clarke. "Early Experience and the Life Path." *The Nature-Nurture Debate: The Essential Readings.* Ed. Stephen J. Ceci and Wendy M. Williams. Malden, MA: Blackwell, 1999. 136–146.

Cleveland, William L. *A History of the Modern Middle East.* 3rd ed. Boulder, CO: Westview Press, 2004.

Coats, Karen. *Looking Glasses and Neverlands: Lacan, Desire and Subjectivity in Children's Literature.* Iowa City: University of Iowa Press, 2004.

Conrad, Joseph. *Heart of Darkness.* Harmondsworth, UK: Penguin, 1973.

Cormier, Robert. *Heroes.* London: Hamish Hamilton, 1998.

Creech, Sharon. *Ruby Holler.* London: Bloomsbury, 2002.

Creed, Barbara. "Horror and the Monstrous-Feminine: An Imaginary Abjection." *Feminist Film Theory: A Reader*. Ed. Sue Thornham. Edinburgh: Edinburgh University Press, 1999. 251–266.

Damodoran, Andal, and Nilima Mehta. "Child Adoption in India." *Intercountry Adoption: Developments, Trends and Perspectives*. Ed. Peter Selman. London: British Association for Adoption and Fostering, 2000. 405–418.

de Lauretis, Teresa. "Queer Theory: Lesbian and Gay Sexualities. An Introduction." *differences* 3.2 (1991): i–xx.

Doty, Alexander. *Making Things Perfectly Queer: Interpreting Mass Culture*. Minneapolis: University of Minnesota Press, 1993.

Douglas, Mary. *Purity and Danger*. London and Boston: Routledge and Kegan Paul, 1969.

Duncan, William. "The Hague Convention on Protection of Children and Co-operation in Respect of Intercountry Adoption: Its Birth and Prospects." *Intercountry Adoption: Developments, Trends and Perspectives*. Ed. Peter Selman. London: British Association for Adoption and Fostering, 2000. 40–52.

Eagleton, Terry. "The Subject of Literature." *The English Magazine* 15 (1985): 4–7.

Edkins, Jenny. "Sovereign Power, Zones of Indistinction and the Camp." *Alternatives* 25 (2000): 3–25.

Egger, Sabine. "Deconstructing Marxist-Leninist Historiography: Memories of National Socialism in East German Poetry." *Cultural Memory: Essay on European Literature and History*. Ed. Edric Caldicott and Anne Fuchs. Bern: Peter Lang AG, European Academic Publishers, 2003. 99–114.

Eisenstein, Zilla. *Against Empire: Feminism, Racism and the West*. Melbourne: Spinifex Press, 2004.

Elliott, John, and Zoe Brennan. *The Sunday Times* 24 Sept. 2006: 16.

"The Empire Writes Back." *Time* 8 Feb. 1993: 46–51.

Fahlberg, Vera I. *The Child's Journey through Placement*. UK ed. London: British Association for Adoption and Fostering, 1994.

Fanon, Frantz. "The Fact of Blackness." Trans. Charles Lam Markmann. *The Post-colonial Studies Reader*. Ed. Bill Ashcroft, Gareth Griffiths, and Helen Tiffin. London: Routledge, 1995. 323–326.

Farmer, Elaine, Sue Moyers, and Jo Lipscombe. *Fostering Adolescents*. London and Philadelphia: Jessica Kingsley Publisher, 2004.

Filipović, Zlata. *Zlata's Diary*. Trans. Christina Pribichevich-Zorić. New York and London: Puffin, 1995.

Fine, Anne. *The Tulip Touch*. Harmondsworth, UK: Puffin, 1997.

Fletcher, John, and Andrew Benjamin, eds. *Abjection, Melancholia and Love: The Work of Julia Kristeva*. London: Routledge, 1990.

Foucault, Michel. "The Abnormals." *Ethics: Subjectivity and Truth: Essential Works of Michel Foucault 1954–1984*. Ed. Paul Rabinow. Trans. Robert Hurley. London: Allen Lane Penguin, 1997. 51–57.

———. *The Archeology of Knowledge*. Trans. A. M. Sheridan Smith. London and New York: Routledge, 1989.

———. *Discipline and Punish: The Birth of the Prison*. Trans. Alan Sheridan. London: Penguin, 1991.

———. *History of Sexuality*. 3 vols. Trans. Robert Hurley. New York: Vintage, 1980.

The French 1795 Declaration of the Rights and Duties of Man and the Citizen, 1795. www.chm.gmu.edu.edu/revolution/browse/texts.

"The Fourth Plinth Project." 7 Nov. 2006 <http://www.fourthplinth.co.uk>.

"Frail Jacko Late for Court Again." *AOL News* 22 Mar. 2005. 20 Nov. 2006 <http://channels.aolsvc.co.uk/news/article.adp?id=20050322032509990002>.

Fraser, Mariam, and Monica Greco. "What Is a Body?" *The Body: A Reader*. Ed. Mariam Fraser and Monica Greco. Abingdon, UK: Routledge, 2005. 43–46.

Freud, Anna, and Sophie Dann. "An Experiment in Group Upbringing." *Psychoanal. Study Child* 6 (1951): 127–168.

Frith, Maxine, and Christopher Thompson. "Madonna Polarises Opinion as David Flies Out." *The Independent* 17 Oct 2006: 2.

Gailey, Christine Ward. "Race, Class and Gender in Intercountry Adoption in the USA." *Intercountry Adoption: Developments, Trends and Perspectives*. Ed. Peter Selman. London: British Association for Adoption and Fostering, 2000. 295–314.

Gibbons, Fiachra. "Children's Author Faces Jewish Wrath." *Guardian* 23 Aug. 2003. 20 Nov. 2006 <http://www.guardian.co.uk/print/0,3858,4739423-103681,00.html>.

Genette, Gérard. *Narrative Discourse*. Trans. Jane E. Lewis. Oxford: Blackwell, 1980.

Gleitzman, Morris. *Boy Overboard*. London and New York: Penguin, 2002.

———. "Epigraph." *Boy Overboard*. By Morris Gleitzman. London and New York: Penguin, 2002.

———. *Girl Underground*. London: Penguin, 2004.

Goldie, Terry. "The Representation of the Indegene." *The Post-colonial Reader*. Ed. Bill Ashcroft, Gareth Griffiths, and Helen Tiffin. London and New York: Routledge, 1995. 232–236.

Golding, William. *The Lord of the Flies*. London: Faber, 1954.

A Good Read. BBC Radio 4. London. 1 Apr. 2006.

Gregory, Derek. *The Colonial Present: Afghanistan, Palestine, Iraq*. Oxford: Blackwell, 2004.

Griffiths, Gareth. "The Myth of Authenticity." *The Post-colonial Reader*. Ed. Bill Ashcroft, Gareth Griffiths, and Helen Tiffin. London and New York: Routledge, 1995. 237–241.

Grosz, Elizabeth. "The Body of Signification." *Abjection, Melancholia and Love: The Work of Julia Kristeva.* Ed. John Fletcher and Andrew Benjamin. London: Routledge, 1990. 80–103.

———. *Space, Time and Perversion: Essays on the Politics of Bodies.* New York and London: Routledge, 1995.

Gubar, Marah. "Species Trouble: The Abjection of Adolescence in E. B. White's *Stuart Little.*" *Lion and the Unicorn* 27.1 (2003): 98–119.

Guest, Tim. *My Life in Orange.* London: Granta, 2004.

Gumblel, Andrew. "US Split by Need for Cheap Labour and a Fear of Outsiders" *The Independent* 31 Mar. 2006: 2.

Haddon, Mark. *The Curious Incident of the Dog in the Night-time.* London: Red Fox, 2004.

Hague Convention on Protection of Children and Co-operation in Respect of Intercountry Adoption (1993). 19 Nov. 2006 <http://www.hcch.net/index_en.php?act=conventions.text&cid=69>.

Hall, Catherine. "Histories, Empires and the Post-colonial Moment." *The Post-colonial Question.* Ed. Iain Chambers and Lidia Curti. London: Routledge, 1996. 65–77.

Hall, Stuart. "Ethnicity: Identity and Difference." *Radical America* 23.4 (1989): 9–20.

———. "Local and Global." *Dangerous Liaisons: Gender, Nation, and Postcolonial Perspectives.* Ed. Anne McClintock, Aamir Mufti, and Ella Shohat. Minneapolis: University of Minnesota Press, 2002. 173–187.

Hanvey, Chris. "The Lessons We Never Learn." *Guardian Unlimited* 26 Jan. 2003: 1+.

Haraway, Donna. *Simians, Cyborgs and Women: The Reinvention of Nature.* New York: Routledge, 1991.

Harding, Jeremy. Review of *I Didn't Do It for You: How the World Used and Abused a Small African Nation. The London Review of Books* 20 July 2006: 13.

Hari, Johann. "How Drugs Brought the Taliban Back to Life." *The Independent* 7 Sept. 2006: 37.

Harpham, Geoffrey Galt. *On the Grotesque: Strategies of Contradiction in Art and Literature.* Princeton, NJ: Princeton University Press, 1982.

Harris, Judith Rich. "How to Succeed in Childhood." *The Nature-Nurture Debate: The Essential Readings.* Ed. Stephen J. Ceci and Wendy Williams. Malden, MA: Blackwell, 1999. 84–95.

Hartnett, Sonya. *Thursday's Child.* London: Walker Books, 2002.

———. "*Thursday's Child*: Author's Note." *Penguin.* 1–3. 24. Sept. 2006 <http://www.penguin.com.au/PUFFIN/TEACHERS/Articles/thursdays_child.cfm>.

Harvey, David. *A Brief History of Neoliberalism.* New York: Oxford University Press, 2005.

———. *The New Imperialism.* Oxford: Oxford University Press, 2004.

Hinton, S. E. *The Outsiders*. New York: Viking Press, 1967.

Hogan, Patrick Colm. "Indigenous Tradition and the Individual Talent." *Empire and Poetic Voice*. Albany: State University of New York, 2004. 197–225.

Holloway, Lester. "Poverty Gap Grows for Black Children." *Black Information Link*. 14 Oct. 2006. <http://www.blink.org.uk/pdescription. asp?key=2789&grp=56&cat=168>.

Hunt, Peter, and Karen Sands. "The View from the Center: British Empire and Post-Empire Children's Literature." *Voices of the Other: Children's Literature and the Postcolonial Context*. Ed. Roderick McGillis. New York: Garland, 2000. 39–53.

International Covenants on Human Rights. 14 Oct. 2006 <http://www.pdhre. org/conventionsum/covsum.html>.

Ishiguro, Kazuo. *When We Were Orphans*. London: Faber and Faber, 2000.

Jallow-Rutherford, S. "The Mask We Wear." *Invisible, Identity, Disability, Culture*. African Caribbean Project Asian Disabled Peoples Group. 14 Oct. 2006. <http://www.cdp.org.uk/art_projects/invisible/poetry01. htm#mask>.

James, Allison, Chris Jenks, and Alan Prout. *Theorizing Childhood*. Cambridge: Polity Press, 1998.

James, Henry. *The Turn of the Screw*. London: Penguin, 1994.

Johnson, David, and Scott Michaelsen, eds. "Border Secrets: An Introduction." *Border Theory: The Limits of Cultural Politics*. Minneapolis: University of Minnesota Press, 1997. 1–39.

Katz, Jonathan. "Dismembership: Jasper Johns and the Body Politic." *Performing the Body / Performing the Text*. Ed. Amelia Jones and Andrew Stephenson. London and New York: Routledge, 1999. 170–185.

Kayser, Wolfgang. *The Grotesque in Art and Literature*. Trans. Ulrich Weisstein. Bloomington: Indiana University Press, 1963.

Kincaid, Jamaica. *A Small Place*. New York: Vintage, 1997.

Kincaid, James R. *Child Loving: The Erotic Child and Victorian Culture*. New York: Routledge, 1992.

Kingsolver, Barbara. *The Poisonwood Bible*. London: Faber and Faber, 1998.

Knowles, Murray, and Kirsten Malmkjaer. *Language and Control in Children's Literature*. London: Routledge, 1996.

Kokkola, Lydia. *Representing the Holocaust in Youth Literature*. New York: Routledge, 2003.

Kristeva, Julia. *Etrangers à nous-même*. Paris: Fayard, 1989. *Strangers to Ourselves*. Trans. Leon S. Roudiez. New York: Columbia University Press, 1990.

———. *The Powers of Horror: An Essay on Abjection*. Trans. Leon S. Roudiez. New York: Columbia University Press, 1982.

———. "Women's Time." *The Kristeva Reader*. Ed. Toril Moi. Oxford: Basil Blackwell, 1986. 187–213.

Kroker, Arthur, and Marilouise Kroker. "Theses on the Disappearing Body in the Hyper-modern Condition." *Body Invaders: Sexuality and the Postmodern Condition.* E. Arthur Kroker and Marilouise Kroker. Houndsmill, UK: Macmillan, 1988. 20–33.

Kutzer, M. Daphne. *Empire's Children: Empire and Imperialism in Classic British Children's Books.* New York and London: Garland, 2000.

Lacan, Jacques. *Écrits: A Selection.* Trans. Alan Sheridan. London and New York: Routledge–Taylor & Francis, 2001.

Laird, Elizabeth. *Kiss the Dust.* London: Egmont, 2001.

———. *A Little Piece of Ground.* London, Macmillan, 2003.

———. Preface. *Kiss the Dust.* By Elizabeth Laird. London: Egmont, 2001.

Laming, Lord Justice. "The Victoria Climbié Inquiry." 20 Nov. 2006 <http://www.victoria-climbie-inquiry.org.uk/finreport/titlepages.htm>.

Lapper, Alison. "The Fourth Plinth Project." 7 Nov. 2006 <http://www.fourthplinth.co.uk/selected_artists.htm>.

Latifa. *My Forbidden Face: Growing Up under the Taliban: A Young Woman's Story.* Trans. Lisa Appignanesi. London: Virago, 2002.

Latour, Bruno. *We Have Never Been Modern.* Trans. Catherine Porter. Hemel Hempstead, UK: Harvester/Wheatsheaf. 1993.

Lechte, John. *Julia Kristeva.* London: Routledge, 1990.

Leder, Drew. *The Absent Body.* Chicago: University of Chicago Press, 1990.

Lee, Nick. *Childhood and Society: Growing Up in an Age of Uncertainty.* London: Open University Press, 2001.

———. "Judgment, Responsibility and Generalized Constructivism." Paper presented at the Conference on the Labour of Division, Centre for Social Theory and Technology, Keele University, Newcastle-under-Lyme, UK, November 1995.

Lesnik-Oberstein, Karín. *Children's Literature: Criticism and the Fictional Child.* Oxford: Clarendon, 1994.

———. "Introduction: New Approaches." *Children's Literature: New Approaches.* Ed. Karín Lesnik-Oberstein. Basingstoke, UK: Palgrave-Macmillan, 2004. 1–24.

Lewis, Kevin. *The Kid: A True Story.* London: Penguin, 2003.

Lingis, Alphonso. *Foreign Bodies.* New York: Routledge, 1994.

———. "The Subjectification of the Body." *The Body.* Ed. Donn Welton. Malden, MA: Blackwell, 1999. 286–306.

Litchfield, John. "Liberté? Égalité? Fraternité?" *The Independent.* 7 Nov. 2005: 1–2.

Lutzeier, Elizabeth. Blurb Note. *No Shelter.* By Elizabeth Lutzeier. London: Blackie and Son Limited, 1984.

———. *Lost for Words.* Oxford: Oxford University Press, 1993.

———. *No Shelter.* London: Blackie and Son Limited, 1984.

Lyotard, Jean-François. *The Postmodern Condition: A Report on Knowledge.* Minneapolis: University of Minnesota Press, 1984.

Macintyre, Donald. "Revealed: Civilian Roll of a Deadly Assault That Has Ravaged Gaza." *The Independent* 19 Sept. 2006: 2.

Mahamdallie, Hassan. "Benjamin Zephaniah: Rage of Empire." *Socialist Review* 281 (2004). 14 Oct. 2006 <http://pubs.socialistreviewindex.org.uk/sr281/mahamdallie.htm>.

Makdisi, Saree. "Diary: Living with the Wall." *The London Review of Books* 3 Mar. 2005. 20 Nov. 2006 <http://www.lrbco.uk/v27/n05/makd01_.html>.

Margaroni, Maria. "The Trial of the Third: Kristeva's Oedipus and the Crisis of Identification." *Julia Kristeva: Live Theory.* Ed. John Lechte and Maria Margaroni. London: Continuum, 2004. 34–62.

McCallum, Robyn. *Ideologies of Identity in Adolescent Fiction.* New York: Garland, 1999.

McClintock, Anne, Aamir Mufti, and Ella Shohat, eds. *Dangerous Liaisons: Gender, Nation, and Postcolonial Perspectives.* Minneapolis: University of Minnesota, 1997.

McGillis, Roderick, ed. *Voices of the Other: Children's Literature and the Postcolonial Context.* New York: Garland, 2000.

Mercer, Kobena. "Black Hair/Style Politics." *Out There: Marginalisation and Contemporary Cultures.* Ed. Rebecca Fergusson, M. Gerver, T. T. Minh-ha, and C. West. Cambridge, MA: MIT Press, 1990. 247–264.

Merleau-Ponty, Maurice. *Phenomenology of Perception.* Trans. Colin Smith. London: Routledge and Kegan Paul, 1962.

Miller, Jane. *Many Voices.* London: Routledge and Kegan Paul, 1983.

Misra, Maria. "Heart of Smugness." *Guardian* 23 July 2002. 20 Nov. 2006 <http://www.guardian.co.uk/comment/story/0,,761626,00.html>.

Mitchell, David T. "The Accent of 'Loss': Cultural Crossings as Context in Julia Alvarez's *How the Garcia Girls Lost Their Accents.*" *Beyond the Binary: Reconstructing Cultural Identity in a Multicultural Context.* Ed. Timothy B. Powell. New Brunswick, NJ, and London: Rutgers University Press, 1999. 165–184.

Mizuma, Chie. "Performativity and Queerness in *Peter Pan.*" *Children's Literature Global and Local: Social and Aesthetic Perspectives.* Ed. Emer O'Sullivan, Kimberly Reynolds, and Rolf Romøren. Oslo: Novis Press, 2005. 117–124.

Montaldo, Charles. "Amy Fisher: The 'Long Island Lolita.'" 24 Sept. 2006 <http://crime.about.com/od/female_offenders/p/amyfisher.htm>.

Moore-Gilbert, Bart, Gareth Stanton, and Willy Maley. "Introduction." *Postcolonial Criticism.* Ed. Bart Moore-Gilbert, Gareth Stanton, and Willy Maley. London: Longman, 1997. 1–72.

———, eds. *Postcolonial Criticism.* London: Longman, 1997.

Naidoo, Beverley. *The Other Side of Truth.* London: Penguin, 2000.

National Adoption Information Clearinghouse. "Adoption Statistics Overview." 19 Nov. 2006 <http://statistics.adoption.com/ information/adoption-statistics-overview.html>.

Natov, Roni. *The Poetics of Childhood*. New York: Routledge, 2003.

Newsnight Review. BBC 2. London. 7 Apr. 2006.

Nikolajeva, Maria. "Imprints of the Mind: The Depiction of Consciousness in Children's Literature." *The Children's Literature Association Quarterly* 26.4 (2002): 173–187.

———. *The Rhetoric of Character in Children's Literature*. Lanham, MD: Scarecrow, 2002.

Nodelman, Perry. "The Other: Orientalism, Colonialism, and Children's Literature." *Children's Literature Association Quarterly* 17.1 (1992): 29–35.

"Off-the-Street Interview." *Channel 4 News*. London. 28 Jan. 2005.

O'Malley, Andrew. *The Making of the Modern Child: Children's Literature and Childhood in the Late Eighteenth Century*. New York: Routledge, 2003.

Orwell, George. *1984*. 1949. New York: Signet, 1977.

Ots, Thomas. "The Silenced Body—the Expressive *Leib*: On the Dialectic of Mind and Life in Chinese Cathartic Healing." *Embodiment and Experience: The Existential Ground of Culture and the Self*. Ed. Thomas J. Csordas. Cambridge: Cambridge University Press, 1994. 116–136.

Paterson, Katherine. *The Great Gilly Hopkins*. London: Puffin, 1981.

Pennell, Beverley, and John Stephens. "Queering Heterotopic Spaces: Shyam Selvadurai's *Funny Boy* and Peter Wells's *Boy Overboard*." *Ways of Being Male: Representations of Masculinities in Children's Literature and Film*. Ed. John Stephens. New York: Routledge, 2002. 164–184.

Petersen, Kirsten Holst, and Anna Rutherford. "Fossil and Psyche." *The Post-colonial Reader*. Ed. Bill Ashcroft, Gareth Griffiths, and Helen Tiffin. London and New York: Routledge, 1995. 185–189.

Petley, Julian. "Monstrous Children." *The Body's Perilous Pleasures: Dangerous Desires and Contemporary Culture*. Ed. Michele Aaran. Edinburgh: Edinburgh University Press. 86–107.

Plumwood, Val. *Feminism and the Mastery of Nature*. London: Routledge, 1993.

Prager, Jeffrey. *Presenting the Past: Psychoanalysis and the Sociology of Misremembering*. Cambridge, MA: Harvard University Press, 1998.

Project for the American New Century. 20 Nov. 2006 <http://www.newamericancentury.org>.

———. 1997. "Rebuilding America's Defenses: Strategy, Forces and Resources for a New Century." *A Report of the Project for the New American Century*. Washington, DC: Project for the New American Century, Sept. 2000. http://www.newamericancentury.org/RebuildingAmericasDefenses.pdf.

Prout, Alan, ed. *The Body, Childhood and Society*. New York: St. Martin's, 2000.

———. *The Future of Childhood*. London: Routledge/Falmer, 2005.

———. "Objective vs. Subjective Indicators or Both? Whose Perspective Counts? Or the Distal, the Proximal and Circuits of Knowledge." Paper delivered to the Workshop on Monitoring and Measuring the State of the Children: Beyond Survival, Jerusalem, January 1996.

Provoost, Anne. *Falling.* Trans. John Nieuwenhuizen. St. Leonards, Australia: Allen and Unwin, 1997.

Quinn, Marc. "The Fourth Plinth Project." 7 Nov. 2006 <http://www.fourth-plinth.co.uk/selected_artists.htm>.

Rabinowitz, Rebecca. "Messy New Freedoms: Queer Theory and Children's Literature." *New Voices in Children's Literature.* Ed. Sebastian Chapelau. Lichfield, UK: Pied Piper Publishing, 2004. 19–28.

Reiss, Johanna. "Epigraph." *The Upstairs Room.* By Johanna Reiss. New York: HarperTrophy-HarperCollins, 1987. v.

———. *The Upstairs Room.* New York: HarperTrophy-HarperCollins, 1987.

Reiter, Andrea. "The Holocaust Seen through the Eyes of Children." *Narrating the Holocaust.* By Andrea Reiter. Trans. Patrick Camiller. London: Continuum, 2000. 230–241.

———. *Narrating the Holocaust.* Trans. Patrick Camiller. London and New York: Continuum, 2000.

Rosaldo, Renato. "Fables of the Fallen Guy." *Criticism in the Borderlands: Studies in Chicano Literature, Culture and Ideology.* Ed. Héctor Calderón and José David Salvadívar. Durham, NC: Duke University Press, 1991. 84–93.

Rosoff, Meg. *How I Live Now.* London: Penguin, 2004.

Russo, Mary. *The Female Grotesque: Risk, Excess and Modernity.* New York: Routledge, 1994.

Rutter, Michael. "Developmental Catch-Up, and Deficit, Following Adoption after Severe Global Early Deprivation." *The Nature-Nurture Debate: The Essential Readings.* Ed. Stephen J. Ceci and Wendy M. Williams. Malden, MA: Blackwell, 1999. 108–133.

Sachar, Louis. *Holes.* New York: Frances Foster Books, 1998.

Said, Edward. "Mind in Winter: Reflections on Life in Exile." *Harper's Magazine* Sept. 1982: 25.

———. *Orientalism.* London: Penguin, 2003.

———. "Orientalism Reconsidered." *Postcolonial Criticism.* Ed. Bart Moore-Gilbert, Gareth Stanton, and Willy Maley. London: Longman, 1997. 126–144.

Salih, Sara, ed. *The Judith Butler Reader.* Oxford: Blackwell, 2004.

Salih, Sara, and Pat Pinsent. "Fame and Fortune in a Modern Fairy Tale: Louis Sachar's *Holes.*" *Children's Literature in Education* 33.3 (2002): 203–212.

Sandhu, Sukhdev. "Pop Goes the Centre: Hanif Kureishi's London," *Postcolonial Theory and Criticism.* Ed. Laura Chrisman and Benita Parry. Cambridge: D.S. Brewer for English Association, 1999. 133–154.

Sara. An Entry of Reader's Comment on Zlata Filipović's *Zlata's Diary* on 16th November 2005. *Reading Matters.* 20 Nov. 2006 <http://www.reading-matters.co.uk/book2.php?id=38>.

Scott, Anne. "The Storyteller's Paradox: Homeopath in the Borderlands." *Exploring the Body*. Ed. Sarah Cunningham-Burley and Kathryn Backett-Milburn. London: Palgrave, 2001. 3–20.

Sedgwick, Eve Kosofsky. *Tendencies*. Durham, NC: Duke University Press, 1993.

Seelinger Trites, Roberta. *Disturbing the Universe: Power and Repression in Adolescent Literature*. Iowa City: University of Iowa Press. 2000.

Selvadurai, Shyam. *Funny Boy: A Novel in Six Stories*. London: Vintage, 1995.

Sergeant, Harriet. *Handle with Care: An Investigation into the Care System*. London: Centre for Young Policy Studies, 2006.

Sharpe, Matthew. *Slavoj Žižek: A Little Piece of the Real*. Aldershot, UK: Ashgate, 2004.

The Soviet Constitution of 1918. 14 Oct. 2006 <http://www.totse.com/en/politics/political_documents/thesovietconst170621.html>.

Spacks, Patricia Meyer. *The Adolescent Idea: Myths of Youth and the Adult Imagination*. New York: Basic Books, 1981.

Spivak, Gayatri Chakravorty. "Can the Subaltern Speak?" *Colonial Discourse and Post-colonial Theory: A Reader*. Ed. Patrick Williams and Laura Chrisman. Hemel Hempstead, UK: Harvester/Wheatsheaf, 1993. 66–111.

———. "Translator's Preface." *Of Grammatology*. By Jacques Derrida. Trans. Gayatri Chakravorty Spivak. Baltimore: Johns Hopkins University Press, 1974. ix–lxxxvii.

Stam, Robert. "Multiculturalism and the Neoconservatives." *Dangerous Liaisons: Gender, Nation, and Postcolonial Perspectives*. Ed. Anne McClintock, Aamir Mufti, and Ella Shohat. Minneapolis: University of Minnesota Press, 1997. 188–203.

Stephens, John, ed. *Representing Masculinities in Children's Literature and Film*. New York: Routledge, 2002.

Swain, Jon. "The Final Word on the Horror of War." Rev. of *Vietnam: The Definitive Oral History Told from All Sides*, by Christian G. Appy. *The Sunday Times* 29 Oct. 2006: culture sec., 45–46.

Swindells, Robert. *Stone Cold*. London: Puffin, 1995.

"System 'Failing Children in Care.'" *BBC News* 23 Aug. 2006. 19 Nov. 2006 <http://news.bbc.co.uk/1/hi/education/5273986.stm>.

Thomson, Rosemarie Garland. "Narrations of Deviance and Delight: Staring at Julia Pastrana, the 'Extraordinary Lady.'" *Beyond the Binary: Reconstructing Cultural Identity in a Multicultural Context*. Ed. Timothy. B. Powell. New Brunswick, NJ, and London: Rutgers University Press, 1999. 81–104.

United Nations. Convention on the Rights of the Child (UNCRC) (20 Nov. 1989). 14 Oct. 2006 <http://www.cirp.org/library/ethics/UN-convention/>.

———. Declaration on Social and Legal Principles Relating to the Protection and Welfare of Children, with Special Reference to Foster Placement and Adoption Nationally and Internationally (3 Dec. 1986). 19 Nov. 2006 <http://www.unhchr.ch/html/menu3/b/27.htm>.

———. General Assembly Document A/RES/44/25 (12 Dec. 1989). 14 Oct. 2006 <http://www.cirp.org/library/ethics/UN-convention/>.

———. Universal Declaration of Human Rights (1948). 14 Oct. 2006 <http://www.cirp.org/library/ethics/UN-human/>.

United Nations High Commissioner for Refugees. UN Refugee Agency. "Asylum Levels and Trends in Industrialized Countries, First Quarter 2006: Comparative Overview of Asylum Applications Lodged in 31 European and Non-European Countries." 21 July 2006. 14 Oct. 2006 <http://www.unhcr.org/statistics/STATISTICS/44d74d9c2.pdf>.

Voigt, Cynthia. *Dicey's Song*. New York: Aladdin, 2003.

———. *Homecoming*. New York: Aladdin, 2003.

Watson, James. "Archbishop Warns of 'Crisis' in Modern Childhood." *The Independent* 18 Sept. 2006. 7 Oct. 2006 <http://news.independent.co.uk/uk/this_britain/article1616811.ece>.

Westwater, Martha. *Giant Despair Meets Hopeful: Kristevan Readings of Young Adult Fiction*. Edmonton, Canada: University of Alberta Press, 2000.

White, Hayden. *Tropics of Discourse: Essays in Cultural Criticism*. Baltimore and London: Johns Hopkins University Press, 1992.

Wilkie, Christine. "Digging Up *The Secret Garden*: Noble Innocents or Little Savages?" *Children's Literature in Education* 28.2 (1997): 73–83.

Wilkie-Stibbs, Christine. *The Feminine Subject in Children's Literature*. New York: Routledge, 2002.

———. "Nina Bawden." *The Oxford Encyclopedia of Children's Literature*. Ed. Jack Zipes. New York: Oxford University Press, 2006.

Willis, Susan. "I Want the Black One: Is There a Place for Afro-American Culture in Commodity Culture?" *New Formations* 10 (1990): 77–97.

Wilson, Jacqueline. *The Dare Game*. London: Corgi Yearling, 2000.

———. *The Illustrated Mum*. London: Corgi Yearling, 2000.

———. *The Story of Tracy Beaker*. London: Corgi Yearling, 1991.

Wrong, Michela. *I Didn't Do It for You: How the World Used and Abused a Small African Nation*. London: Harper Perennial, 2005.

Wyile Schwenke, Andrea. "*Thursday's Child*: Expanding the View of First Person Narratives." *Children's Literature in Education* 30.3 (1999): 185–202.

Xie, Shaobo. "Rethinking the Identity of Cultural Otherness: The Discourse of Difference as an Unfinished Project." *Voices of the Other: Children's Literature and the Postcolonial Context*. Ed. Roderick McGillis. New York: Garland, 1999. 1–16.

Young, Iris Marion. "Abjection and Oppression: Dynamics of Unconscious Racism, Sexism and Homophobia." *Crises in Continental Philosophy*. Proc. Society of Phenomenology and Existential Philosophy meeting of Northwestern University, 1988. Ed. Arleen B. Dallery and Charles E. Scott with Holley Roberts. Albany: State University of New York Press, 1990. 201–204.

"Young Killers." *Crime Library.* 20 Nov. 2006 <http://www.crimelibrary.com/notorious_murders/young/index.html>.

Zenatti, Valérie. *When I Was a Soldier.* Trans. Adriana Hunter. London: Bloomsbury, 2002.

Zephaniah, Benjamin. *Face.* London: Bloomsbury, 1999.

———. "Interview." *The Independent Education Supplement* 29 June 2006: 10.

———. *Refugee Boy.* London: Bloomsbury, 2001.

Zipes, Jack. *Breaking the Magic Spell.* London: Heinemann, 1979.

Žižek, Slavoj, ed. *Mapping Ideology.* London: Verso, 1994.

———. *Tarrying with the Negative.* Durham, NC: Duke University Press, 1993.

———. *The Ticklish Subject: The Absent Centre of Political Ontology.* London: Verso, 1999.

Zornado, Joseph L. *Inventing the Child: Culture, Ideology and the Story of Childhood.* New York: Garland, 2001.

NOTES

CHAPTER 1

1. For an interesting analysis of feminized characterization in Peter Pan, see Mizuma.
2. Robert Stam points out how books like *The Official Politically Correct Dictionary and Handbook* have been endlessly satirized by new Right neoconservatives who also ridicule and portray multiculturalists as "puritanical party poopers, an unpleasant people anxious to spoil the good times of fun-loving Americans," in such epithets as "self-righteous," "censorious," "pious," "cranky," and "sanctimonious," while simultaneously portraying them as "irresponsible hedonists, the heirs to the permissive 1960s" (Stam 197).
3. See also Butler, "Bodily Inscriptions," 106–107.
4. See also Scott, 4–5.
5. See also Butler, *Gender Trouble*, 13–31; and *Case*, 1–20.
6. Doty asserts, however, that by using the term "queer" in his cultural studies work, he wanted to "recapture and reassert a militant sense of difference that views the erotically 'marginal' as both (in bell hooks's words) a consciously chosen 'site of resistance' and a 'location of radical openness and possibility'" (3).
7. See for example Ceci and Williams, *The Nature-Nurture Debate*.
8. See also Sharpe 89.
9. See, for example, James, Jenks, and Prout; Prout, *The Future of Childhood*; Prout, *The Body, Childhood and Society*; and Lee, *Childhood and Society: Growing Up in an Age of Uncertainty.*
10. This topic is part of the focus of chapter 4.
11. For an elaboration on these conceptions of character, see Nikolajeva, *The Rhetoric of Character and "Imprints of the Mind."*
12. I discuss this epigraph and its relevance to the question of whether adult insider authors have a right to seem to speak on behalf of child outsider subjects in chapter 2.
13. See "Young Killers" and Montaldo.

14. Lingis says,

    The incarceration of infancy in the power systems of pedagogy has constituted the child's body as vulnerable and an object of power operations.... The sado-masochist, pederast, gerontophile, homosexual, fetishist, etc. are made by the psychiatrists and by the accomplices—the pastors, the pedagogues, the police—just as the delinquent is produced by the penitentiary archipelago and pursues a career within it which feeds its knowledge and serves its power. (Foreign Bodies 303)

15. In August 2006, the United Kingdom's Blair government floated the idea of a "Children's Index" that will be set up to identify and register on a national database established for the purpose predictive indicators of delinquency in children, even before they are born.

16. See also, in relation to savagery, wildness, and nature, Hayden White, 150–151.

17. See also Edward Said, *Orientalism*, 40; and Catherine Hall, "Histories, Empires and the Post-colonial Moment."

18. See Boaz; Wilkie; James, Jenks, and Prout; and Prout, *The Future of Childhood*.

19. White points out that "the Noble Savage" stands in opposition to the term "savagery" that is synonymous with "wildness.

    The notion of "wildness" (or, in its Latinate form "Savagery") belongs to a set of culturally self-authenticating devices which includes, among many other things, the idea of "madness" and "heresy" as well. These terms are used not merely to designate a specific condition or site of being but also to confirm the value of their dialectical antitheses "civilization," "sanity," and "orthodoxy," respectively. Thus they do not so much refer to a specific thing, place, or condition as dictate a particular attitude governing a relationship between a lived reality and some area of problematical existence that cannot be accommodated easily to conventional conceptions of the normal or familiar. (White 151)

20. See James, Jenks, and Prout, 142–145. They refer to the "distal" and "proximal" representations of childhood: the former, they say, characterizes a set of research practices that offers a fixed, unitary view of childhood favored by policy makers who produce the "executive summary," the "table of results"—whose very format distills "(certainly at the cost of reduction) complex realities into forms which can be taken in at a glance, and ordered and controlled. Distal knowledges present a neat and tidy outline: they can be acted upon." The proximal view, on the other hand, they argue, characterizes the "'close-up' complexity of more ethnographic comparative research." The latter is heterogeneous and untidy: "The result can be that children slip between the spaces of these competing claims to knowledge." See also Prout, "Objective vs. Subjective Indicators"; Lee, "Judgment, Responsibility"; and Bauman.

CHAPTER 2

1. The United Kingdom's Conservative Party canvassed in the 2005 general election on a campaign that included opposition to current UK immigration policies and appealed to the need for tighter border controls to curb illegal immigration. These quotations from "Tory" politicians on the campaign trail were reproduced in the article "Are You Thinking What They're Thinking?" on the front page of *The Independent*:

   Last year in London Colney, five illegal immigrants were arrested but later freed … under instructions from the Home Office. Nobody knows if these people were criminals carrying disease, or even where they went [Anne Main].

   What bit of "send them back" don't you understand Mr. Blair? [Bob Spinks].

   Immigration is sufficient to create a city 10% larger than Oxford each year [Lorraine Fullbrook].

   I have actively campaigned to try to make people recognize the real problems … the strain put on local schools by bogus asylum-seekers, rising levels of MRSA in our hospitals, and soaring violent crime in our once safe and peaceful areas [Nick De Bois]. (Brown, Morris, and Woolf 1)

2. Pity is described as "repugnance refined" in Thomson, "Narrations of Deviance and Delight" 100.

3. It is ironic that the West, which once exported disease as well as manufactured goods to the lands they "discovered," now sees ex-colonies as sources of diseases as well as manufactured goods.

4. The second paragraph of the American Declaration of 1948 reads "The fulfillment of duty by each individual is a prerequisite to the rights of all," and its Article XXXVII says, "It is the duty of every person to work, as far as his capacity and possibilities permit …" The 1918 Soviet Constitution's Article 18 says, "He who does not work, neither shall he eat."

5. On the other hand, illegal economic migrants, not usually distinguished in popular "host" perception either from refugees and asylum seekers or from legal economic migrants such as migrants to the United Kingdom from Eastern European countries that are newly members of the European Community, do have something with which, in theory, they could earn civic rights. The first of two stories entitled "US Split by Need for Cheap Labour and a Fear of Outsiders" on one page (Gumblel 2) of the UK newspaper *The Independent* of 31 March 2006 tells how the half million or so illegal immigrants to the United Kingdom contribute an estimated £6 billion per annum to the economy without them earning as much as the minimum wage (or paying taxes) or deriving any of the state benefits of legal residents. The second story tells how there is a growing demand to felonize and deprive of welfare rights the 12 mil-

lion or so undocumented but economically "irreplaceable" immigrants to the United States. Both stories also record a rise in hostility and racism directed at illegal immigrants, and the UK story reports how they are blamed for crime and terrorism. The issue of economic migrants, or "guest workers" as they are known in some countries, is picked up again in chapter 6, "Colonized."

6. See for example, *Australia, A Last Resort? National Inquiry into Children Immigration in Detention*, 55–86.

7. See United Nations High Commissioner for Refugees, "Asylum Levels and Trends in Industrialized Countries First Quarter 2006: Comparative Overview of Asylum Applications Lodged in 31 European and Non-European Countries."

8. For a discussion and criticism of the implications of how Spivak's position seems to silence any speech on behalf of subalterns, see Bart Moore-Gilbert, Gareth Stanton, and Willy Maley, "Introduction," in *Postcolonial Criticism*, 28–32.

9. See Madeleine Brand, "Profile: Controversy over Children's Book *A Little Piece of Ground*."

10. Jeremy Harding, reviewing Michela Wrong's *I Didn't Do It for You: How the World Used and Abused a Small African Nation*, says that "meddling and cynicism on the part of Eritrea's neighbours, the colonial powers and chiefly the two Cold War adversaries, created the moral and political catastrophe of which so few outsiders had an inkling" (13).

11. It is an irony that one of Alem's surviving cultural connections to his origins should be a liking for a colonial import. As Jeremy Harding, reviewing Michela Wrong's *I Didn't Do It for You: How the World Used and Abused a Small African Nation*, says, "Colonisation is an assertion of foreign culture, and Italian colonial rule was a reality for the assimilated and unassimilated alike" (13).

12. In March 2006, French President Jacques Chirac walked out of a European session in protest at the use of English by a French speaker, Ernest-Antoine Seillière, because Seillière said that English was "the language of business" ("Chirac Upset").

13. See Aijaz Ahmad, writing of intellectuals rather than unskilled workers but, still pertinently, on the difference between forced and chosen migration.

CHAPTER 3

1. The "Fourth Plinth" is a project for the promotion of contemporary art. It was originally designed by Sir Charles Barry and built in 1841 to display an equestrian statue. There were insufficient funds to create such a

statue, and so the plinth remained empty. Marc Quinn's *Alison Lapper Pregnant* was unveiled on September 15, 2005, and on display for eighteen months. See "The Fourth Plinth Project."
2. See chapter 1.
3. There are resonances in this with the concept of the abject discussed in chapter 4.
4. This point relates also to the notion of the borderlands of abjection in chapter 4.
5. The subtitle is taken from Judith Butler's introduction to her book *Undoing Gender.*
6. The novel is discussed by Beverley Pennell and John Stephens, who refer to these chapters as "episodes." See Pennell and Stephens, "Queering Heterotopic Spaces."
7. See Wolfgang Kayser, *The Grotesque in Art and Literature.*
8. The metaphor breaks down, however, when the male and female bodies are considered in relation to the pregnant female body of, for example, Lapper.
9. See Harpham, who describes gargoyles as grotesque figures of meaninglessness:

> Gargoyles could be considered images of the "screen," figures for the world we perceive with earthly eyes. Compounded of multiple natures, they body forth the multiplicity of the world, and remind us that unity lies beyond our grasp. Their meaning is that they do not mean; we understand them by failing to understand. (81)

CHAPTER 4

1. They are Nina Bawden's *Squib* (1973), Anne Fine's *The Tulip Touch* (1997), Sonya Hartnett's *Thursday's Child* (2002), Johanna Reiss's *The Upstairs Room* (1987), Louis Sachar's Holes (1998), and Elizabeth Lutzeier's *No Shelter* (1984).
2. One of the appropriations of abjection in the wider field of literary studies has been to the literature of atrocity. For critical approaches to the literature of atrocity and children's literature studies, see Kokkola; and Bosmajian.
3. For alternative readings of some of these novels, see Salih and Pinsent; Coats 133–136; Wyile Schwenke; and Armstrong and Rudd.
4. For consideration of the status of the child and childhood in children's literature, see Natov; Lesnik-Oberstein, *Children's Literature: Criticism and the Fictional Child*; James R. Kincaid; O'Malley; and Zornado.
5. There are a number of precedents within and beyond the field of children's literature criticism. See Coats (138). Other studies drawing on Kristevan theories include Gubar; Westwater; Wilkie-Stibbs, *The Feminine Subject in Children's Literature*; and Spacks. Westwater's interpretation of some

of Kristeva's work is heavily nuanced with Christian interpretation in ways that her title's allusion to *The Pilgrims' Progress* suggests. In relation to issues of power in adolescent fiction, see Seelinger Trites.

6. The psychosocial-sociocultural resonances and implications of Kristeva's work are ongoing, particularly in the field of cultural-feminist criticism, and especially in relation to the Oedipal paradigm on which her work is premised in the realm designated by her as the "semiotic." Her insistence on relegating the maternal body, including the maternal chora, as unsignifiable and/or prior to culture and language, which then raises questions about maternal agency, is much debated and criticized. Butler, in "Subversive Bodily Acts," argues on grounds that corporeal borders are as much culturally determined inscriptions as they are psychic necessity and that the former then deliver certain, formalized, hegemonic subjectivities as the consequence of a series of necessary foreclosures (79–93). See also Chanter 1–23; and Margaroni. Butler talks about the instability of the paternal metaphor in *Antigone's Claim* (22). Political theorist Slavoj Žižek relates the erosion in contemporary society of the "givenness" of the paternal authority (*Ticklish Subject* 374). Butler points out how Žižek has shown that the work of Lacan "can be understood through popular culture and how popular culture conversely indexes the theory of Lacan" ("Competing Universalities" 268).

7. See Coats 137–160. It is also worth bearing in mind that Anne Fine wrote *The Tulip Touch* to explore the idea of childhood evil in the wake of the child killing of baby James Bulger in 1993.

8. For further details of Nina Bawden's depiction of outsider children, see Wilkie-Stibbs, "Nina Bawden."

9. Social and anthropological theorists of childhood studies are now questioning the nature versus culture dichotomy, and the dualistic thinking it perpetuates and on which it is premised, by acknowledging and theorizing the multiple and hybrid character of social life and its inextricable relation to the child's body as a biological field. See Prout, *The Future of Childhood* 83–111; and Latour 7, 96, 105–109.

10. *The Kid* is Kevin Lewis's autobiography that recounts his childhood of persistent abuse at the hands of his parents and exposes the weaknesses in state child protection provision that allowed the abuses to continue unchecked. The book is now required reading for many child education and social welfare programs in the United Kingdom.

11. There is a well-developed critical discourse deriving from Kristeva's work on abjection and the semiotic chora. See Creed; and Chanter.

12. Butler has since shifted her earlier position in relation to the subject's interpellation in language per se and now advocates a more radical approach that challenges rather than occupies dominant forms: deconstruction, translation, and metalanguage, she says, comprise the "dem-

ocratic project of contestation where the terms that constitute us are simultaneously deployed, deconstructed and reiterated" ("Competing Universalities" 259).

CHAPTER 5

1. According to Andal Damodoran and Nilima Mehta, "In India, there is no uniform law of adoption that is applicable to all Indians, irrespective of their religious affiliation" (409).
2. In 1986, the UN General Assembly made the Declaration on Social and Legal Principles relating to the Protection and Welfare of Children, with special reference to Foster Placement and Adoption Nationally and Internationally, which was cited in the preamble to the UNCRC in 1989. And in 1993, the Hague Conference on Private International Law made the Convention on Protection of Children and Co-operation in Respect of Intercountry Adoption, which more particularly attempts to regularize intercountry adoption, including adoption between countries which have different cultures, adoption customs, and degrees of legal and administrative development, and turns the relevant ethical ambitions of UNCRC into specific requirements. See also Duncan 40–52.
3. See, for example, Ceci and Williams, "Born vs. Made" 1–9.
4. According to the statistics provided by the British Association for Adoption and Fostering (BAAF), in 2005, in England most adoptions from care are of children four years old and under.
5. The implications of "attachment theory" for potential later emotional and cognitive difficulties in adopted children, and the significance of age of adoption, are discussed later in this chapter.
6. In 2005, in England, 68 percent of children in the care of local authorities were, in accordance with UK policy on looked-after children, living with foster carers rather than in residential homes (BAAF). According to the National Adoption Information Clearinghouse, it is harder to make statistical generalizations about where children in care in the United States are looked after, because of its federal structure: "Since 1980 ... information on the foster care system [is collected] through the Voluntary Cooperative for Information system ... data is submitted by States on a voluntary basis, leading to incomplete information compared under inconsistent data definitions."
7. Elaine Farmer, Sue Moyers, and Jo Lipscombe say that the disruption rate for the placements of adolescents is very high.... We do know that most studies confirm that children's behavior problems play a major part in the breakdown of foster placement ... and behavioural difficulties are particularly likely to be an issue with adolescents. (9)

8. Farmer, Moyers, and Lipscombe point out that almost a third of young people [in their UK Department of Health Survey on Supporting Parents] were rated by the[ir] foster carers as having little or no attachment to any adult at the start of the placement. This lack of emotional ties predicted later placement disruption. (57)

9. Farmer, Moyers, and Lipscombe observe that in the USA and Canada since the mid 1980s, pressures on child care agencies have led to increasing numbers of children being placed with the extended family.... The proportion of children fostered with relatives or friends in the UK has been rising in recent years ... to 12% in 2002.... It is also clear that relatives and friends are increasingly looking after young people between the ages of 10 and 15. (24)

10. According to the statistics provided by BAAF, in March 1955, 11 percent of looked-after children in England were in children's homes.

11. Parallels between the stories in the novels in this chapter and those of fairy tales are frequent, for the obvious reason that so many fairy tales as we know them originated in societies where it was commonplace for children to be orphaned and even abandoned. See Jack Zipes, *Breaking the Magic Spell* 32–33.

12. For example, see Barnardo's [children's charity] 2006 report *Failed by the System* cited in BBC News "System 'Failing Children in Care.'"

13. In the survey for the UK Department of Health project on Supporting Parents, respondents gave the following as main reasons for beginning to foster: liking the company of children, feeling they could help, knowing a child who needed care, and wanting a job they could do at home (Farmer, Moyers, and Lipscombe 69–70).

14. Christine Ward Gailey discusses the covert motives of intercountry adoptions in her study of intercountry adoption into the United States, and links between it and the consequences of US covert operations and Cold War activities.... "Often the US has attempted to assimilate or incorporate the 'enemy other.' The zeal with which the US as an imperial power attempts to promote what is termed 'the American way of life' or 'democratic society' (i.e. a particular configuration of capitalism with a non-social state apparatus, particular forms of gender hierarchy, and beliefs in individualism) is widely recognized." (298–299)

15. According to Fahlberg, "A child's identity is usually strongly tied to his or her first name. Changing the first name infers [sic] that his/her identity is not acceptable" (214).

CHAPTER 6

1. See, for example, Žižek *Ticklish*, 352–359; Butler, Laclau, and Žižek, 223–225; and Sharpe 174.

2. *Falling* was first published in Dutch in 1995 (Vallen) and has since been translated into English, German, Danish, Swedish, Norwegian, Finnish, French, Spanish, Catalan, Portuguese, Polish, and Slovak. It has won five literary awards, including being named as an International Board on Books for Young People (IBBY) honor book, and was made into an English-spoken feature film in 1994. The English translation is published in Australia. It is available internationally through Amazon.com, and/or in Canada and the United States through numerous outlets, including azbooks.com, bookconcern.com, a1books.com, pbshopus.com, super-bookdeals.com, and caiman.com.

3. For an explication of the supremacy of Western modernity and imperialist constructions of "otherness," see especially Xie 1–16. For postcolonial readings in children's literature see Nodelman; and Kutzer.

4. *Heart of Darkness* projects the image of Africa as "the other world, the antithesis of Europe and therefore of civilization, a place where man's vaunted intelligence and refinement are finally mocked by triumphant bestiality" (Achebe 114). For postcolonial readings of children's literature, see Kutzer; the essays in McGillis; and Nodelman.

5. See also Hunt and Sands 49.

6. For further examples of postcolonial readings of children's literature, see the other essays in this volume. See also Nodelman; and Kutzer.

7. The phrase originates from the title of the seminal work edited by Bill Ashcroft, Gareth Griffiths, and Helen Tiffin, *The Empire Writes Back: Theory and Practice in Post-colonial Literatures*, a collection of critical essays that explicates how the new body of postcolonial literature constituted a radical critique of the assumptions underlying Eurocentric notions of literature and language. See also "The Empire Writes Back."

8. Gregory quotes "Heart of Smugness" here from Misra, "Heart of Smugness."

9. Robert Stam points out that one of the achievements of neoconservatives has been in relation to those groups that it wishes to isolate politically "to associate individual attributes (self-righteousness, censoriousness, p.c. attitudes) that are democratically spread along the political spectrum with one group alone ... the right-wing portrayed all politicized critique as the neurotic effluvium of whiny malcontents" (197–198). He also accuses them of "euphemization" in terms such as "collateral damage" and in the use of "code words like 'welfare queen,' 'criminals,' 'inner city,' and 'underclass' when they actually mean 'black'" (Stam 197).

10. Stuart Hall makes this point when he says,

   The homogenization is never absolutely complete, and it does not work for completeness. It is not attempting to produce miniversions of Englishness everywhere or little versions of Americanness. It wants to recognize those differences within the larger, overarching framework of what is essentially an American conception of the world.... It is now a form of capitalism that recognizes that it can rule only through other local capitals, rule alongside and in partnership with other economic and political elites. It does not attempt to obliterate them; it operates through them. It has to hold the whole framework of globalization in place and simultaneously police that system: it stage-manages independence within it, so to speak. ("Local and Global" 179)

11. Harvey says,

While economic power seemed to be highly concentrated in the United States, other territorial concentrations of financial power could and did arise [for] almost any rentier class that positioned itself correctly within the matrix of capitalistic institutions…. Privileged classes could seal themselves off in gilded ghettos in Bombay, Sao Paulo, and Kuwait while enjoying the fruits of their investment on Wall Street. (*New Imperialism* 186)

12. I am using the term "hyperborder" here as an adaptation of Jean Baudrillard's concept of the "hyper-real," because it usefully appropriates to the nonreferential nature of political borders in the liberal capitalist economy. In his notion of the hyperreal, Baudrillard described a situation in which any pretension to an idea of an objective reality is occluded in contemporary discourse in a series of nonreferential signifiers and a circulation of meanings filtered through and repositioned in a panoply of media messages in a degree to which the image, the word, or the message no longer connect with or are located in the event from which they derive or to which they refer. Images, then, become themselves the reality, defined as more "real" than the "reality" to which they refer (Baudrillard 166–184). So it is in this sense that I am coining the term "hyperborders" in relation to the idea of borders that are constructed through the saturation of sociopolitical messages: "borders" are thus reinscribed to demarcate any manifestations of physical or geographical or temporal or, indeed, ideological alterity that are deemed to be outside the particular frames of reference the messages themselves set up.

13. The book is distributed internationally through Penguin Books. It has won nine literary awards, including the American Library Association (ALA) Young Adult (2005) and Horn Book Fanfare (2004) awards.

14. See Stuart Hall's quote in note 10, above.

15. For a detailed thesis of current political inscriptions of these terminologies, see Gregory 47–75.

16. An audience of ethnically diverse young people in conversation with Blackman admitted to being taken aback to discover the ethnic inversions of Noughts and Crosses when they reached page 50 (*A Good Read*).

17. Multiple and alternating narrator voices are a feature of young adult fictions. Melvyn Burgess adopts a multiple-voice strategy in *Bloodtide* (1999), as he did in his earlier novel, *Junk* (1997). Alternating-voice nar-

rative was used by Robert Swindells in *Stone Cold* (1995) to effect a switch of voice and viewpoint between his homeless hero "Link" and the serial killer "Shelter," who stalks Link and his kind to their deaths.

18. The Hadley speech resonates with Bush's 2001 pronouncement of the neocon policy of trade and economic expansion that masqueraded as political altruism, rather than the self-interested driving force behind the expansion of the U.S. empire that it actually was: "Open trade is not just an economic opportunity, it is a moral imperative. Trade creates jobs for the unemployed. When we negotiate for open markets, we're providing new hope for the world's poor. And when we promote open free trade, we are promoting political freedom" (quoted in Burbach and Tarbell 129).

19. The point was made by John Harris in relation to the newly released Palestinian movie *Paradise Now* (2005; *Newsnight Review*).

20. See Harvey, *New Imperialism*. Harvey discusses one of the side effects of neoliberalism and the global market economy that provoked an "ease and fluidity of capital mobility over space and the networks of spatial interdependency that increasingly ignored state borders" (185). He also states,

> Neo-liberal imperialism abroad tended to produce chronic insecurity at home.... The racism and nationalism that had once bound nation-state and empire together re-emerged at the petty bourgeois and working-class level as a weapon to organize against the cosmopolitanism of finance capital. Since blaming the problem on immigrants was a convenient diversion for elite interests, exclusionary politics based on race, ethnicity, and religion flourished, particularly in Europe where neo-fascist movements began to garner considerable popular support. (188)

21. See Hogan 197–225.

22. I have adapted the term from the neocon Project for the New American Century. The New American Century website describes itself as follows: "The Project for the New American Century is a non-profit educational organization dedicated to a few fundamental propositions: that American leadership is good both for America and for the world; and that such leadership requires military strength, diplomatic energy and commitment to moral principle."

23. See Madeleine Brand's recorded interview with Elizabeth Laird, "Profile: Controversy over Children's Book *A Little Piece of Ground*," joined by Linda Silver. A part of the recorded interview is quoted as follows:

> Ms. Laird: ...And what I've tried to do in my book is to be as true as possible to what it is like to be a Palestinian child today. Brand: But what is truthful depends on which side of the Green Line you're standing on.... For Linda Silver, a children's book critic for Jewish Book World here in the US, Laird has been anything but truthful. Ms Linda Silver: It's as though the Israelis were invaders from outer space who are simply

motivated by malicious desire to make people's lives miserable. They're just mindless killing machines. Brand: The owner of Canada's largest bookstore says she won't sell the book because she's so offended.... Phyllis Simon said she was disgusted at the irresponsible decision to publish what she feels is a racist, inflammatory and totally one-sided piece of propaganda, and she's called on Macmillan to reconsider publishing it. Silver says authors of children's books have a particular responsibility to portray multiple sides of a sensitive political situation because children don't have the same critical faculties as adults. Ms Silver: It is at least dishonest to portray a political conflict in totally unpolitical terms, particularly when it's written for kids who can't be assumed to know what the political context is. The author in that case has some responsibility, I think, to supply some, and she doesn't. " Compare Mordecai Briemberg, "canpalnet: Canada –Palestine Support Network": "If the child is Kurdish, their experiences, their visions of the injustices in their world, are fit to be described by Elizabeth Laird, and published and distributed and read. ... But if the child is Palestinian, their experiences of living today under Israeli occupation, their visions of the injustices in their world, are not fit to be described by Elizabeth Laird. ... And should Laird dare to do so, they are unfit for publication and distribution by Macmillan Children's books. ... Her (Phyllis Simon's) fear of that child's telling of their experiences is so deep that she is not even capable of a fair reading of the text."

24. See "Children's Author Faces Jewish Wrath." *Guardian*, 23 August 2003:

   "Children's writer Ann Jungman, a member of the liberal Jews for Justice in Palestine group, said that she admired the book but still found it biased. 'It's not what is in there that I object to. It's what has been left out. There should have been a broader picture. All the Palestinians are reasonable, and all the Israelis are monsters.' ... Laird denies the story is anti-Israeli[:] "I did expect comeback, but to say that any criticism of Israel is anti-semitic is doing Israel a disservice. ...... There is already a great deal of understanding of Israel. All western people have felt sympathetic to Israel, for good reason often; and I don't think that should stop. The voice of the Palestinian child, on the other hand, has not been heard." ... Laird claimed *A Little Piece of Ground* was not meant to explain politics. "It's true, lots of Israelis are trying to come to an accommodation with the Palestinians, and many refuse to serve in the West Bank. But the book is written through the eyes of a 12-year-old who just sees men with guns. It would not have been true to characters to do otherwise." ... Laird insisted that everything in the book was drawn from real events. "A lot of the incidents have come from the main Israeli human rights website," while others were taken from the experiences of her collaborator, Sonia Nimir, a lecturer at Bir Zeit university on the West Bank. ...

Laird said ... "the motivation for suicide bombing had to be tackled.... 'Suicide bombings are going on in the background, and in one scene I have Karim's uncle questioning his (Karim's) hunger for vengeance after his father is humiliated by the soldiers. He tells him: "Does that make it right for us to go and bomb them?"'"

25. See Butler, *Bodies* 13; and Butler, "Performative Acts and Gender Constitution" 270.

26. See Foucault, *The Archeology of Knowledge*.

27. See Butler, *Bodies* 13; and Butler, "Performative Acts and Gender Constitution" 270.

28. See Sara, *Reading Matters*.

29. He draws attention to *Homo Sacer: Sovereign Power and Bare Life*, the work of Giorgio Agamben, who, Gregory says, maintained that "the formation of a political community turns not on inclusion—on 'belonging'—but on exclusion" (62). "The juridico-political ordering of space is not only a 'taking of land', Agamben continues, but above all a 'taking of the outside,' an exception" (62). Agamben drew attention to the figure of the "*homo sacer*," those figures who were considered by Roman law to be beyond ritual sacrifice because their deaths were not valuable to the gods, but who, therefore and nevertheless, could still be killed with impunity.

30. See Gregory 282. He refers to the work of Jenny Edkins, who has noted that the figure of the *homo sacer* is more than nominally male, but that many in this position (in Afghanistan and elsewhere) are women. See Jenny Edkins, "Sovereign Power.".

31. See, for example, Gregory, *Colonial Present* 30–46 and 77–106; *Cleveland, A History of the Modern Middle East*; and David Harvey, *A Brief History of Neoliberalism*.

INDEX

DATE DUE
